BENEDETTO CROCE:
COLLECTED WORKS

Volume 1

FREEDOM

FREEDOM

Its Meaning

Edited by
RUTH NANDA ANSHEN

LONDON AND NEW YORK

First published in 1942 in Great Britain by George Allen & Unwin Ltd

This edition first published in 2019
by Routledge
2 Park Square, Milton Park, Abingdon, Oxon OX14 4RN

and by Routledge
52 Vanderbilt Avenue, New York, NY 10017

Routledge is an imprint of the Taylor & Francis Group, an informa business

© 1940 Harcourt Brace Inc.

British Library Cataloguing in Publication Data
A catalogue record for this book is available from the British Library

ISBN: 978-0-367-10994-3 (Set)
ISBN: 978-0-429-05271-2 (Set) (ebk)
ISBN: 978-0-367-13848-6 (Volume 1) (hbk)
ISBN: 978-0-367-13928-5 (Volume 1) (pbk)
ISBN: 978-0-429-02920-2 (Volume 1) (ebk)

Publisher's Note
The publisher has gone to great lengths to ensure the quality of this reprint but points out that some imperfections in the original copies may be apparent.

Disclaimer
The publisher has made every effort to trace copyright holders and would welcome correspondence from those they have been unable to trace.

FREEDOM

ITS MEANING

by BENEDETTO CROCE · CHARLES A. BEARD
JACQUES MARITAIN · BERTRAND RUSSELL · GAETANO SALVEMINI
VILHJALMUR STEFANSSON· HENRY A. WALLACE · HENRI BERGSON
ALFRED NORTH WHITEHEAD · THOMAS MANN · FELIX BERNSTEIN
HAROLD J. LASKI · JOHN MACMURRAY · ALBERT EINSTEIN
J. B. S. HALDANE · LANCELOT HOGBEN · FRANK KINGDON
FRANZ BOAS · JOHN DEWEY

PLANNED AND EDITED BY
RUTH NANDA ANSHEN

GEORGE ALLEN·AND UNWIN *AU* LONDON

Copyright in the U.S.A.

First published in Great Britain 1942

Printed in Great Britain by

SIMSON SHAND LTD

HERTFORD

Acriores autem morsus sunt intermissae
libertatis quam retentae.

Freedom suppressed and again regained bites
with keener fangs than freedom never
endangered.
—Cicero *De Officiis* ii.7.24.

ACKNOWLEDGMENTS

For important suggestions and criticisms the Editor wishes to express her deep gratitude to Felix Bernstein.

The Editor also wishes to make grateful acknowledgments for permission to use the following copyright material: to The Macmillan Company for the use of Professor Whitehead's contribution from *Adventures of Ideas;* to George Allen and Unwin Ltd., and G. P. Putnam's Sons for Professor Dewey's contribution from *Freedom and Culture;* to Henry Holt and Company for Professor Bergson's contribution from *Morality and Religion.*

CONTENTS

PAGE

Ruth Nanda Anshen: PROLOGUE: ORIGIN AND AIM   I

Charles A. Beard: FREEDOM IN POLITICAL THOUGHT   7

Henri Bergson: FREEDOM AND OBLIGATION   24

Felix Bernstein: THE BALANCE OF PROGRESS OF FREEDOM IN HISTORY   43

Franz Boas: LIBERTY AMONG PRIMITIVE PEOPLE   50

Benedetto Croce: THE ROOTS OF LIBERTY   56

John Dewey: THE PROBLEM OF FREEDOM   75

Albert Einstein: FREEDOM AND SCIENCE   91

J. B. S. Haldane: A COMPARATIVE STUDY OF FREEDOM   94

Lancelot Hogben: THE CONTEMPORARY CHALLENGE TO FREEDOM OF THOUGHT   120

Frank Kingdon: FREEDOM FOR EDUCATION   131

Harold J. Laski: NATIONALISM AND THE FUTURE OF CIVILIZATION   148

John Macmurray: FREEDOM IN THE PERSONAL NEXUS   176

Thomas Mann: FREEDOM AND EQUALITY   194

Jacques Maritain: THE CONQUEST OF FREEDOM   210

Bertrand Russell: FREEDOM AND GOVERNMENT   229

Gaetano Salvemini: DEMOCRACY RECONSIDERED   245

Vilhjalmur Stefansson: WAS LIBERTY INVENTED?   265

Henry A. Wallace: THE GENETIC BASIS FOR DEMOCRACY AND FREEDOM   293

Alfred North Whitehead: ASPECTS OF FREEDOM   303

Ruth Nanda Anshen

ORIGIN AND AIM

MAN alone, during his brief existence on this earth, is free to examine, to know, to criticize and to create. In this freedom lies his superiority over the resistless forces that pervade his outward life. But Man is only Man—and only free—when he is considered as a being complete, a totality concerning whom any form of segregation is artificial, mischievous, and destructive, for to subdivide Man is to execute him. Nevertheless, the persistent inter-relationship of the processes of the human mind has been, for the most part, so ignored as to create devouring distortions in the understanding of Man to the extent that one begins to believe that if there is any faith left in our seemingly moribund age it clings in sad perversion, in isolated responsibility, and with curious tenacity to that ancient tenet: "Blessed is he who shall not reveal what has been revealed unto him".

The mutual unintelligibility among most contemporary thinkers, their apparent inability to communicate the meaning and purpose of their ideas to those of differing opinions, the paucity of their knowledge pertaining to the subjects and researches of others, all this has grown to be as profound as it is ominous for the future of mankind, and the possibility of clarifying the confusion and of dissipating the distortions seems to be desperately remote. The subdivision, specialization, nay, atomization increasingly characteristic of religious, philosophic, and scientific ideas, of political events and social movements

B

during the last two centuries, have proved to be an almost implacable impediment to an adequate correlation of these very ideas and movements which, in truth, are in perpetual inter-play. The postulates, categories, dialectical promptings, fecund analogies, or decisive doctrines which first appear in one eminent province of human thought may, and frequently do, penetrate, through their inevitable divagations, into a diversity of other realms; and to be cognizant of only one of them is to misunderstand the character, kinship, logic, and operation of the entire organism and to obscure, and even eclipse, the illumi-nating inter-relations.

Human thoughts and knowledge have never before been so abundant, so kaleidoscopic, so vast, and yet, at the same time, never so diffused, so inchoate, so directionless. And human anxiety and restlessness, the dark loneliness of man amid hostile forces, exist commensurately. There has been little recognition of the importance of a synthetic clarification of modern know-ledge and of the affinity of ideas, a kind of encyclopedic synthesis, indispensable if, in the future, human affairs are to be handled with any hopeful freshness. We seem to have forgotten that all great changes are preceded by a vigorous intellectual reorganization, and that nothing new can be attempted in collective human thought and action without a reinterpretation of the fundamental values of mankind. Is there no hope for Man to live a well-ordered life, to be able to depend upon the help of his fellow-beings, especially upon those who by their ideas direct and interpret the course of his existence? And is the knowledge which Man most requires, namely, the knowledge of himself, only to be found in terms of Delphian ambiguity or in erroneous and cruel understanding?

Out of such considerations as these and a concern for the integrity of the intellectual life, its moral and spiritual meaning, the plan to bring about a correlation of those contemporary ideas which are concerned not with sense data and logical universals, but with the status of values and the bearing of these values on conduct, had its genesis. Those humanistic thinkers in the various branches of scholarly inquiry (and the contributors to this volume) with whom this plan was discussed seemed to be poignantly aware of the principal ailment of mankind—of the disjunction of empirical approach from theory, of methods of observation from speculative doctrine, and of the grave lacunae existent in the study of the nature of Man. They seemed to know that values are eternally present, to question how they might be discovered, to wonder why they are often confused, and to be anxious to determine in what sense they are present when they are not recognized.

It was deemed desirable to establish a series of books, each devoted to the discussion, from diverse and important contemporary points of view, of a single, well-defined question, the object being to make clear, first, how much agreement there is and on what specific points, pertinent to the question, and to make, also, as explicit as possible the points of disagreement and their real grounds. Such volumes (collectively known as the "Science of Culture Series," of which *Freedom* is the first book) could do much to clarify the present situation with respect to the questions defined, and such clarification should be an aid towards eventual agreement. A co-operative effort to accomplish this, to exhibit with all possible clarity where representatives of differing schools of opinion agree and precisely where and precisely why they disagree, and to do this fairly concisely could, it was hoped, be of some significance and importance. Just as Diderot and the other humanists of the eighteenth century were imbued with a new vision of Man in their encyclopedic integration of knowledge, so the "Science of Culture Series" will endeavour to synthesize fundamental contemporary ideas which, by virtue of their dispersion, have been rendered comparatively ineffectual.

Although such a synthesis could have no judicial or political power of any kind, it could, perhaps, exert such an influence on the peoples of the world that no ruling caste could afford to defy the moral judgment of this "conscience" of humanity, living in the thoughts of the thinkers and represented and expressed by the contributors of this volume.

One of the values of such a correlation of contemporary knowledge could be the formulation of a cultural directory for the guidance of mankind, the creation of a systematic circumspection compatible with democratic principles, the discernment of possible alternatives in a social crisis, leading to a genuine social democracy in which collective intelligence is so highly developed as to make individuality not only possible but fruitfully effective.

The material necessities of existence and the spiritual values of the contemporary world, which co-exist in the same complex social totality, are functionally dependent upon each other and must be co-ordinated to assure the stability of our civilization. This work has been undertaken in the hope that it will be the corporeal manifestation of the spirit of science and culture prevailing in the conduct of human affairs; that it will be a laboratory for the discussion of important and earnest contemporary problems—with an end to direct the thought and action of mankind; that by gathering in a synthetic crucible knowledge pertaining to values, it may at least in part bring back into human society that humanity which has been so rudely eliminated; and that, finally, it may, in the words of Bergson, help us to think as men and women of action and to act as men and women of thought.

The subject of this volume, a problem of unsurpassed and critical importance for our age, is, happily, one on which most "intellectuals," however various their opinions on other matters, are of one mind. It has two distinct aims: one, a discussion of the problem of freedom from diverse points of view; the other, the promulgation of an authoritative, or at least broadly representative, synthesis or conspectus of issues and conclusions pertaining to this subject, as a basis for a programme of action.

The passionate concern of the present book is the freedom of Man, the autonomy of the rational being developing to ripe maturity and achieving self-fulfilment. The question of freedom is one of the fundamental principles of Being, since the very perception of Being depends upon freedom which is itself prior to Being. This book is a positive estimation of freedom not only as embodied in institutions, but also as moral and spiritual power; it is a consideration of the personal responsibility of Man which the freedom and dignity of choice place upon him in his every decision. And above all, it is an apotheosis of

Reason which, in the final analysis, is the real mark of freedom and beyond which there is no true unifying force.

If the slumbering consciousness of man can be awakened to a clear, rational discernment of the value of Freedom and Reason, both so seriously endangered, if Man with his mind and with his heart can embrace the universal cause of humanity whose radiant synonym is liberty, if he can know the truth about freedom and its wisdom, then we may still have some tremulous hope for society, and some pride in Man's decision as to what his destiny will be. For in the words of Pico della Mirandola, Man is neither earthly nor divine, neither mortal nor immortal, but has the power to form himself into whatever shape he may desire as a free former and sculptor of himself. He can degenerate into the lower things which are brute or can be regenerated by the very sentence of his soul into the higher things which are divine. But first he must institute the radical reform of an order that is one of darkness and peril, assailed by bewilderment and demonic forces, and destructive of human personality and of true freedom. He must recognize (since means must be consonant with the ends they are intended to serve) that the means to be used must be worthy of the splendour of the end in view and commensurate with the renewal of an order of society on a truly spiritual basis.

With Promethean fidelity let us fiercely resist a prostrate submission to Moloch, let us defy the blind evil of Force and the wanton creed of Militarism; let us worship only that god attained by the inspiration and insight of our love and respect for truth, for beauty and for the ideal of perfection, and with a new intensity and tenderness rekindle a resurrected vision of mankind.

It is to those men and women who realize that there is now the gravest need to bring things back to the fertile, changeless source of truth, to reintegrate that desire for justice and that nostalgia for communion through which the world can find some clear, sincere, and basic meaning and purpose, thereby creating a cultural force of freedom—that unchanging freedom to which Plato aspired—with power to act in history and come to the aid of mankind, it is to those who demand freedom with unremitting insistence, who not only cherish it but who wish to comprehend it, who seek a *modus vivendi* compatible with the dignity of Man, who long to experience the overpowering beauty of human existence, and who say, "Here stand I, I can do no other," that this volume is faithfully dedicated.

Honour to those heroic warriors who have preserved for us the priceless heritage of freedom and have kept undefiled the sanctity and divine fire of the essence of Man!

Charles A. Beard

Visiting Professor of Government, Columbia University

FREEDOM IN POLITICAL THOUGHT

IN the vocabulary of political thought, the two words "free-dom" and "liberty" are interchangeable. Although there has been a tendency in the English-speaking world to treat "liberty" as "something French, foolish and frivolous," and "freedom" as "English, solid, and sensible," there is no ground whatever for the distinction. Freedom is, of course, older in the Anglo-Saxon tongue, but the two words have been employed in English thought as substantially identical in meaning since the fourteenth century. In their deeper origins, in fact, they possessed strikingly similar characteristics.

Liberty stems from the Latin word *liber*, which had a double meaning: (1) free or unrestrained, and (2) especially in plural form "the free members of a household." In Old English "free" meant in the ordinary sense "dear" as applied to the free members of a household. It stemmed from *fréon*, to love, whence the current word "friend;" and freedom has carried the double meaning of *liber* from time immemorial. Neither origin nor historical usage warrants any material distinction between freedom and liberty.

In persistent usage, it is significant to note, freedom and liberty have had negative and positive features. Both have meant exemption or release from bondage, servitude, and arbitrary power—as among the ancient Romans and the early English. At the same time both have meant a given condition for human beings—the positive enjoyment of rights and privi-

7

leges in the household or family of human beings. All through
written history to the latest hour, negative and positive connotations have been associated with freedom and liberty. On
the one side is protection against the arbitrary power of government and persons, and on the other side is the enjoyment of
rights belonging to human beings conceived as something more
than the beasts of the field. To lose sight of either connotation
is to miss both the substance and power of freedom.

On the negative side exists a vast body of laws, customs, and
practices safeguarding freedom, that is, the emancipation of
persons from bondage and from the arbitrary power of government. Under this head come the age-long efforts to establish
the rule of law, as distinguished from wilful, irregular, and
uncontrolled acts of sheer force exerted by rulers, bandits,
wandering soldiers, and mobs. The results of such efforts are
incorporated in various declarations of rights, in the limitations
on government incorporated in the Constitution of the United
States and in the constitutions of the several States, and extended
by legislation and by judicial interpretation. The bare summary
of the elements of freedom from arbitrary action would fill a
volume. These features are well known and, despite variations
of detail in interpretation, are generally agreed upon.

Such rules of law and practice are negations on power. They
forbid legislatures to trespass upon freedom of press and speech,
to deprive any person of life, liberty, or property without due
process of law, to pass any *ex post facto* law, to impose penalties
on any person by bill of attainder, to enact any laws respecting
the establishment of a state religion. To be sure, such limitations protect persons in the positive enjoyment of certain rights,
privileges, and immunities, but in essence they are negative as
expressions of law. And as recent experiences with dictatorships
show, they may be brushed aside by governments based upon
the exercise of sheer and arbitrary power.

There is profound truth in Alexander Hamilton's statement
in Number 84 of *The Federalist*, to the effect that such principles
as freedom of the press cannot be forever guaranteed by mere
constitutional provisions. "Security of the press," he said,
"whatever fine declarations may be inserted in any constitu-

tion respecting it, must altogether depend on public opinion and on the general spirit of the people and the government." No doubt the very existence of declarations of rights in solemn documents of public law does act as a salutary force in restraining public officials; yet the well-framed proclamations of the Weimar Constitution were easily swept into the discard by Adolf Hitler and his Storm Troopers. Something more is needed to preserve freedom than verbal proclamations. Underlying all practice in this respect are the thought, scheme of values, and resolve of a sufficient body of people in every country to sustain assertions of freedom made in the form of law.

If we are to get at the sustaining convictions which give force to paper formulations of freedom, we must examine the thought that has accompanied the rise, growth, assertion, and defence of freedom. How have asserters and defenders of freedom looked upon the world of human beings? What assumptions have they made respecting humanity? What values have they accepted as primordial? What promises of freedom have they found in the very nature or constitution of mankind?

Witnesses for freedom start with a conviction respecting human nature, for it is with human beings, not material things, that they are primarily concerned. They assume and believe that the human being is, in fact, not a mere beast of the field despite all the animal characteristics which unite humanity with the animal kingdom. Whatever men and women are, they are not apes, lions, tigers, or elephants. The products of invention, accumulated cultural goods, and "the funded wisdom of the race" support the conclusion.

Though obvious, the distinction is fundamental. It forms a starting point for considering all the features of freedom, such as capacity for self-restraint, consciously directed effort, or conformity with the requirements of common interest. It recognizes the fact that human beings are to some extent educable, despite all physical and biological determinism. It makes all mere animal analogies, such as the habits of bees and ants, merely illustrative at best, and inapplicable to human affairs in any case. Even if the whole Darwinian hypothesis respecting human origins be accepted, it yet remains a fact that there is a break between the highest of the anthropoids and human beings. Whether this break should be ascribed to "sports" or accidents in nature, to a struggle for existence in peculiar circumstances, to physical developments, such as the apposition of the thumb and forefinger, matters little for practical purposes. Whatever their origins, human beings are differentiated from the rest of the animal kingdom by physical and psychic characteristics of their own. This is not academic. It means, in thought about human freedom, a certain degree of emancipation from the mechanism of biology, if contemporary biology may be called mechanical.

Starting with the human being so conceived, advocates of freedom assert that human life has a value in itself, and that the human being should not be used for purposes alien to humanity, as other animals are brought into servitude. To some extent this assumption is an ethical imperative, but to a large extent it represents the realism of experience. The story of "man's inhumanity to man" is certainly long and makes painful reading. Cold-blooded murders, endless slaughters in war, the cruelties often associated with chattel slavery, and endless violations of liberty, do present glaring contradictions to the assumption that human life has a value in itself. This is undeniable, and human conduct to the latest moment provides brutal illustrations.

Yet on the other side is the record of manifestations supporting the assertion—all the arts and practices of peace, industries, institutions of beneficence, the pronouncements of ethical teachers, the essences of the great religions, the endless striving for human good. Even under chattel slavery, save in its most barbaric form, the slave was accorded some rights of humanity. They were meagre enough; but such as they were they indicated a break with mere bestiality. And chattel slavery has been almost completely outlawed by civilization. Nor is it without significance that this outlawry has accompanied the development of the spirit of freedom in Western civilization. So the assumption that human life has a value in itself and must be accorded some rights not granted to other animals is not a mere theory, a mere ethical imperative; it is rooted in vast experience.

Associated with the assumption and belief that human life has a value in itself, and that human beings are and must be accorded rights appropriate to humanity, is another conception —a conception of human nature itself. In extreme form this conception represents the human being as innately good, and therefore worthy and capable of enjoying and preserving freedom. In this form it is placed in contrast with the conception of the human being as an animal or as innately evil and unworthy of liberty. Those who uphold the one side point to the manifestations of good, of sacrifice, and of mutual aid in history. Those who uphold the other side point to the evil, the selfishness, and "tooth and claw struggle" in history. But neither side can really strike a balance and demonstrate what the proportions are. And since history is not and cannot be an exact science, the problem must forever remain unsolved.

Does the evil in human nature outweigh the good in substance and in practice? The question is unanswerable, no matter what assertions are made under that head. Yet good there is, and advocates of freedom who hold their ground without taking on the airs of omniscience lay emphasis on the good; and by so doing doubtless aid in bringing forth the good in creating the reality asserted by their belief. Nothing is more clearly established in historical experience than the fact that even a myth may help to create the very substance of things hoped for and dreamed of That which is affirmed by experience, such as the former universality of chattel slavery, may be hastened to destruction by the constant reiteration that it is contrary to human rights asserted and assumed; and the rights asserted against experience may be realized. Whatever the future may hold, advocates of freedom do lay emphasis on the good that is in human nature.

Implicit in the conception of human rights and innate goodness is the idea of moral equality. The term "equality" is unfortunate, but no other word can be found as a substitute. Equality means "exactly the same or equivalent in measure, amount, number, degree, value, or quality." It is a term exact enough in physics and mathematics, but obviously inexact when applied to human beings. What is meant by writers who have gone deepest into the subject is that human beings possess, in degree and kind, fundamental characteristics that are common to humanity. These writers hold that when humanity is stripped of extrinsic goods and conventions incidental to time and place, it reveals essential characteristics so widely distributed as to partake of universality. Whether these characteristics be called primordial qualities, biological necessities, residues, or any other name matters little. No one can truthfully deny that they do exist. It is easy to point out inequalities in physical strength, in artistic skill, in material wealth, or in mental capacity, but this too is a matter of emphasis. At the end it remains a fact that fundamental characteristics appear in all human beings. Their nature and manifestations are summed up in the phrase "moral equality."

Emphasis must be placed on the term "moral." From time immemorial it has been the fashion of critics to point out the obvious facts that in physical strength, talents, and wealth, human beings are not equal. The criticism is both gratuitous and irrelevant. No rational exponent of moral equality has ever disputed the existence of obvious inequalities among human beings, even when he has pointed out inequalities which may be ascribed to tyranny or institutional prescriptions. The Declaration of Independence does not assert that all men are equal; it proclaims that they are "created" equal.

In essence the phrase "moral equality" asserts an ethical value, a belief to be sustained, and recognition of rights to be respected. Its validity cannot be demonstrated as a problem in mathematics can be demonstrated. It is asserted against inequalities in physical strength, talents, industry, and wealth. It denies that superior physical strength has a moral right to kill, eat, or oppress human beings merely because it is superior. To talents and wealth, the ideal of moral equality makes a similar denial of right. And indeed few who imagine themselves to have superior physical strength, talents, and wealth will withhold from inferiors all moral rights. In such circumstances government and wealth would go to superior physical strength;

while virtue and talents would serve the brute man, as accomplished Greek slaves served the whims, passions, and desires of Roman conquerors. When the last bitter word of criticism has been uttered against the ideal of moral equality, there remains something in it which all, except thugs, must accept and in practice do accept, despite their sneers and protests. A society without any respect for human personalities is a band of robbers, and there is reputed to be honour even among thieves.

This doctrine of moral equality implicit in the ideal of freedom is no new-fangled creation of modern times, designed as cynics have it to authorize the weak to prey upon the strong. It is as old as civilization itself. Indeed we may regard it as older, even if we dismiss the cosmogony expressed in the medieval lines:

"When Adam delved and Eve span
Who was then the gentleman?"

In ancient Greece the conception of moral equality, if with qualifications, appeared in the Hellenistic age. As Crane Brinton[1] admirably sums up the state of thought on the subject: "Herodotus is emphatic on the contrast between irresponsible Persian rule and Greek *isonomia*, equality before the law. Athenian *isotimia*, equal respect for all, and *isegoria*, equal freedom of speech and hence of political action, together with that regard for equal opportunity so evident in Pericles' funeral speech make up a conception of equality not unlike that of the early, hopeful days of the French Revolution." In short, civilized Greeks proclaimed and adhered to an idea of moral equality and, amid glaring contradictions, applied it to some extent in practice. And at no time were the leading philosophers unaware of the glaring contradictions.

Even from Rome, with all its ruthless force and stratification of classes, the idea of equality was not absent. The idea crept into Roman law, especially in the later days when jurists had to deal with all sorts and conditions of people who were not Roman citizens. In the application of *jus gentium*—the law of

[1] Article in *Encyclopedia of the Social Sciences*, Vol. V, p. 574, to which I am heavily indebted.

Peoples—they came to see that all peoples had qualities in common, and they reached the conclusion that nature had originally decreed equality, though institutions and disobedience had marred it. As Roman thought broadened beyond immediate things, it betrayed a belief in the essential oneness of humanity, despite glaring contradictions. Epictetus taught that we are all children of God and are in duty bound to cherish love for, and practise forbearance toward one another. Weakness has its inherent rights and strength its moral limitations. Although nowhere in Roman history appeared a solemn declaration of the rights of man, all the elements of it could be gathered from the scattered works of Roman thinkers and leaders. And great as was the superstructure of force, it could not perpetuate itself, but crumbled to earth leaving naked humanity to. begin over again the work of social and State rebuilding. To the multitudes bereft of their imperial rulers, the teachings of Roman moralists were more significant than the memories of the glittering eagles once carried before conquering armies.

As the empire of force crumbled, as the doctrines of Roman moralists were forgotten, as their written works were buried in dust, a new faith in moral worth and equality furnished both inspiration and a guiding principle for the re-ordering of human affairs. Or perhaps it would be more correct to say that the doctrines of Roman moralists had prepared the way for the triumph of the new faith.[1] Seneca had said that "we are all akin by nature, which has formed us of the same elements and placed us here together for the same end." To a similar conclusion the tragic Marcus Aurelius had come: "If our reason is common, there is a common law. . . . And if there is a common law we are fellow-citizens; if this is so, we are members of some political community—the world is in a manner a State." In such writings had been foreshadowed the elaboration of the teachings of Jesus Christ. And in this new faith the

[1] Harold Laski, Speaking of Stoicism, rightly says: "Christianity added little to this notion by way of substantial content; but it added to its force the impetus of a religious sanction, not improbably the more powerful because Christianity was in its original phase essentially a society of the disinherited, to whom the idea of the eminent dignity of human personality as such would make an urgent appeal." *Encyclopædia of the Social Sciences*, Vol. IX, pp. 442 ff.

moral worth of the human personality and the principle of equality were clearly and categorically asserted. "Of one blood are all nations of men." "There is neither Jew nor Greek, neither bond nor free, neither male nor female; for yet are all one in Christ Jesus." If some later theologians tended to shift this equality from earth to heaven, early Christians did not take their faith in this supermundane sense alone. They brought it down to practice in the communities of the early churches, some going so far as to share the fruits of their property. So potent was the Christian faith, so powerful were the energies inspired by it, that it contributed to sapping and undermining the empire of force into which it was introduced. Although later entangled in the vested interests of accumulating property and confronted by a feudal hierarchy of class orders, Christian teachers never entirely abandoned the early doctrine of human equality. In monastic movements, and in popular tumults such as those led by Savonarola in Florence and John Ball in England, appeared the primitive passion for the unprivileged and for the mere humane.

In Protestantism of the levelling variety, moral equality flamed up in a sacrificial ardour. It produced forms of religious organization which, on account of equalitarian principles, have rightly been placed by students of the subject among the fore-runners of modern democracies. In them was an assertion of the right of individual conscience demanding respect. In them was a comradeship and a deep attachment to common good. As communities, religious congregations stood together against the oppressions and persecutions of State and Established Church. As communities many of them migrated to America in search of freedom for their way of life. Of the Pilgrims at Plymouth it was written: "We are knit together as a body in the most sacred covenant of the Lord . . . by virtue of which we hold ourselves tied to all care of each other's good and of the whole." Thus was expressed, on the barren coasts of New England, the ancient cry: "And the multitude of them that believed were of one heart and one soul." Despite all formalisms, all conformity to power, and all giant masquerades, the flame of this faith and conviction has never been extinguished.

Closely associated with the levellers in religious organization, if not stemming from that source, were the levellers in politics and economics who threatened Cromwell's iron despotism in England, no less than the power of kings. This obscure and despised party, thrown up in the Puritan Revolution, united divinity and nature in the formulation of its doctrines. "All men," they taught, "are by nature the sons of Adam, and from him have legitimately derived a natural propriety (property), right, and freedom. . . . By natural birth all men are equally and alike born to like propriety, liberty, and freedom, and as we are delivered of God by the hand of nature unto this world, every one with a natural innate freedom and propriety, even so we are to live, every one equally and alike, to enjoy his birthright and privilege."

Here, indeed, is evidence of the link of faith in common humanity that united Christian teachings with the reliance on nature, and later became the support of equalitarian democracy and equal rights. Thus, all the elements of the Declaration of Independence in America and of the Declaration of the Rights of Man in France were formulated more than a century before those documents appeared, by the English levellers working in the traditions of Puritan Christianity. Thus, although to some there seems to be a break in the movement of historic idealism —a sharp antithesis between divinity and nature, there was no such break or antithesis in fact. As the great humane teachings of Greece and Rome, which combined divinity and nature, merged easily with the humane teachings of Christianity, so the great teachings of the Christian tradition were merged with the eighteenth-century philosophy of nature. If clerical monopoly on *divine* right encouraged an emphasis on *natural* right, the two sources of knowledge and inspiration were in truth never separated. Rather were they interwoven in the stream of mental and moral energies which drove institutions and mankind in the direction of a larger freedom; so forcibly indeed and so swiftly, that the creed of the despised sect proclaimed in the seventeenth century became within two hundred years the creed of a great Respectability.

So it came about that when the philosophers of the eighteenth century resorted to Nature and applied what they deemed the cold analysis of reason to royal, feudal, and clerical institutions of prescriptive and vested rights, they actually had behind them more than twenty centuries of Greek, Roman, and Christian idealism. If God had not created all human beings free and equal, as Stoics and Christians had long maintained, at least Nature and Nature's God had done just that very thing. In any case a humane idealism historically rooted in divinity and nature, equipped with the weapon of reason and the sharp edge of scientific analysis, sapped and undermined institutions founded on prescriptive force, overthrew them in thought, and presided over the revolutions that ushered in modern liberty. Nothing could be more superficial, therefore, than the idea and belief that liberty came into being as the result of a temporary fit of uninformed reason, soon to be submerged forever in a wave of eternal unreason, emotion, and sheer force. It was, in truth, governments founded on violence—Alexandrian, Roman, and royal, that had proved temporary; while the movement of human idealism had been continuous; now underground, now sweeping to victories, now retreating, now advancing.

Hence, unless knowledge is a delusion, the inescapable conclusion: The dogma of human worth, with its implicit equalitarianism and liberalism, is as old as civilization and is irrevocably rooted in the very substance of things, whether that very substance be regarded as a realization of the divine idea or as a mere result of the material conditions of economic production. And the force of the ideal forever undermines the force of brute strength, challenges it, and overthrows it. This seems to be the very essence of Western history, of which our own times are a fleeting expression.

Holding to the assumption of human worth and the conception of moral equality, advocates of freedom contend that human effort can create material and moral conditions in which human worth, human equality, and human liberty may become more perfectly revealed and made more evident in the arrangements of life. It would be possible to amass a mountain of evidence on this contention from writings strewn through the centuries, from Greek antiquity to our own times. But no writer associated with the rise and growth of liberty in the United States expressed it with more precision than Thomas Jefferson. In a remarkable paper he contrasted his conceptions with the theories of government generally prevailing in Europe.

"The doctrines of Europe were," Jefferson said, "that men in numerous associations cannot be restrained within the limits of order and justice, but by forces physical and moral, wielded over them by authorities independent of their will. Hence their organization of kings, hereditary nobles, and priests. Still further to restrain the brute force of the people, they deem it necessary to keep them down by hard labour, poverty, and ignorance, and to take from them, as from bees, so much of their earnings, as that unremitting labour shall be necessary to obtain a sufficient surplus thereby to sustain a scanty and miserable life. And these earnings they apply to maintain their privileged orders in splendour and idleness, to fascinate the eyes of the people, and excite in them an humble adoration and submission, as to an order of superior beings.

"Although few among us had gone to all these lengths of opinion, yet many had advanced, some more, some less, on the way. . . . Ours, on the contrary, was to maintain . . . the will of the people themselves. We believed . . . that man was a rational animal, endowed by nature with rights, and with an innate sense of justice; and that he could be restrained from wrong and protected in right, by moderate powers, confided in persons of his own choice and held to their duties by dependence on his own will. We believed that the complicated organization of kings, nobles, and priests was not the wisest or best to effect the happiness of associated man; that wisdom and virtue were not hereditary; that the trappings of such a machinery consumed by their expense those earnings of industry they were meant to protect, and by the inequalities they produced exposed liberty to sufferance. We believed that men, enjoying in ease and security the full fruits of their own industry, enlisted by all their interests on the side of law and order, habituated to think for themselves and to follow reason as their guide, would be more easily and safely governed, than with minds nourished in error, and vitiated and debased, as in

Europe, by ignorance, indigence, and oppression."

Holding fast to conceptions of human nature, human rights, moral equality, and of conditions favourable to the flowering of these virtues, advocates of liberty have demanded that such virtues be permitted to unfold against all the handicaps of legal and economic privileges. This has been regarded all along as an aspect of the equalitarian trend, and in practice the rise of political liberty has been accompanied by an upswing of talents from among the once obscure, unprivileged, and subjugated. In the Middle Ages the flowering of talents was marked in handicrafts among the guilds which were, within their limits, petty democracies endowed with large rights of self-government. Moreover, the Roman Catholic Church drew its monks, nuns, priests, and bishops from various walks of life. If the higher posts often went to persons of the privileged classes, they were by no means closed to the sons and daughters of the unprivileged. No small part of the Church's strength has been, and is derived from the fact that its authorities look for talents and draw talents from every section of its membership, and it is surely no accident that, despite its defeats on many fronts, the Church has survived the revolutions that unhorsed kings and nobles.

In modern times the upswing of talents, favoured by the doctrine of freedom, appears in every field of human activity—in invention, business enterprise, industrial management, labour organizations, the arts, sciences, and letters. When all due respect is paid to the perfections of medieval art, architecture, and handicrafts, and the demerits of the modern "cheap and nasty" are recognized, the achievements in all the enterprises and arts that sustain humanity and adorn human nature in the centuries that witnessed the rise of political freedom stand unimpeachable. Comparisons of particular merits may yield no general conclusions. Indications of particular shortcomings prove no moral. The flowering of individual talents has been and remains an aspect of freedom—one of its asserted and cherished values.

Such are broad tendencies of thought and conviction respecting the nature of humanity which underlie the modern conception of freedom and its corollary—self-government as distinguished from government superimposed by force. In these tendencies mankind has been deemed fundamentally worthy of freedom and rightfully destined to enjoy freedom within the circle of law expressing the sentiments and ideas of self-government. Freedom has been deemed a value in itself, attached to the status and dignity of the human being. It has been deemed also an eternal force, a sacred fire in the human breast, working forever, even in prisons and dungeons, against despotism in every form.

Will this thought and this conviction perish from the earth and give place to the thought and conviction that a self-chosen and self-constituted few are now to extinguish the idea of freedom and make some kind of Asiatic tyranny the final shape of government and social living throughout the world? There is no exact science of society which enables us to answer that question. We have only the lamp of experience to guide us—our own experience and the records of history.

Since the beginning of civilization there has been a struggle between sheer force and humanity, between the few who have sought dominance by physical might and the many who have sought to protect and govern themselves under customs and rules of their own making. The contest has been waged under many names, with varying phrases of justification and defence, but in fact it has continued through the centuries. Sheer force has clothed itself in different forms at different ages. In early times it put forward no ethical pretensions. The war lord and his companions, for love of plunder and excitement, fell upon their neighbours, seized their lands and goods, conquered them, and settled down upon them, without making any explanations or claiming to bestow any benefits. In the beginning was the deed, and the deed was sufficient for the victor. No highflown phrases represented the act as good. No system of world philosophy made it appear both necessary and beneficial to conqueror and victim. No religious sanctions covered it with the will or mercy of God. The records of such acts of power appear in the early passages of the Anglo-Saxon Chronicle which describes deeds of conquest and plunder without any embellishments of morality or learning.

After sheer force took on the habiliments of civilization it was decorated by various titles. The war lord became the absolute monarch and claimed to rule by the grace of God. Huge volumes were written in justification of the power so exercised. At other times and in various places, sheer force appeared under the name of dictatorship. "Every man the least conversant in Roman story," wrote Alexander Hamilton in *The Federalist*, "knows how often that republic was obliged to take refuge in the absolute power of a single man, under the formidable title of dictator, as well as against the intrigues of ambitious individuals who aspired to the tyranny, and the seditions of whole classes of the community whose conduct threatened the existence of all government, as against the invasions of external enemies who menaced the conquest and destruction of Rome."

At other times sheer force appeared as the *imperator*, the military commander raised to supreme power in civil government through the support of his soldiers. Caesar and Napoleon were examples. Once installed, the *imperium* was clothed with insignia and called divine, and efforts were made to give it the appearance and substance of eternity. Whether it was the war lord of the naked deed, the absolute monarch by divine right, the dictator prolonging his temporary assignment, the tyrant, or the emperor, sheer force meant the subjection of the multitudes, high and low, to the will, the passions, and the distempers of the master. Fear might check him. The peril of assassination might moderate his despotism. In his greed he might overreach himself and pull down his own system. But the people whom he ruled were subjects obeying his orders, yielding their labour and goods to his agents, fighting his wars, building monuments to his glory, and accepting his laws. Submission and servitude were their lot.

Yet accompanying the manifestations of sheer force have been, in many times and places since the beginning of civilization, institutions of check and control set up in the name of freedom. The stark war lord did not fight his battles alone. He had companions with whom he took some counsel. The king

in early England had his council, which developed into the
Witenagemot, or assembly of wise men. The emperor Napoleon
I had his four-chambered legislature in which even "clodhop-
pers," as he called them, had a weak and ineffectual voice.
Napoleon III, raised to power by a plebiscite and seeking to
emulate his uncle, was compelled to make concessions to parliamentary government on the eve of his downfall in war. Where
absolutism did not yield, bend, and make concessions, it was in
many times and places overthrown by revolution from below:
the British Revolution of 1649, the French Revolution of 1789,
the Russian Revolution of 1917. Indeed it is impossible to find
in history anywhere back of the twentieth century a despotism
which did not disappear in violence or was not, like the British
monarchy, tempered down into weakness by revolution and
institutions of popular control, with varying degrees of popular
freedom. If the fullness of truth be our goal, it is necessary
therefore to parallel the history of sheer force with the history
of endless efforts, more or less popular, to subdue it to institutions of control directed by a portion of the people in the
interest of freedom.

At the opening of the twentieth century it appeared that
popular government accompanied by checks and balances conceived in the interest of freedom was destined to spread to all
quarters of the globe. Then came a reaction, such as had
punctuated the whole movement for freedom since the beginning of the Renaissance. Now we are in the midst of that
reaction, and there are prophets engaged in foretelling the
complete and final triumph of that reaction.

We cannot discover in the nature of history anything that
enables us to make out of knowledge unequivocal predictions
such as the chemist can make when an event is precipitated in
a chemical compound. But in the very nature of history we do
observe the long and tenacious struggle between humanity
and brute force, between freedom and arbitrary power; and
we can scarcely escape the conclusion that this struggle will
not be closed either immediately or in the distant future by any
acts of any despots. If we know anything about history we
know that its continuous flowing into the future will not be

halted by new Alexanders, Caesars, Napoleons. Death is as merciless to them as it is to common clay. Their mortal coil is shuffled off. Their governments collapse. Their empires dissolve. Their despotisms sink into the dust. That much seems to be, indeed is, established by the record of long human experience.

We know also that humanity alone survives amid the decay and collapse of royal families and dictatorial dynasties. If history goes on, it will continue to survive. If humanity goes on, the thought and conviction respecting the worth, values, and freedom of humanity that have accompanied the rise of civilization will unfold, here weakly, there strongly. Those, then, who believe in freedom as restraints on arbitrary power and as a good in itself may take courage. The very stars may not be marshalled on their side, but undying forces of humanity march with them. Despair and defeat may threaten them, but the conviction that the noblest thought of thirty centuries belongs to them, and not to tyrants, sustains them in a conflict that is never won triumphantly and yet never lost beyond hope of recovery. If this is an illusion, they may at least draw inspiration from the knowledge that tyrants also are passing shadows.

Henri Bergson

Professor Emeritus of Philosophy, Collège de France

FREEDOM AND OBLIGATION

THE remembrance of forbidden fruit is the earliest thing in the memory of each of us, as it is in that of mankind. We should notice this, were not this recollection overlaid by others which we are more inclined to dwell upon. What a childhood we should have had if only we had been left to do as we pleased! We should have flitted from pleasure to pleasure. But all of a sudden an obstacle arose, neither visible nor tangible: a prohibition. Why did we obey? The question hardly occurred to us. We had formed the habit of deferring to our parents and teachers. All the same we knew very well that it was because they were our parents, because they were our teachers. Therefore, in our eyes, their authority came less from themselves than from their status in relation to us. They occupied a certain station; that was the source of the command which, had it issued from some other quarter, would not have possessed the same weight. In other words, parents and teachers seemed to act by proxy. We did not fully realize this, but behind our parents and our teachers we had an inkling of some enormous, or rather some shadowy thing that exerted pressure on us through them. Later we would say it was society. And speculating upon it, we should compare it to an organism whose cells, united by imperceptible links, fall into their respective places in a highly developed hierarchy, and for the greatest good of the whole naturally submit to a discipline that may demand the sacrifice of the part. This, however, can only be a comparison, for an organism subject to inexorable laws is one thing, and a society composed of free wills another. But once these wills are organized, they assume the guise of an organism; and in this more or less artificial organism habit plays the same rôle as necessity in the works of nature. From this first standpoint, social life appears to us a system of more or less deeply rooted habits, corresponding to the needs of the community. Some of them are habits of command, most of them are habits of obedience, whether we obey a person commanding by virtue of a mandate from society, or whether from society itself, vaguely perceived or felt, there emanates an impersonal imperative. Each of these habits of obedience exerts a pressure on our will. We can evade it, but then we are attracted towards it, drawn back to it, like a pendulum which has swung away from the vertical. A certain order of things has been upset, it *must be* restored. In a word, as with all habits, we feel a sense of obligation.

But in this case the obligation is immeasurably stronger. When a certain magnitude is so much greater than another that the latter is negligible in comparison, mathematicians say that it belongs to another order. So it is with social obligation. The pressure of it, compared to that of other habits, is such that the difference in degree amounts to a difference in kind. It should be noted that all habits of this nature lend one another mutual support. Although we may not speculate on their essence and on their origin, we feel that they are interrelated, being demanded of us by our immediate surroundings, or by the surroundings of those surroundings, and so on to the uttermost limit, which would be society. Each one corresponds, directly or indirectly, to a social necessity; and so they all hang together, they form a solid block. Many of them would be trivial obligations if they appeared singly. But they are an integral part of obligation in general, and this whole, which is what it is owing to the contributions of its parts, in its turn confers upon each one the undivided authority of the totality. Thus the sum total comes to the aid of each of its parts, and the general sentence "do what duty bids" triumphs over the hesitations we might feel in the presence of a single duty. As a matter of fact, we do not explicitly think of a mass of partial duties added together and constituting a singly total obligation. Perhaps there is really not an aggregation of parts. The strength which one obligation derives from all the others is rather to be compared to the breath of life drawn, complete and indivisible, by each of the cells from the depths of the organism of which it is an element. Society, present within each of its members, has claims which, whether great or small, each express the sumtotal of its vitality. But let us again repeat that this is only a comparison. A human community is a collectivity of free beings. The obligations which it lays down, and which enable it to subsist, introduce into it a regularity which has merely some analogy to the inflexible order of the phenomena of life.

And yet everything conspires to make us believe that this regularity is comparable with that of nature. I do not allude merely to the unanimity of mankind in praising certain acts and blaming others. I mean that, even in those cases where moral precepts implied in judgments of values are not observed, we contrive that they should appear so. Just as we do not notice disease when walking along the street, so we do not gauge the degree of possible immorality behind the exterior which humanity presents to the world. It would take a good deal of time to become a misanthrope if we confined ourselves to the observation of others. It is when we detect our own weaknesses that we come to pity or despise mankind. The human nature from which we then turn away is the human nature we have discovered in the depths of our own being. The evil is so well screened, the secret so universally kept, that in this case each individual is the dupe of all: however severely we may profess to judge other men, at bottom we think them better than ourselves. On this happy illusion much of our social life is grounded.

It is natural that society should do everything to encourage this idea. The laws which it promulgates and which maintain the social order resemble, moreover, in certain aspects, the laws of nature. I admit that the difference is a radical one in the eyes of the philosopher. To him the law which enunciates facts is one thing, the law which commands, another. It is possible to evade the latter; here we have obligation, not necessity. The former is, on the contrary, unescapable, for if any fact diverged from it we should be wrong in having assumed it to be a law; there would exist another one, the true one, formulated in such a way as to express everything we observe and to which the recalcitrant fact would then conform like the rest. True enough; but to the majority of people the distinction is far from being so clear. A law, be it physical, social, or moral —every law—is in their eyes a command. There is a certain order of nature which finds expression in laws: the facts are presumed to "obey" these laws so as to conform with that order. The scientist himself can hardly help believing that the law "governs" facts and consequently is prior to them, like the Platonic Idea on which all things had to model themselves. The higher he rises in the scale of generalizations the more he tends, willy-nilly, to endow the law with this imperative character; it requires a very real struggle against our own prepossessions to imagine the principles of mechanics otherwise than as inscribed from all eternity on the transcendent tables that modern science has apparently fetched down from another Sinai. But if physical law tends to assume in our imagination the form of a command when it attains to a certain degree of generality, in its turn an imperative which applies to everybody, appears to us somewhat like a law of nature. The two ideas, coming against each other in our minds, effect an exchange. The law borrows from the command its prerogative of compulsion; the command receives from the law its inevitability. Thus a breach of the social order assumes an anti-natural character; even when frequently repeated, it strikes us as an exception, being to society what a freak creation is to nature.

And suppose we discern behind the social imperative a religious command? No matter the relation between the two terms: whether religion be interpreted in one way or another, whether it be social in essence or by accident, one thing is certain, that it has always played a social rôle. This part, indeed, is a complex one: it varies with time and place; but in societies such as our own the first effect of religion is to sustain and reinforce the claims of society. It may go much further. It goes at least thus far. Society institutes punishments which may strike the innocent and spare the guilty; its rewards are few and far between; it takes broad views and is easily satisfied; what human scales could weigh, as they should be weighed, rewards and punishments? But, just as the Platonic Idea reveals to us, in its perfection and fullness, that reality which we see only in crude imitations, so religion admits us to a city whose most prominent features are here and there roughly typified by our institutions, our laws, and our customs. Here below, order is merely approximate, being more or less artificially obtained by man; above, it is perfect and self-creative. Religion, therefore, in our eyes, succeeds in filling in the gap, already narrowed by our habitual way of looking at things, between a command of society and a law of nature.

We are thus being perpetually brought back to the same comparison, defective though it be in many ways, yet appropriate enough to the point with which we are dealing. The members of a civic community hold together like the cells of an organism. Habit, served by intelligence and imagination, introduces among them a discipline resembling, in the interdependence it establishes between separate individuals, the unity of an organism of anastomotic cells.

Everything, yet again, conspires to make social order an imitation of the order observed in nature. It is evident that each of us, thinking of himself alone, feels at liberty to follow his bent, his desire, or his fancy, and not consider his fellow-men. But this inclination has no sooner taken shape than it comes up against a force composed of the accumulation of all social forces; unlike individual motives, each pulling its own way, this force would result in an order not without analogy to that of natural phenomena. The component cell of an organism, on becoming momentarily conscious, would barely have outlived the wish to emancipate itself when it would be recaptured by necessity. An individual forming part of a community may bend or even break a necessity of the same kind, which to some extent he has helped to create, but to which, still more, he has to yield; the sense of this necessity, together with the consciousness of being able to evade it, is none the less what he calls an obligation. From this point of view, and taken in its most usual meaning, obligation is to necessity what habit is to nature.

It does not come then exactly from without. Each of us belongs as much to society as to himself. While his consciousness, delving downwards, reveals to him, the deeper he goes, an ever more original personality, incommensurable with the others and indeed undefinable in words, on the surface of life we are in continuous contact with other men whom we resemble, and united to them by a discipline which creates between them and us a relation of interdependence. Has the self no other means of clinging to something solid than by taking up its position in that part of us which is socialized? That would be so if there were no other way of escape from a life of impulse, caprice, and regret. But in our innermost selves, if we know how to look for it, we may perhaps discover another sort of equilibrium, still more desirable than the one on the surface. Certain aquatic plants as they rise to the surface are ceaselessly jostled by the current: their leaves, meeting above the water, interlace, thus imparting to them stability above. But still more stable are the roots, which, firmly planted in the earth, support them from below. However, we shall not dwell for the present on the effort to delve down to the depths of our being. If possible at all, it is exceptional; and it is on the surface, at the point where it inserts itself into the close-woven tissue of other exteriorized personalities, that our ego generally finds its point of attachment; its solidity lies in this solidarity. But, at the point where it is attached, it is itself socialized. Obligation, which we look upon as a bond between men, first binds us to ourselves.

It would therefore be a mistake to reproach a purely social morality with neglecting individual duties. Even if we were only in theory under a state of obligation towards other men, we should be so in fact towards ourselves, since social solidarity exists only in so far as a social ego is superadded, in each of us, to the individual self. To cultivate this social ego is the essence of our obligation to society. Were there not some part of society in us, it would have no hold on us; and we scarcely need seek it out, we are self-sufficient, if we find it present within us. Its presence is more or less marked in different men; but no one could cut himself off from it completely. Nor would he wish to do so, for he is perfectly aware that the greater part of his strength comes from this source, and that he owes to the ever recurring demands of social life that unbroken tension of energy, that steadiness of aim in effort, which ensures the greatest return for his activity. But he could not do so, even if he wished to, because his memory and his imagination live on what society has implanted in them, because the soul of society is inherent in the language he speaks, and because even if there is no one present, even if he is merely thinking, he is still talking to himself. Vainly do we try to imagine an individual cut off from all social life. Even materially, Robinson Crusoe on his island remains in contact with other men, for the manufactured objects he saved from the wreck, and without which he could not get along, keep him within the bounds of civilization, and consequently within those of society. But a moral contact is still more necessary to him, for he would be soon discouraged if he had nothing else to cope with his incessant difficulties except an individual strength of which he knows the limitations. He draws energy from the society to which he remains attached in spirit; he may not perceive it, still it is there, watching him; if the individual ego maintains alive and present the social ego, he will effect, even in isolation, what he would with the encouragement and even the support of the whole of society. Those whom circumstances condemn for a time to solitude, and who cannot find within themselves the resources of a deep inner life, know the penalty of "giving way," that is to say, of not stabilizing the individual ego at the level prescribed by the social ego. They will therefore be careful to maintain the latter, so that it shall not relax for one moment its strictness towards the former. If necessary, they will seek for some material or artificial support for it. You remember Kipling's Forest Officer, alone in his bungalow in the heart of the Indian rukh? He dresses every evening for dinner, so as to preserve his self-respect in his isolation[1].

We shall not go so far as to say that this social ego is Adam

---

[1] "In the Rukh," in *Many Inventions*.

Smith's "impartial spectator," or that it must necessarily be identified with moral conscience, or that we feel pleased or displeased with ourselves according as it is favourably or unfavourably affected. We shall discover deeper sources for our moral feelings. Language here groups under one name very different things. What is there in common between the remorse of a murderer and that racking, haunting pain, also a remorse, which we may feel at having wounded someone's pride or been unjust to a child? To betray the confidence of an innocent soul opening out to life is one of the most heinous offences for a certain type of conscience, which is apparently lacking in a sense of proportion, precisely because it does not borrow from society its standards, its gauges, its system of measurement. This type of conscience is not the one that is most often at work. At any rate it is more or less sensitive in different people. Generally the verdict of conscience is the verdict which would be given by the social self.

And also, generally speaking, moral distress is a throwing out of gear of the relations between the social and the individual self. Analyze the feeling of remorse in the soul of a desperate criminal. You might mistake it at first for the dread of punishment, and indeed you find most minute precautions, perpetually supplemented and renewed, to conceal the crime and avoid being found out; at every moment comes the awful thought that some detail has been overlooked and that the authorities will get hold of the tell-tale clue. But look closer: what the fellow wants is not so much to evade punishment as to wipe out the past, to arrange things just as though the crime had never been committed at all. When nobody knows that a thing exists, it is almost as if it were non-existent. Thus it is the crime itself that the criminal wants to erase, by suppressing any knowledge of it that might come to the human ken. But his own knowledge persists, and note how it drives him more and more out of that society within which he hoped to remain by obliterating the traces of his crime. For the same esteem for the man he was, is still shown to the man he is no longer; therefore society is not addressing him; it is speaking to someone else. He, knowing what he is, feels more isolated among his fellow-men than he would on a desert island; for in his solitude he would carry with him, enveloping him and supporting him, the image of society; but now he is cut off from the image as well as the thing. He could reinstate himself in society by confessing his crime: he would then be treated according to his deserts, but society would then be speaking to his real self. He would resume his collaboration with other men. He would be punished by them, but, having made himself one of them, he would be in a small degree the author of his own condemnation; and a part of himself, the best part, would thus escape the penalty. Such is the force which will drive a criminal to give himself up. Sometimes without going so far he will confess to a friend, or to any decent fellow. By thus putting himself right, if not in the eyes of all, at least in somebody's eyes, he re-attaches himself to society at a single point, by a thread; even if he does not reinstate himself in it, at least he is near it, close to it; he no longer remains alienated from it; in any case he is no longer in complete rupture with it, nor with that element of it which is part of himself.

It takes this violent break to reveal clearly the nexus of the individual to society. In the ordinary way we conform to our obligations rather than think of them. If we had every time to evoke the idea, enunciate the formula, it would be much more tiring to do our duty. But habit is enough, and in most cases we have only to leave well enough alone in order to accord to society what it expects from us. Moreover, society has made matters very much easier for us by interpolating intermediaries between itself and us: we have a family; we follow a trade or a profession; we belong to our parish, to our district, to our county; and, in cases where the insertion of the group into society is complete, we may content ourselves, if need be, with fulfilling our obligations towards the group and so paying our debts to society. Society occupies the circumference; the individual is at the centre; from the centre to the circumference are arranged, like so many ever widening concentric circles, the various groups to which the individual belongs. From the circumference to the centre, as the circles grow smaller, obligations are added to obligations, and the individual ends by finding himself confronted with all of them together. Thus obligation increases as it advances; but, if it is more complicated, it is less abstract, and the more easily accepted. When it has become fully concrete, it coincides with a tendency, so habitual that we find it natural, to play in society the part which our station assigns to us. So long as we yield to this tendency, we scarcely feel it. It assumes a peremptory aspect, like all deep-seated habits, only if we depart from it.

It is society that draws up for the individual the programme of his daily routine. It is impossible to live a family life, follow a profession, attend to the thousand-and-one cares of the day, do one's shopping, go for a stroll, or even stay at home, without obeying rules and submitting to obligations. Every instant we have to choose, and we naturally decide on what is in keeping with the rule. We are hardly conscious of this; there is no effort. A road has been marked out by society; it lies open before us, and we follow it; it would take more initiative to cut across country. Duty, in this sense, is almost always done automatically; and obedience to duty, if we restrict ourselves to the most usual case, might be defined as a form of non-exertion. passive acquiescence. How comes it, then, that on the contrary this obedience appears as a state of strain, and duty itself as something harsh and unbending? Obviously because there occur cases where obedience implies an overcoming of self. These cases are exceptions; but we notice them because they are accompanied by acute consciousness, as happens with all forms of hesitation—in fact consciousness is this hesitation itself; for an action which is started automatically passes almost unperceived. Thus, owing to the interdependence of our duties and because the obligation as a whole is immanent in each of its parts, all duties are tinged with the hue taken on exceptionally by one or the other of them. From the practical point of view this presents no inconvenience, there are even certain advantages in looking at things in this way. For, however naturally we do our duty, we may meet with resistance within ourselves; it is wise to expect it and not take for granted that it is easy to remain a good husband, a decent citizen, a conscientious worker, in a word an honest fellow. Besides, there is a considerable amount of truth in this opinion; for if it is relatively easy to keep within the social order, yet we have had to enroll in it, and this enrollment demands an effort. The natural disobedience of the child, the necessity of education, are proof of this. It is but just to credit the individual with the consent virtually given to the totality of his obligations, even if he no longer needs to take counsel with himself on each one of them. The rider need only allow himself to be borne along; still he has had to get into the saddle. So it is with the individual in relation to society. In one sense it would be untrue, and in every sense it would be dangerous, to say that duty can be done automatically. Let us then set up as a practical maxim that obedience to duty means resistance to self.

But a maxim is one thing, an explanation another. When, in order to define obligation, its essence and its origin, we lay down that obedience is primarily a struggle with self, a state of tension or contraction, we make a psychological error which has vitiated many theories of ethics. Thus artificial difficulties have arisen, problems which set philosophers at variance and which will be found to vanish when we analyze the terms in which they are expressed. Obligation is in no sense a unique fact, incommensurate with others, looming above them like a mysterious apparition. If a considerable number of philosophers, especially those who follow Kant, have taken this view, it is because they have confused the sense of obligation, a tranquil state akin to inclination, with the violent effort we now and again exert on ourselves to break down a possible obstacle to obligation.

After an attack of rheumatism, we may feel some discomfort and even pain in moving our muscles and joints. It is the general sensation of a resistance set up by all our organs together. Little by little it decreases and ends by being lost in the consciousness we have of our movements when we are well. Now, we are at liberty to fancy that it is still there in an incipient, or rather a subsiding, condition, that it is only on the lookout for a chance to become more acute; we must indeed expect attacks of rheumatism if we are rheumatic. Yet what should we say of a philosopher who saw in our habitual sensations, when moving our arms and legs, a mere diminution of pain, and who then defined our motor faculty as an effort to resist rheumatic discomfort? To begin with, he would thus be giving up the attempt to account for motor habits, since each of these implies a particular combination of movements, and can be explained only by that combination. The general faculty of walking, running, moving the body, is but an aggregation of these elementary habits, each of them finding its own explanation in the special movements it involves. But having only considered the faculty as a whole, and having then defined it as a force opposed to a resistance, it is natural enough to set up rheumatism beside it as an independent entity. It would seem as though some such error had been made by many of those who have speculated on obligation. We have any number of particular obligations, each calling for a separate explanation. It is natural, or, more strictly speaking, it is a matter of habit to obey them all. Suppose that exceptionally we deviate from one of them, there would be resistance; if we resist this resistance, a state of tension or contraction is likely to result. It is this rigidity which we objectify when we attribute so stern an aspect to duty.

It is also what the philosophers have in mind, when they see fit to resolve obligation into rational elements. In order to resist resistance, to keep to the right paths when desire, passion or interest tempt us aside, we must necessarily give ourselves reasons. Even if we have opposed the unlawful desire by another, the latter, conjured up by the will, could arise only at the call of an idea. In a word, an intelligent being generally exerts his influence on himself through the medium of intelligence. But from the fact that we get back to obligation by rational ways it does not follow that obligation was of a rational order. Let us say that a tendency, natural or acquired, is one thing; another thing the necessarily rational method which a reasonable being will use to restore to it its force and to combat what is opposing it. In the latter case the tendency which has been obscured may reappear; and then everything doubtless happens as though we had succeeded by this method in re-establishing the tendency anew. In reality we have merely swept aside something that hampered or checked it. It comes to the same thing, I grant you, in practice: explain the fact in one way or another, the fact is there, we have achieved success. And in order to succeed, it is perhaps better to imagine that things did happen in the former way. But to state that this is actually the case would be to vitiate the whole theory of obligation. Has not this been the case with most philosophers?

Let there be no misunderstanding. Even if we confine ourselves to a certain aspect of morality, as we have done up to now, we shall find many different attitudes towards duty. They line the intervening space between the extremes of two attitudes, or rather two habits: that of moving so naturally along the ways laid down by society as barely to notice them; or on the contrary hesitating and deliberating on which way to take, how far to go, the distances out and back we shall have to cover if we try several paths one after another. In the second case new problems arise with more or less frequency; and even in those instances where our duty is fully mapped out, we make all sorts of distinctions in fulfilling it. But, in the first place, the former attitude is that of the immense majority of men; it is probably general in backward communities. And, after all, however much we may reason in each particular case, formulate the maxim, enunciate the principle, deduce the consequences, if desire and passion join in the discussion, if temptation is strong, if we are on the point of falling, if suddenly we recover ourselves, what was it that pulled us up? A force asserts itself which we have called the "totality of obligation:" the concentrated extract, the quintessence of innumerable specific habits of obedience to the countless particular requirements of social life. This force is no one particular thing and, if it could speak (whereas it prefers to act), it would say: "You must because you must." Hence the work done by intelligence in weighing reasons, comparing maxims, going back to first principles, was to introduce more logical consistency into a line of conduct subordinated by its very nature to the claims of society; but this social claim was the real root of obligation. Never, in our hours of temptation, should we sacrifice to the mere need for logical consistency our interest, our passion, our vanity.

Because in a reasonable being reason does indeed intervene as a regulator to assure this consistency between obligatory rules or maxims, philosophy has been led to look upon it as a principle of obligation. We might as well believe that the flywheel drives the machinery.

Besides, the demands of a society dovetail into one another. Even the individual whose decent behaviour is the least based on reasoning and, if I may put it so, the most conventional, introduces a rational order into his conduct by the mere fact of obeying rules which are logically connected together. I freely admit that such logic has been late in taking possession of society. Logical co-ordination is essentially economy. From a whole it first roughly extracts certain principles and then excludes everything which is not in accordance with them. Nature, by contrast, is lavish. The closer a community is to nature, the greater the proportion of unaccountable and inconsistent rules it lays down. We find in primitive races many prohibitions and prescriptions explicable at most by vague associations of ideas, by superstition, by automatism. Nor are they without their uses, since the obedience of everyone to laws, even absurd ones, assures greater cohesion to the community. But in that case the usefulness of the rule accrues, by a kind of reverse action, solely from the fact of our submission to it. Prescriptions or prohibitions which are intrinsically useful are those that are explicitly designed for the preservation of well-being of society. No doubt they have gradually detached themselves from the others and survived them. Social demands have therefore been co-ordinated with each other and subordinated to principles. But no matter. Logic permeates, indeed, present-day communities, and even the man who does not reason out his conduct will live reasonably if he conforms to these principles.

But the essence of obligation is a different thing from a requirement of reason. This is all we have tried to suggest. Our description would, we think, correspond more and more to reality as one came to deal with less developed communities and more rudimentary stages of consciousness. It remains a bare outline so long as we confine ourselves to the normal conscience, such as is found to-day in the ordinary decent person. But precisely because we are in this case dealing with a strange complex of feelings, of ideas and tendencies all inter-penetrating each other, we shall avoid artificial analyses and artibtrary syntheses only if we have at hand an outline which gives the essential. Such is the outline we have attempted to trace. Conceive obligation as weighing on the will like a habit, each obligation dragging behind it the accumulated mass of the others, and utilizing thus for the pressure it is exerting the weight of the whole: here you have the totality of obligation for a simple, elementary, moral conscience. That is the essential; that is what obligation could, if necessary, be reduced to, even in those cases where it attains its highest complexity.

This shows when and in what sense (how slightly Kantian!) obligation in its elementary state takes the form of a "cate-gorical imperative." We should find it very difficult to discover examples of such an imperative in everyday life. A military order, which is a command that admits neither reason nor reply, does say in fact: "You must because you must." But, though you may give the soldier no reason, he will imagine one. If we want a pure case of the categorical imperative, we must construct one *a priori* or at least make an arbitrary abstraction of experience. So let us imagine an ant who is stirred by a gleam of reflection and thereupon judges she has been wrong to work unremittingly for others. Her inclination to laziness would indeed endure but a few moments, just as long as the ray of intelligence. In the last of these moments, when instinct regaining the mastery would drag her back by sheer force to her task, intelligence at the point of relapsing into instinct would say, as its parting word: "You must because you must." This "must because you must" would only be the momentary feeling of awareness of a tug which the ant experi-ences—the tug which the string, momentarily relaxed, exerts as it drags her back. The same command would ring in the ear of a sleepwalker on the point of waking, or even actually beginning to wake, from the dream he is enacting; if he lapsed back at once into a hypnotic state, a categorical imperative would express in words, on behalf of the reflection which had just been on the point of emerging and had instantly disappeared, the inevitableness of the relapse. In a word, an absolutely categorical imperative is instinctive or somnambulistic, enacted as such in a normal state, represented as such if reflection is roused long enough to take form, not long enough to seek for reasons. But, then, is it not evident that, in a reasonable being, an imperative will tend to become categorical in proportion as the activity brought into play, although intelligent, will tend to become instinctive? But an activity which, starting as intelligent, progresses towards an imitation of instinct is exactly what we call, in man, a habit. And the most powerful habit, the habit whose strength is made up of the accumulated force of all the elementary social habits, is necessarily the one which best imitates instinct. Is it then surprising that, in the short moment which separates obligation merely experienced as a living force, from obligation fully realized and justified by all sorts of reasons, obligation should indeed take the form of the categorical imperative: "You must because you must?"

Let us consider two divergent lines of evolution with societies at the extremities of each. The type of society which will appear the more natural will obviously be the instinctive type; the link that unites the bees of a hive resembles far more the link which holds together the cells of an organism, co-ordinate and subordinate to one another. Let us suppose for an instant that nature has intended to produce, at the extremity of the second line, societies where a certain latitude was left to individual choice: she would have arranged that intelligence should achieve here results comparable, as regards their regularity, to those of instinct in the other; she would have had recourse to habit. Each of these habits, which may be called "moral," would be incidental. But the aggregate of them, I mean the habit of contracting these habits, being at the very basis of societies and a necessary condition of their existence, would have a force comparable to that of instinct in respect to both intensity and regularity. This is exactly what we have called the "totality of obligation." This, be it said, will apply only to human societies at the moment of emerging from the hands of nature. It will apply to primitive and to elementary societies.

But, however much human society may progress, grow complicated and spiritualized, the original design, expressing the purpose of nature, will remain.

Now this is exactly what has happened. Without going deeply into a matter we have dealt with elsewhere, let us simply say that intelligence and instinct are forms of consciousness which must have interpenetrated each other in their rudimentary state and become dissociated as they grew. This development occurred on the two main lines of evolution of animal life, with the Arthropods and the Vertebrates. At the end of the former we have the instinct of insects, more especially the Hymenoptera; at the end of the second, human intelligence. Instinct and intelligence have each as their essential object the utilization of implements: in the first case, organs supplied by nature and hence immutable; in the second, invented tools, and therefore varied and unforeseen. The implement is, moreover, designed for a certain type of work, and this work is all the more efficient the more it is specialized, the more it is divided up between diversely qualified workers who mutually supplement one another. Social life is thus immanent, like a vague ideal, in instinct as well as in intelligence; this ideal finds its most complete expression in the hive or the anthill on the one hand, in human societies on the other. Whether human or animal, a society is an organization; it implies a co-ordination and generally also a subordination of elements; it therefore exhibits, whether merely embodied in life or, in addition, specially formulated, a collection of rules and laws. But in a hive or an anthill the individual is riveted to his task by his structure, and the organization is relatively invariable, whereas the human community is variable in form, open to every kind of progress. The result is that in the former each rule is laid down by nature and is necessary; whereas in the latter only one thing is natural, the necessity of a rule. Thus the more, in human society, we delve down to the root of the various obligations to reach obligation in general, the more obligation will tend to become necessity, the nearer it will draw, in its peremptory aspect, to instinct. And yet we should make a great mistake if we tried to ascribe any particular obligation, whatever it might be, to instinct. What we must perpetually recall is that, no one obligation being instinctive, obligation as a whole *would have been* instinct if human societies were not, so to speak, ballasted with variability and intelligence. It is a virtual instinct, like that which lies behind the habit of speech. The morality of a human society may indeed be comparable to its language. If ants exchange signs, which seems probable, those signs are provided by the very instinct that makes the ants communicate with one another. On the contrary, our languages are the product of custom. Nothing in the vocabulary, or even in the syntax, comes from nature. But speech is natural, and unvarying signs, natural in origin, which are presumably used in a community of insects, exhibit what our language would have been, if nature in bestowing on us the faculty of speech had not added the function which, since it makes and uses tools, is inventive and called intelligence. We must perpetually recur to what obligation *would have been* if human society had been instinctive instead of intelligent. This will not explain any particular obligation; we should even give of obligation in general an idea which would be false, if we went no further; and yet we must think of this instinctive society as the counterpart of intelligent society, if we are not to start without any clue in quest of the foundations of morality.

From this point of view obligation loses its specific character. It ranks among the most general phenomena of life. When the elements which go to make up an organism submit to a rigid discipline, can we say that they feel themselves liable to obligation and that they are obeying a social instinct? Obviously not; but whereas such an organism is barely a community, the hive and the anthill are actual organisms, the elements of which are united by invisible ties, and the social instinct of an ant—I mean the force by virtue of which the worker, for example, performs the task to which she is predestined by her structure—cannot differ radically from the cause, whatever it be, by virtue of which every tissue, every cell of a living body, toils for the greatest good of the whole. Indeed it is, strictly speaking, no more a matter of obligation in the one case than in the other, but rather of necessity. It is just this necessity that we perceive, not actual but virtual, at the foundations of moral obligation, as through a more or less transparent veil. A human being feels an obligation only if he is free, and each obligation, considered separately, implies liberty. But it is necessary that there should be obligations; and the deeper we go, away from those particular obligations which are at the top, towards obligation in general, or, as we have said, towards obligation as a whole, which is at the bottom, the more obligation appears as the very form assumed by necessity in the realm of life, when it demands, for the accomplishment of certain ends, intelligence, choice, and therefore liberty.

Felix Bernstein

Professor of Biometrics, New York University

THE BALANCE OF PROGRESS
OF FREEDOM IN HISTORY

"IT has always been a grave question," says Abraham Lincoln, "whether any government not too strong for the liberties of its people, will be strong enough to maintain its existence in grave emergencies." This remark goes to the root of one of the most important problems of human history. There is a balance between cultural freedom and freedom in the political and economic spheres. There is a balance between the independence of the individual and the power of the State. To strike the balance which secures sufficient stability without checking progress in freedom has been the greatest problem of statesmanship from the dawn of history to the present day.

There is a great factor to be considered in the obvious slowing up of the progress of mankind. There are conditioned reflexes which not only govern the psychology of the individual but also that of the social group at large. Not only the individual habits are built upon them, but also the customs and *mores* which rule the habits of group life. If progress routs out one evil habit, it throws into jeopardy at least ten indifferent and perhaps a certain number of good ones. It is due to our psychological nature that we must act by the use of conditioned reflexes, partly in the unconscious sphere, and only to a very small extent through conscious choice under the rule of reason.

Any progress really made by mankind cannot endure unless

43

it becomes thoroughly anchored in the existing culture so that its processes can be performed largely through unconscious conditioned reflexes by the great mass of the people. It is for this reason that much progress attempted and successful for a short span of time, but not sufficiently anchored in the minds of the people, has been subsequently lost. And at any time that progress has been lost, an older but more stable equilibrium has reappeared. The fate of all religious reformers who tried to erect a totalitarian religious state lies buried beneath this simple truth. But also the fate of the French Revolution, as a political, not a spiritual, movement, can be described in these terms.

What did liberty, equality, fraternity mean to the degraded impoverished populace of Paris after one century of oppression? Adapted to a slave existence they lost, together with the oppressive regulations, the conditioned reflexes with which the normal functioning of their morality was bound up. The effect could only be a release of the unbridled instincts of animal life, out of which no higher organized social life could be formed. The historical results are well known. On the contrary, the frontiersman of the American Commonwealth at the same period in history already enjoyed the benefits of unregimented liberty, of personal equality, or co-operative fraternity. The American Revolution only confirmed his way of life and sanctioned and hallowed his practical convictions. It is no wonder that the Declaration of Independence and the Bill of Rights completely failed to unleash such excesses as France exhibited to a stunned world.

Nevertheless, the French Revolution did not end in complete retrogression. In the July Revolution of 1830 the democratic France was born. But this revolution aimed at much less than the great revolution of 1789. It meant the ideological confirmation of the way of life of the French *bourgeoisie*, as it had developed in the period from 1789 to 1830, and it brought the ethical principles of cultural and political freedom of that period to domination.

The great French Revolution meant the end of a period of a disproportionate civilization. Sorel, influenced by Taine's aesthetic resentments, tried to prove that the revolution could have been halted if only the leading classes would have resorted to force. This thesis, taken up by Pareton, has had the unfortunate consequence of giving rise to the fascist creed and its glorification of force. Let us therefore examine the case fairly.

Under Louis XIV the feudal system of medieval France had been destroyed by the King, who tried to centralize all power by making the court the only place of life for the ruling class. Cultures of this kind make prestige the dominating power of life, prestige in this case to be won only under the shining rays of the central royal sun. We know from the observation of the disproportionate culture of the North-west Indians to-day, in their potlatch game, whose essence is not to have but to squander, to what consequences such a distorted culture leads. The dominating psychological tendency in time swallows up all others. La Bruyère in his *Caractères* has sketched the most lively picture of the psychological effects of such a situation. At that time the unavoidable reaction ensued not in France, but in the rest of Europe under the leadership of William of Orange. While in France the young nobility was completely absorbed in playing the game of prestige—very much like the Nazi Fuehrer—William of Orange and the Burgomaster of The Hague formed for the defence of independence and Protestant cultural freedom the formidable League which broke the power of Louis XIV in the War of the Spanish Succession.

That war lasted for approximately eleven years, and for nearly a century longer the broken and defeated system dragged on its cadaver-like existence. Why did the aristocrats of 1789 not use force against the revolution—as Sorel and Pareton believe they could have done? Simply because a system based on prestige cannot last, if it has lost that prestige. The prestige was based on military and kingly glory. It had been challenged by a modest king and a kingly burgher of a small Protestant country which had won its freedom from the domination of the Spanish autocrat. And again the small country of freedom had won against overwhelming odds. This was the verdict against that French culture of prestige, and late but inevitably that culture died under the blow. This is the answer to the question why the French aristocrats did not fight. They could have fought only for a restoration of the kingdom of Louis XIV, for a renewal of its prestige, for a destruction of the victorious civil liberty in Holland, and in the whole Protestant world. Since such restoration of prestige, like that of the Sun King, was impossible, they could not fight. What they could hope for at best was what Mirabeau tried: to cross the bridge to a democratic world before it was too late. It is correct to say that if Mirabeau had not died, this possibility might have become a reality, and the French Revolution might have taken a constructive turn, bringing to France that freedom which Holland owed to its decisive victory over the French system nearly a century before.

Let us view another example of our thesis, namely, that progress in freedom not sufficiently anchored in the culture of the people must fail. Prussia, the Prussia of Frederick the Great, could continue the feudal system until the World War because it had under Frederick's father blended carefully the centralizing system of Louis XIV with the cultural liberty of Holland. This blending of traditions made possible the complete separation of justice from executive power under the great King. In Prussia one could sue the sovereign without his consent, a right not conceded to the American citizen by the Constitution, and the miller of Sans Souci in doing so saved his mill from condemnation by the King himself.

Prussia in this blending of power with right could develop during the nineteenth century, with some oscillations, a system of cultural progress in which academic freedom was paramount. Through the defeat of the World War, however, the element of historic prestige in this blended culture was wiped out. Certainly the democratic Republic achieved progress in freedom. However, the republic then erected through defeat, in contrast to the republics in Switzerland and in the United States founded on victory, lacked a necessary element of prestige from its very beginning. It entirely lacked emotional appeal. A monarchical reaction, if a suitable pretender had existed, might have meant a milder retrogression, bringing back the stimuli which were lacking in every field, because of the disappearance of a power of prestige such as the former monarchy had represented.

There came instead an attempt, grown out of the World War and first seen in Italy, to create a system of democratized prestige, namely, the Nazi system in which the prestige was flowing from one central source in an unheard of ramified system of smaller and smaller channels. The destruction of democratic freedom, therefore, was due to the fact that it did not fill the void left by the fall of monarchy. This lesson must be drawn: that progress in human freedom cannot be made, that restraints to political or economic or cultural freedom cannot be removed, if these restraints satisfy cultural and political needs which are imperative, and contribute to the stability of society.

Only by winning a great prestige, for instance, by establishing a union of Germany with Austria, which Chancellor Bruening attempted, could the freedom of the German Republic have been saved and the progress in freedom have been preserved. And what is true for progress in political freedom is not less true for economic freedom, and also to a certain extent, for cultural freedom. As soon as too many restraints are removed at the same time, the cycles of conditioned reflexes break down in an unexpected manner and the gain in freedom is not preserved. The sum of progress in freedom at any time in history is limited by the very psychological nature of Man.

It was advantageous for the building of the system of political freedom in the United States that the economic and cultural field at the time of its growth was relatively problemless. This, of course, only means that the restraints present were little felt. Puritanism was still so powerful that men did not yearn for a life which was abundant in the European way. Not all taboos were respected by all at all times, but this was a private, not a public problem. Hence the possibility arose of removing further and further the restraints of political freedom. It was characteristic that the problem of slavery, though well before the minds of the fathers of the Constitution, was not touched at the time of its creation.

Let us still consider a final example, where the over-emphasis

on cultural freedom destroyed the freedom in the economic and
the political sphere: the example of the Greeks in the classic
age and in Byzantium. The Greeks had by indulging in personal cultural refinement prematurely weakened their will to
defend their independence. The result of this pitiful development was the educated Greek slave of the rough but brave
Roman master, and in the Orient the unhappy Byzantine serf
of the barbaric system of the Turks. To blame some unique
characteristic of the Greeks for this is entirely misleading. As
long as they were independent, the Greeks were in no way of a
different character from other independent people. But the
rapid emancipation of the mind as visible in character destroys
the stability of character on which independence rests. And
with the loss of independence the ethical character of Greek
culture completely disintegrated.

From these observations the consequence can be drawn that
the Marxian contention that political freedom without economic
freedom is worthless is incorrect. We see, in fact, that the practical attempt to achieve the Marxian economic freedom has
first destroyed cultural freedom and has not produced political
freedom. Grave doubts must prevail whether they will be
regained in any foreseeable future. Perhaps a further example,
analogous to those we have mentioned, will be developed illus-
trating that any disproportionate progress in one direction will
cause a complete loss of liberty and independence in another.
The safer way for progress in freedom is the way of the gradual
removal of barriers and restraints one after another with the
full conservation of all gains already made. In the United
States political freedom does not need further improvement at
this time, in our opinion, but economic freedom and cultural
freedom call for progress. The unequal distribution of opportunity for economic rise is probably the very reason for the
present stagnation, and it is in this field that greater freedom
must be achieved in the near future.

The Historic Position of the Problem of Freedom

We are at the end of this discussion, and in conclusion we
may call attention to the fact that no matter how successfully

the empirical science of the nineteenth century has increased positive knowledge, the synthesis leads back to the speculative thought of the eighteenth. Such romantic ideas as those of Rousseau, that man must only be freed from the shackles of culture to be perfect, find no justification in our present-day knowledge. We know that man freed from some shackles will produce new ones for himself. Human nature has no natural equilibrium which is strong enough to support itself. Reason and morals are necessary to support social equilibrium and to prevent society from becoming a disproportionate structure with eventually Hippocratic traits.

Cultural anthropology has shown that many a culture which we believed primitive is full of exaggerated social growth and has become self-blocked against progress. But in one respect, the standpoint of the eighteenth century was correct, the potentiality for progress in freedom is everywhere present in human nature. With a slight modification in the formulas of the thinkers of that period who used the language of Deism, we can establish the principles of freedom on nearly the same basis. The fundamental difference consists only in the position of evolution. But it is noteworthy that the German thinker, G. E. Lessing, aimed at something quite comparable when he tried to synthesize the liberal principles of the century by the idea of a cosmic education of mankind. Say evolution instead of education, and the difference in standpoint becomes infinitesimal.

Franz Boas

Professor Emeritus of Anthropology, Columbia University

LIBERTY AMONG PRIMITIVE PEOPLE

MANY years ago, I lived alone with a tribe of Eskimos. I travelled about, generally accompanied by a family with whom I had made friends, a man and his wife. Sometimes I travelled alone for days on a dog sledge. Those were days of the most joyful feeling of freedom, of self-reliance: ready to meet the dangers of the ice, sea, and wild animals; on the alert to meet and overcome difficulties; no human being there to hinder or help. Still, there were restraints that in the exuberance of youth I did not feel. Nature interposed insurmountable obstacles to my plans. Food had to be provided for myself and for the dogs. A dread disease had reduced the number of available dogs, which hindered me from going where I wished. More than this, the very task which took me to the Arctic, although freely chosen, was imposed upon me by the cultural pattern in which I had grown up. My Eskimo friends wondered why I should choose to climb mountains where there was no game, why I should gather up useless plants and stones, and do other things that have no sensible use in their lives. Maybe they thought that somebody, or some strange compelling habit, made me do things that could be understood only as due to compulsion, not to free choice.

My Eskimo friends felt absolutely free. There was no one to command them, no one to tell them what to do and what not to do. They settled and hunted wherever they chose. The only restraints felt by them were those imposed by the forces of nature; but my observation of their habits showed me how subject they were to the rigorous demands of custom. They were not allowed free choice of their food; the hunter had to observe the strictest regulations to secure success; sickness and death in a family disturbed the regular life of the whole community in which it occurred; the breach of customary observances by a single individual was believed to affect the life of everyone who came into contact with the transgressor; in short, I found their freedom restricted at every step. Still, their customs were to them so natural, so self-evident, and the only possible way of living known to them, that they were not felt as a restraint of freedom.

The life of the Eskimo as seen from my point of view, as well as my life seen from the Eskimo point of view, was not free, for objective observation from the point of view of one culture shows the restraints imposed by life in another type of culture. At the same time, the individual who is thoroughly in harmony with the culture in which he lives does not feel these restraints and will feel free.

Freedom is a concept that has meaning only in a subjective sense. A person who is in complete harmony with his culture feels free. He accepts voluntarily the demands made upon him. He does not feel them as imposed upon him. They are his natural reactions to the events of daily life. Obedience to a ruler, law, or custom is not exacted but rendered freely.

For this reason, the concept of freedom can develop only in those cases where there are conflicts between the individual and the culture in which he lives. The more uniform the culture, that is, the more intensely all the individuals of a community are subject to the same customs, the stronger will be the feeling of lack of restraint.

Nevertheless, one form of subjection may be felt in a culturally uniform society: the impotence of man against fate, against fate as determined by the forces of nature, by supernatural powers, or by predestination.

We may call those cultures primitive in which little differentiation between classes has developed. Even in those groups in which the mode of life of everyone is practically the same, where everyone has to obtain sustenance in the same manner by his own efforts, where no economic classes exist, except those developed by different degrees of ability to provide for one's needs, there are differences according to sex and age, but these are so deeply embodied in the cultural pattern that in the course of everyday life they are seldom felt as restrictions of freedom. Although in most cultures of this type children are generally treated with great indulgence, there will always be cases in which they are disciplined and compelled to obey until in the course of their individual development they become completely assimilated to the culture of the tribe.

Still, in a loosely organized society like the one just described, individual tyrants may occur, individuals of unusual strength, skill, and will-power who interfere with the lives of their fellow-tribesmen. Such are the "strong men" of the Chukchee and Eskimo who tyrannize a village until the people rise against them, do away with them, and free themselves of the fear of their torturers.

More complex societies embrace classes with different privileges and functions, and different standards of behaviour. The relations between the classes may be so institutionalized that the restraints imposed upon each of them are accepted as a "natural" arrangement. When the privileged group is felt as a valuable asset for the whole community the lower class may be eager to protect and to maintain its privileges, in a way quite similar to conditions in feudal times, or in modern monarchies. An example of this kind occurs among certain Indians of British Columbia. Although the people have to pay tribute to the chief, the possession of a respected chief's family is valued so highly that the people rise against a chief who weakens his own family by causing the death of his successor.

The consciousness of restraint, and hence the concept of freedom, cannot arise where there is no conflict between the wishes of the individual and his freedom of action. He must be conscious of a freedom of choice. As long as he feels that there is no possible mode of behaviour except that prescribed by social custom which keeps his activities in standard bounds, there can be no concept of freedom.

Interference with the freedom of action or the personal comfort of an individual by fellow-tribesmen may occur even in the simplest societies. Such interference is generally based on personal conflicts. Two individuals may strive for possession of the same object. If the customs of the community permit, the conflict may be decided by combat between the antagonists and may also involve their friends. Unfriendly gossip may create a condition against which the individual cannot successfully contend and which limits his freedom of action within the social group. In some forms of culture, opportunity is given to him to free himself, at least partly, by a show of valour or power which silences the gossip for a while, in others he is entirely at the mercy of his personal enemies without any means of redress. Such conflicts between individuals, or between individuals and society as a whole, or between groups unfriendly to each other, may encroach seriously upon the freedom of the individual.

Unless personal conflicts are regulated in some way by custom, they are liable to disrupt society. In many primitive societies customary law, which restrains excesses of hostility between individuals, holds these disruptive forces in check. In more complex societies law regulates the rights of individuals and checks license.

The problem of freedom is different when the wishes of an individual go counter to the customary behaviour of the community, for instance, when a couple desire to marry against the strict rule of choice of mates. In such a case it is not only the disapproval of the community, or the forcible method by which such a marriage is prevented, that affects those concerned, but even more the restraint of their freedom of choice, enforced by a custom rejected by them.

Only when this revolt against custom occurs can a feeling for the meaning of intellectual freedom develop. In primitive society this conflict is rare. Passionate love between man and woman who belong to groups forbidden to intermarry is about as rare as in our society passionate love between brother and sister, father and daughter, or mother and son. Obviously the traditional *mores* exert a strong restraining influence upon the wishes of the individual.

It is, however, certain that intellectual freedom is not entirely absent even in societies in which rigid dogmatic belief pervades the whole life. Among tribes in which the life-histories of individuals are known in some detail, we find disbelievers who disregard sacred teachings and who come into conflict with their fellow-tribesmen. More frequently we find those given to speculation who develop or reform the tribal dogma. It would be difficult to understand the complex ceremonial life, and the systematic mythology of many peoples, if we did not assume that priests or other thinkers have shaped a heterogeneous mass of ceremonial actions, myths, and religious teachings into a more or less consistent whole. A communal growth of such phenomena without individual initiative is unthinkable. More than this, primitive cultures, the history of which we do not know, appear to us as stable, frozen; but this impression is erroneous. All cultures are in a state of flux, slow among primitive groups, rapid when differentiation reaches a higher degree. Whatever the stimulus may be that brings about changes, it can become manifest only through the thoughts and actions of individuals whose concepts deviate from the cultural norm of their time. In this sense they are free, so far as they modify the existing forms. When no outer forces break the continuity of tribal life, the changes are generally slight. Not so when the life of the people undergoes violent changes. This may be observed most readily in the contact between primitive cultures and European civilization, when inter-tribal warfare is suppressed, new products of our industry are imported, and new standards of life and thought are observed. Under these conditions we see new ideas develop that are neither the old nor the new, but a result of the interaction of both.

Similar observations may be made in the study of art. In a stable society the artist is bound to a traditional style, not absolutely, as is proved by the development of local styles in each art area and wherever we can trace historical changes in style. With the introduction of new art forms and new techniques, radical changes may develop which are due to the free inventive genius of gifted individuals.

With all this, the *concept* of freedom is not found in primitive society. The individual, on account of the lack of knowledge of diverse forms of thought and action, cannot form by himself the concept of something new, not intimately connected with the range of his experience, and, therefore, the possibility of a free choice does not exist. We believe that we have such freedom and are not aware of our own limitations founded on our participation in our culture, which does not permit us to feel its limitations. In this sense we may say that absolute freedom does not exist. We are free in so far as the limitations of our culture do not oppress us; we are unfree when we become conscious of these limitations and are no longer willing to submit to them. This is true, no matter whether the constraint put upon us is due to our subjection to individuals or to the manifold restraints that law and custom impress upon us.

Benedetto Croce

Senator of the Kingdom of Italy; Minister of Public Instruction

THE ROOTS OF LIBERTY[1]

EVERYBODY can see, everybody admits, that in the period since the beginning of the Great War the love of freedom has sensibly weakened throughout the world, while the idea of freedom has progressively lost its clarity. Liberal systems that were once regarded as solidly established have collapsed in many countries, and everywhere and in general liberal convictions have been shaken, liberal enthusiasms have cooled, people have grown lukewarm toward an ideal of freedom that has ceased to fill hearts, inspire conduct, and give direction to outlooks on the future.

It should nevertheless be apparent to everybody that this so-called decadence of the liberal idea, or, as others say, this crisis that at present confronts it, is a strange sort of decadence, a strange sort of crisis, in that it is illumined by no flash of a new ideal that is to subsume, replace, outmode the old, in that no new order is put forward to replace the order that is being attacked or overthrown. The liberal ideal is a moral ideal, expressing an aspiration toward a better humanity and a higher civilization. The new ideal that is to triumph should, therefore, present itself with promise of a newer, richer, deeper humanity and civilization.

Now the one alternative to freedom that is being practically suggested in our day cannot be regarded as offering any such

---

[1] Translated from the Italian by Arthur Livingston, Professor of Romance Languages, Columbia University.

promise. It is the alternative of violence, and violence, in whatever name it be exercised, whether of race, of country or proletariat, can have no status as morality. Violence contains within itself none of those energies that enhance civilized human living. It is capable at best of expanding in a very problematical future the physical living of a few individuals, while narrowing the physical living of all others. Violence may punch to the floor and silence a person, for instance, who is trying to solve a problem in mathematics, but no one will claim that the silence thus brutally obtained will provide the solution for the mathematical problem. All we shall have will be a man on the floor and a problem still pending—it will pend till some mathematician is allowed to speak and solve it.

Hence the barrenness in terms of thought, science, art, civic virtues, human relations, that systems based on violence—or on what amounts to the same thing, on authority—commonly show. Everything sound and productive that still survives, or flourishes in them in the directions mentioned, survives and flourishes either through the survival of free minds or through the persistence of acquired habits. But these latter gradually weaken for lack of sustenance and replenishment and through the passing of the human beings who possess them. Meanwhile none of the new formulas or ideals is allowed to defend itself in orderly discussion, to justify itself by critically tested arguments, by interpretations of history, in a word by perspicacious, cautious, sober research. It is forced to drone its arid mechanical assertions over and over again, without variations, without proofs, without elaborations, deriving such animation as it can from an accompaniment of threats. There is talking in plenty, there is much brandishing of clubs and swords; but while scorn and ridicule are heaped upon it, the ideal of freedom stands substantially intact and intangible, since it can be overthrown and replaced only by a better and sounder ideal—and such an ideal cannot even be conceived.

Our experience of the present world, therefore, can lead only to one conclusion: that the so-called crisis of liberalism is not the crisis of any particular ideal—as, for instance, of the ancient *polis* as compared with imperial forms of government, or of feudalism as compared with absolute monarchy, or of absolute as compared with constitutional monarchy, and so on; but a crisis of the ideal itself. It is a bewilderment, a degeneration, a corruption, a perversion, of the moral sense, of that moral enthusiasm which ennobles the individual life and glorifies the history of humanity, marking the latter off into its great periods.

How this degeneration has come about is made clear enough by history, and the history more particularly of the period fol-lowing 1870, when the policies, the pronouncements, and the whole spirit of Bismarck combined with the theories and the influence of Marxian socialism to discredit the ideal of freedom, and the lives of the peoples turned in predominantly economic and material directions, though liberal constitutions were kept and in fact proved very serviceable to the new materialism.

This historical development, which has not yet ended and in fact is probably in its most acute stage, I have examined else-where, and from the point of view just mentioned; but if I were to summarize its significance in a single sentence I might say that it lies in the anguish and the travail incident to the growth of a new religious faith, and to the quest for such a faith on the part of humanity or at least on the part of the civilized peoples. The old religions have worn out before the religion of freedom has spread widely enough abroad and taken a sufficiently firm hold. Not only has the religion of freedom failed to translate itself into conviction and accepted opinion in the masses—clothing itself meantime in more or less of a myth, as inevitably happens. Even among the educated the religion of freedom has not attained such a solid theoretical elaboration as to render it impregnable to attacks frontal or treacherous.

But we should not lose heart on that account, we should not give way to pessimism—pessimism is by definition incoherent and profitless. We have no reason despondently to resign our-selves to a new aeon-long era of barbarism such as a number of apocalyptic writers of our day foresee and foretell—such fancies, like all structures of the imagination, have their empty possibility, they have no certainty whatever.

We should not lose heart in the first place because it is the lot and the duty of man to work on and fight on. But then again human society has lived through other periods when moral sentiments have waned and materialisms have waxed triumphant, and in every such case it has recovered through a spontaneous rekindling of enthusiasm and idealism, through an ever re-blossoming spiritual exuberance, through the words and the examples of apostles aflame with the religious spirit who sooner or later have recaptured the ears of men. As regards our scholars and thinkers of the present time, it is their task to keep the concept of freedom precise and clear, to broaden it and work out its philosophical foundations. That is the contribution that may properly be required of us in the many-sided struggle that is laid upon us to resurrect the ideal and restore life under freedom.

There are those who smile at this sort of contribution and doubt its necessity and its utility. The tree of theory, we are told in the words of the poet, is gray, while the tree of life is green. We are told that ideas and arguments do not create the passion or the flaming resolve that alone counts in practice. But the notion that thought and action are separate things, that they are indifferent to each other and without influence upon each other, is a hasty judgment based upon superficial observation. In the living and concrete spiritual act the two terms stand perfectly united. The act of thought is at the same time an act of willing, since it derives from nothing less than a moral urge, from the torment, the pain, the necessity, of removing an impediment to the flow of life; and it eventuates in nothing else than a new disposition of will, a new attitude and demeanour, a new manner of acting in the practical field. A thinker who does not suffer his problem, who does not live his thought, is not a thinker; he is a mere elocutionist, repeating thoughts that have been thought by others. Rarely enough, to be sure, has the thinker also been the statesman, the warrior, or the leader of parties or peoples; but that fact depends on the specification of human activities, each of which, for that matter, evolves in its particular sphere but with an outlook upon life as a whole. Within its sphere, the labour of speculation does not stand cut off from life; rather it gathers there the energy that it requires for functioning in the world at large; and it so functions not merely by communicating the logical processes involved in it to those who accept it, rethink it in compendious form, and make it their own, but also, and very particularly, through the fact that in many people conclusions that are products of the thinker's labour are transmuted into axioms, commonplaces, proverbs and, stripped of the proofs that justify them, become articles of faith and trusted guides of conduct.

So the educated and the so-called ruling classes are formed. Without such classes no human society has ever been able to endure, and their strength is the strength of society as a whole. There is, to be sure, a class now large, now very large, that lives on from day to day indifferent to moral questions and to problems of public life, devoting neither thought nor attention to them and speaking, when it speaks, only to voice its satisfactions or dissatisfactions in respect of its needs and comforts. Such are the so-called "masses," to whom a demagogic romanticism ascribes mysterious and mystical virtues and pays a worship corresponding. The potency of ideas being at its minimum among the uneducated, it is certainly not to be expected that the truths that are discovered by thinkers, and become part of the common patrimony of civilization, should be easily carried down to the masses. But we must nevertheless do our best to educate them, and enable them on the one hand to replenish the ruling classes with fresh forces, new workers, new members; and on the other to bring themselves progressively into harmonious accord with the educated. Whenever and wherever this is not possible the masses must be handled with the political wisdom that the special case requires, in order to prevent them from ruining the conquests that society has made —in other words, from ruining civilization. Civilization has been ruined a number of times in the course of history, but always, sooner or later, now with more, now with less difficulty, the dismantled dykes have been repaired and the stream has resumed its regular flow.

For a full and clear discussion of the philosophical theory of freedom, three aspects, or levels, had better be kept distinct.

Under the first aspect, freedom may be regarded as the force that creates history—indeed this is so truly its real and proper function that one might say, in a sense somewhat different from the Hegelian, that history is the history of freedom. In fact, everything the human being does or creates is done or created freely—actions, political institutions, religious conceptions, scientific theories, the productions of poetry and art, technical inventions, instruments for increasing wealth and power. Illiberal systems, as just indicated, are barren. Their counterfeit achievements have the traits of the so-called imitations, or artificial reworkings, of poetry and art, which retrace through more or less grotesque or repulsive recombinations, poems or paintings that already exist, and which, devoid as they are of anything truly new or original and therefore devoid of aesthetic reality, are thrust aside and ignored by the critic or the historian. So in civic history all those things that are done under constraint, even though they may help to some extent to meet individual needs of patronage, livelihood, or comfort, belong to physiological living and not to the moral or civic living which they fraudulently ape. Periods of suppressed or oppressed liberty contribute to the general productivity of history only in so far as the suppression or oppression cannot be and never is absolute and complete, since the very violence of the oppression provokes multifarious reactions in an opposite direction. On the one hand, therefore, we often see oppressors inclined to favour or promote labours of freedom, not because they like the freedom— indeed the reverse—but because they come to see that for the particular social or political systems that they have instituted, whatever these may be, they need certain services and certain kinds of support. They cannot, for instance, dispense with doctors, engineers, scientists, or writers; and, soon discovering that such experts cannot be produced by mechanical processes, they find themselves obliged to leave them more or less free in their training and in the prosecution of their work. On the other hand we always observe efforts and activities on the part of an opposition, now overt and talkative, now secret and silent, but which are never lacking and which to some extent fertilize the barren present and attenuate its despair by planting seeds for a more or less immanent future. If human affairs did not develop in this manner, ages of oppression would be altogether sterile—they would be periods of death and not of life, or at least of no civilized living—they would represent vacuums in the historical process. Such a thing is unthinkable and that it does not take place is evidenced by the little or much that ages, which for one reason or another are considered ages of oppression, have nevertheless produced, and even more emphatically by the joyous resilience which spreads abroad in the succeeding ages, which must therefore have been prepared for by the earlier and so after a fashion have existed in them.

The historian looks at things and judges them otherwise than people who are in the thick of the fight and feel all its passions, whether these be the oppressors who gloatingly imagine they have stamped out liberty, or the oppressed who mourn liberty as dead and would fain resurrect her. The historian knows that the issue in the struggle is never whether freedom shall live or die—freedom, after all, being naught else but humanity, a humanity that is at war with itself. He knows that the question always is of a more or a less, of a more rapid rhythm or a slower rhythm, and that the contrasting beliefs just mentioned are illusions, mistaken impressions, reflecting the share which the opponents of freedom and the lovers of freedom severally have in the struggle.

Under its second aspect, on its second level, freedom is thought of not as the force that creates history but as a practical ideal which aims to create the greatest possible freedom in human society, and therefore to overthrow tyrannies and oppressors and establish institutions, laws, ethical systems, that will successfully uphold it. If one plumbs this ideal to the bottom one finds it in no sense different or distinguishable from conscience and moral behaviour, and one observes that the will to freedom, as conscience expresses the sum and the synthesis of all the moral virtues and of all the definitions which have been given of ethics. However variously these may describe the moral ideal—placing it now in respect for one's neighbour, now in the general welfare, now in an enhancement of the spiritual life, now in a striving for a better and better world, and so on— they all agree on one thing: on a resolve that freedom shall triumph over the obstacles that rise in its path and over the aversions that beset it, and give full expression to its life-creating power. When we go to the rescue of a person who is ill and quiet or lessen his pain, we are striving, in effect, to restore a source of activity, in other words a source of freedom, to society. When we educate a child, we aim to make of him a person able to go his own way as a free, autonomous being. When we defend the just against the unjust, the true against the false, we do so because the unjust and the false represent servitude to passion and to mental inertia, whereas the true and the just are acts of freedom.

Altogether inappropriate, therefore, is the fear—nay the terror—that some people manifest when it is proposed to foster or recognize the full and unlimited freedom of the human being. Their thoughts turn at once to the abuses that the wicked, the criminal, the insane, the young and inexperienced, may make of unlimited freedom—as though to control or to help those sorts of people there were no moral judgments and condemnations on the part of society, no penal sanctions, sanatoria, asylums, schools, and the like, on the part of the State. They ignore, or pretend to ignore, the fact that when we speak of the need of freedom we are thinking strictly and exclusively of ways of facilitating the activities of people who are neither wicked nor criminal nor insane nor inexperienced and immature, and not of ways of facilitating the excesses of people who are subject, in one way or another, to bestial unrestraint, madness, childishness, ignorance, or the like. It should be clear that only with the former in mind do we assert that all obstacles that are set in the way of free activity are harmful to human society.

Since, as we have seen, the liberal ideal is one and the same with conscience, that ideal in one form or another, and to a greater or lesser degree, exerts its influence in all ages and cannot therefore be regarded as a historical phenomenon that appears at a certain moment, endures for a certain length of time and then, like all historical phenomena, wanes and disappears. It is of course true that, as we commonly say, the liberal ideal is a product of modern times, that it had its beginnings in the seventeenth century and reached its full blossoming in the first half of the nineteenth. In strict exactness, however, we could not say that the sense of freedom or the ideal of liberty originated and developed during that period or any other particular period. What we should say is that during that period people became strongly and growingly conscious of the essential character of freedom and of its status as a supreme principle. That perception had not been so easy in earlier periods, because of the prevalence of transcendental conceptions, and the strings of commandments and prohibitions ordained on high which went with transcendental systems and were upheld against dissenters by punishments and persecutions, now of Protestants by Catholics, now of Catholics by Protestants, and so on.

But with the end of the religious wars and the advent of religious tolerance, people began to see the importance of not suppressing unpopular ideas but of meeting them with opposite ideas. This liberty gradually brought all other liberties in its train, till the principle that underlay and upheld them all was finally perceived in its completeness. Thus a higher, more comprehensive ideal made its way to triumph, breaking through beliefs in the transcendental, subsuming, replacing them, warming, enlightening, re-shaping the soul of the modern man, which is a very different soul from the soul of the medieval or ancient man.

This was a movement of moral liberation and of moral ascension. To imagine, after the fashion of the economic-interpretationists and their imitators, that it can be explained by the simultaneous rise of an economic social class, the *bourgeoisie*, and the rise of capitalism, industry, and free commercial competition, in other words to regard it as an economic phenomenon, is to misunderstand it altogether. Nor, really, are we any better served by attempts, such as have been made, to explain it as a strictly psychological derivation from a Calvinistic concept of vocation or mission.

This deliberate, self-conscious aspiration for freedom as a supreme and fundamental good, exerted a tremendous influence upon the generations of men who witnessed and provoked 1830, 1848, and 1860. In those days, and indeed long afterwards, it seemed to be a permanent acquisition of the human spirit, an abiding conquest of civilization. Now, as we have seen, it is the sentiment that has faltered and weakened to a greater or lesser extent in all parts of the present world.

Under a third aspect, on a third level, one may think of freedom in terms of the process by which the ideal of freedom and the aspiration to freedom have been worked into a philosophical concept, and brought under a general conception of reality that defines and justifies them; and here we perceive the intimate connections that subsist between the history of the theory of freedom and the history of philosophy which has so strongly influenced, as it is still influencing, the former.

During the long period when metaphysical, transcendental philosophies prevailed in Europe, the concept of freedom as the law of life and history did not find the place that rightfully belonged to it, and it experienced no end of difficulty and labour in making its way forward. Even when the sense of freedom was very keen it was a matter of feeling and conduct rather than of theory. Now, one might ask, what was needed in order that the ideal of freedom might find larger reference and support in a philosophy? The need, evidently, was that the same negation of the transcendental that liberalism was making in the practical field it should also make in the logical field and in more and more comprehensive form. Philosophy, in other words, had to be a philosophy of absolute immanentism, an immanentism of the spirit and therefore not naturalism and not materialism, and not, either, a dualism of spirit and nature but an absolute spiritualism. Moreover, since the spirit is a dialectic of distinctions and oppositions, since the spirit is perpetual growth, perpetual progress, philosophy had to be absolute historicism.

Such a conception was very far indeed from ways of thinking in the country where the ideal of freedom found its first and noblest expressions, and was so embodied in institutions and in public and private morals as to supply most stimulating examples to the rest of the world. English philosophy in those days was what it was to remain for two centuries more or less: sensistic, utilitarian, empirical, and, in the religious field, agnos-

F

tic and possibilistic. The first-born offspring of liberalism was therefore of all philosophies the one least qualified to provide a philosophical justification of the ideal and the practice of freedom.

To measure the full scope of this deficiency one has only to glance again at John Stuart Mill's famous treatise *On Liberty*. Of the author's sincere libertarian faith there can be no slightest doubt. But what cheap, what ignoble arguments he is provided with by his concepts of public welfare, happiness, wisdom, opportuneness, human frailty! In view of this last, Mill argues, as long as men are what they are, we had better allow free play to differing individual opinions and traits, provided their exercise involves no harm to one's neighbour!

To wretched and fallacious reasonings of this type we owe a widespread belief that liberalism is identical with utilitarian individualism, with "social atomism," as Hegel said, and that it regards the State as a mere instrument for helping individuals in their quest for comforts and pleasures. If at all, one might identify liberalism with moral individualism, viewing the State as an instrument for attaining a nobler plane of living and therefore, in the light of that assumption, requiring the individual to love it, serve it, and if need be die for it. Unfortunately, in thinking along that line, not even the concept of the individual is analyzed critically enough. Utilitarian theory continues to substantialize the individual as a monad, to naturalize him as a physical person to be respected and guaranteed as a physical person; whereas the individual should be resolved into the individuality of doing, into the individuality of the act, in other words into the concreteness of universality.

Lack of definiteness in the moral ideal and superficial conceptions of history have meantime led people to drowse fondly in beliefs of a rosy progressive hue. It is assumed that such things as elections, parliaments, and free discussion have once and for all opened to mankind a royal road, a *chemin de velours*, leading to higher and higher levels of existence, ever more abundant comforts, ever greater wealth and power, a steadily increasing culture and refinement, a greater and greater splendour of civilization. On that theory the days of harsh conflicts and cruel devastations are supposed to be over. There are to be no more wars and revolutions, no further danger of relapses to lower forms of political and social living. There may be some slight disturbance, but in the end everything will be smoothed out in agreements arrived at through good-humoured conference. Actually, achievement of the moral ideal requires unremitting effort and vigilancy on our part. We are obliged continuously to re-achieve with our labour and with our sufferings all that we have inherited from those who have gone before us. The course of history—the "education of the human race," as Lessing called it—advances over roads that are rough and rugged, roads that are broken by precipices and pitfalls and strewn with killed and wounded. Just as the course of history never ends in a finer and static condition of happiness, so it is never able to signboard and utilize a way of progress that is safe and sheltered from all mishap. All the worst in the worst past can always return. But we should remember it will always return under new conditions and, for that very reason, once we have again mastered it, we will find that it has lifted us to a higher and nobler plane. The epic of history stands closer to the tragedy than to the idyll.

The fact that people have not grasped this truth, the fact that they so readily succumbed to fatuous optimism, is the main cause of the pessimism and the lack of confidence that prevail so widely in the world to-day. The world is indeed beset by difficulties, but instead of thinking of these as natural aspects of the individual life and of history as a whole, as manifestations so to say, of life's eternal rhythm, instead of ridding themselves of their illusions and correcting their childish errors, such people adopt the easier course of dropping the ideal itself—in other words, the ideal of freedom—by swiftly denying it, only to be left in a sort of stupor where they fall prey to one or another of the political forms that are provided in a whirling dance about us.

In another direction, in Germany, philosophy had gone far beyond sensism, hedonism, utilitarianism, empiricism, and associationism, but in the major philosophical systems ancient metaphysical and theological elements survived among new and original ideas. The tendency, therefore, was to subject the idea of freedom to pre-established historical schemes and, in the political field, in view of the weakness of the liberal tradition in German life, to smother it under the idea of the State, which in turn was conceived as a sort of personified abstraction possessing many of the attributes and attitudes of the Hebrew God.

Worse yet, in the second half of the nineteenth century, Darwinism and evolutionism came to the fore and the liberal ideal began to be justified with concepts deriving from such doctrines as the struggle for existence or the survival of the fittest, and from the habit of thinking of men as mere animals. Therewith the dialectic, the thesis, antitheses, and syntheses, the alternating victories and defeats, the progressive solutions, which liberalism had regarded as part and parcel of its spiritual conception of life, gave way to picturings and admiring descriptions of wild beasts clawing at one another and devouring and destroying one another.

The fact that a theory gives an inadequate or inappropriate account of a thing by no means implies that the thing is not enjoying a fulsome and exuberant prosperity, so long as the vital force that is at work within it is vigorous and inspiring. Often excellent paintings, poems, or sculptures are produced by men who hold fantastic, conventional, or outmoded theories on art, and acts of the highest morality and nobility are performed quite unpretentiously by men who profess the crudest and most hardhearted materialisms. For a person to act in one way and think in another involves, of course, incoherence and lack of balance. There are such cases, however, and we see that there must be, once we remember that we reach coherence through our incoherences; we attain our balance from our frequent stumblings. The fiery and fruitful development of liberalism in England and all over Europe in the nineteenth century dashed the absolutisms to earth, liberated oppressed peoples from foreign dominion and united them into great States. It created a supple form of living that enjoyed an intense interchange among the nations of economic but also of moral, intellectual, and aesthetic values.

It is in no way surprising that the theory of liberty, mean-time, should have grovelled on the wretched planes just described. A Cavour was so deeply and devoutly inspired by the ideal of freedom that in him the word and the deed seemed a living theory, so that nothing more was needed. But that is not the case when the practical urge has weakened, when the vision is veiled or is growing dim, when action falters, draws back, or even renounces and betrays its ideal to fall in with the current that it once combated. And meantime false ideas, mistaken opinions, mendacious histories, step forward as though to deliver an unflattering obituary for the liberty that is reported dead or to inscribe a condemnatory epitaph upon her waiting tomb. At such times it becomes imperative to have a truly adequate theory of freedom. As he stands waiting for the practical revival to dawn again the thinker should start things going in his own field, he should scatter the clouds that are gathering above it and bring clear skies back into the domain of thought. The time when freedom is dead or dying in others is the time when she should resume the weaving of her tapestry before the thinker's mind.

This reconsideration of the problem of freedom, this con-struction or reconstruction of the foundations of the theory of liberty, should also help us to correct a number of mistaken impressions that more directly affect the life of our times. One of these regards the relationship—not very adequately under-stood as yet—between "moral liberalism,"–liberalism proper, and "economic liberalism," or free trade. This is not a relation-ship of cause and effect, of principle and consequence, of premise and conclusion. It is a relationship of form and matter. The economic life becomes matter as compared with con-science, and matter are the various systems that economic life proposes—free trade, protectionism, monopoly, planned econ-omy, economic autarchy, and the like. No one of these systems can claim moral status as against the other, since they are all economic and non-moral and can each, in the various situations that eventuate in history, be either adopted or rejected by the moral man. The same may be said of property systems, capital-istic, communistic, or otherwise, which are necessarily variable and can never be fixed on by reference to any moral law. It might seem possible to fix on one or the other of them with reference to some dream of a general and permanent state of comfort or welfare. But such a dream would not only be Utopian. Intrinsically it would have nothing to do with ethics. Morals envisage no impossible state of individual or general comfort. They are exclusively concerned with an *excelsius*.

Another mistaken notion comes to us from the opposite direction—not from *laissez faire* and free trade, but from the communists. This is the distinction that is drawn between a "legal" or "formal" or "theoretical" freedom and an "actual" or "real" freedom. The first sort of freedom is the one that was allegedly bestowed upon the peoples by the Revolution of 1789 and which has been made deceptive and unreal because it has not been accompanied by the second and, worse yet, has been used as a pretext to resist propaganda or action for the second. On careful examination, freedom of the first sort, the allegedly "legal" or "formal" freedom, turns out to be the real and actual freedom—freedom as a moral principle and therefore the only freedom. The other sort, which is called "actual" and "real," is not freedom at all, but just a name for a communist and equalitarian system of economic organization. The fact that the two things have, with revolting callousness to facts, been subsumed under one concept by exponents of the economic interpretation of history, is just another instance of the obtuseness which that school of thought has encouraged towards everything pertaining to the spiritual and moral life.

It cannot be argued, in rebuttal, that the communist ideal, as merely economic, is, among the various possible or plausible ideals, adapted to certain conditions and more or less permanent in relation to them. The communist system, to begin with, is very improperly called a system of "equality" and "justice," but that is not the point here. What we must reject is the assertion that represents that system of economic organization as the foundation, and liberty as the pinnacle, of the social edifice. Liberty is not dependent on any particular economic system, or on either of the two systems here contrasted. It calls all systems to the bar of judgment and accepts or rejects any or all according to the case. If, therefore, one insists in the face of the facts on conceiving the relationship upside down, there is nothing to do except to begin by founding the equalitarian economic order, without reference to freedom and consent, and resorting to violence. Then, in line with the principle that states are upheld by the same forces that create them, one can only go on and uphold the equalitarian order by violence and suppress freedom.

The truth of this contention is so obvious, from the standpoint of reason and logic, that it would hardly be necessary to seek a verification of it in the facts. Yet the verification has been supplied, and in no doubtful terms, by a number of the so-called proletarian dictatorships of our time. These systems can pretend to establish liberty in their written constitutions. They cannot achieve it in the fact, any more than they can divest themselves of their dictatorial character—divest themselves, that is, of their actual selves. As in the case just mentioned, therefore, the real relationship is the reverse one: first and fundamental, freedom, which judges, accepts, or rejects either or any system of economic organization according as the latter shows itself to be morally the more salutary, and thereby economically, the more advantageous in the conditions supplied at the given historical moment.

One might touch briefly, also, on a third misapprehension which comes to us not from the battle of conflicting economic systems but from the more strictly political field, the field of diplomacy. There we find a formula of "non-intervention," which decks itself out in a halo of liberalism and declares humble deference to the rights particular countries have of freely working out their problems and fighting out their domestic quarrels even by civil war.

In the background of such propositions lurks a very important truth, the truth that the government of a given country is in duty bound to consider the vital interests entrusted to it, and to concern itself with the affairs of other countries only as these affect those interests in line of prospect or menace, advantage or harm. This truth, however, is never the predominant con-

sideration with those who use the formula. The pious respect
that is professed for the self-determination of the peoples must
be classed with the political hypocrisies. The principle is
evidently not applied, and is in fact inapplicable, to the so-
called backward or uncivilized peoples and cannot be applied,
either, to peoples who fall into temporary conditions of civic
inferiority. The interests that the given government is called
upon to protect all by itself cannot be conceived in terms of an
exclusive and abstract particularity. All countries participate
in the common life of Europe, or of the world. To refuse to
consider the moral vicissitudes of peoples beyond one's own
country's frontiers involves, first of all, exposing one's country
to the danger of the *proximus ardet Ucalegon*. But then again such
policies are definitely unhealthy to the sense that a people must
have of itself. This sense cannot be satisfied by the mere idea of
power. It has to be re-enforced by a persuasion that the power
is beneficial to humanity—otherwise the country shrinks into a
sort of cynical selfishness that works against the country itself.

In the light of this truth a friend and co-worker of mine[1]
saw fit, with some reason, to accuse the English sense of freedom of narrowness, in that the English seem to conceive of
liberty as a private, personal, or national possession of their
own, not as a universal human value which it is their duty to
spread abroad and with which the destinies of their own
liberties are necessarily bound up.

This reluctance—a very understandable reluctance—to
embrace and apply an active international morality rests in
part on historical memories—memories of the Crusades, for
instance, which were so idealistic in their dreams and so
un-idealistic in their realities and which anyhow failed; memories of certain Catholic crusades, which were so unwisely
undertaken by the Spain of the Hapsburgs; or memories of
the religious wars, which laid Europe waste, drowned a continent in blood, and ended not in the victory of one faith or
the other, but in a return to the *cuiusregioeius religio*, followed
by a general outburst of rationalism and illuminism before
which both Catholicism and Protestantism gave ground.

---

[1] Osmodeo, review of Fisher's *History of Europe*, *La Critica*, Vol. XXXVI (1938).

This reluctance tends, at any rate, to lose sight of the fact that morality, and the ideal of freedom which is the political expression of morality, are not the property of a given party or group, but a value that is fundamentally and universally human, to diffuse and enhance which all of us must devote our efforts of good will in the ways that are most appropriate to the given case and which political wisdom must advise and guide. No people will be truly free till all peoples are free.

I confess that I am not a little alarmed at the scant attention, if any at all, that is being paid to the problem of freedom in the philosophical literature of our time, and at the little interest that is being shown in the vicissitudes and destinies of freedom throughout the world. One can say the same, for that matter, of literature in general—of the drama, of the novel, of historical writing.

This is just the opposite of what went on during the first half of the nineteenth century, though it should be going on even more intensely to-day when the liberties which were then won are in danger of being lost and of having to be won again. Actually, philosophy and literature seem to be indifferent to the distress of those who love our sacred heritage of freedom and fear its passing. Philosophy is turning back to the old and faraway problems of the schools, and literature to irrelevant sentiments and impulses; when indeed both philosophy and literature are not being placed at the service of adversaries of the liberal ideal in an effort to construct a body of doctrine that will help the oppressions that are being exercised and the various attempts that are being made to brutalize the world.

For my part, for some two decades I have been trying to revive interest in the subject of freedom through a number of philosophical or historical treatises; and in the course of those labours I have been impressed by the relatively imperfect state in which the doctrine of liberty has been left by thinkers of the past. The lightness of the armour, the ancientness and inadequacy of the weapons, with which they provided freedom may in part account for the ineffectiveness of the defence that it has made against the surprises and attacks that have of late been hurled upon it. I have therefore set down here a few of the outlines of a doctrine of freedom that seem to me essential; but I cannot end these pages without observing that the subject has so many and such varied aspects, that it intertwines with so many of the gravest problems of life and history, as to require all the energy and talents that any number of scholars can devote to it.

John Dewey

Professor Emeritus of Philosophy, Columbia University

THE PROBLEM OF FREEDOM

WHAT is freedom and why is it prized? Is desire for freedom inherent in human nature or is it a product of special circumstances? Is it wanted as an end or as a means of getting other things? Does its possession entail responsibilities, and are these responsibilities so onerous that the mass of men will readily surrender liberty for the sake of greater ease? Is the struggle for liberty so arduous that most men are easily distracted from the endeavour to achieve and maintain it? Does freedom in itself, and in the things it brings with it, seem as important as security of livelihood; as food, shelter, clothing, or even as having a good time? Did man ever care as much for it as we in this country have been taught to believe? Is there any truth in the old notion that the driving force in political history has been the effort of the common man to achieve freedom? Was our own struggle for political independence in any genuine sense animated by desire for freedom, or were there a number of discomforts that our ancestors wanted to get rid of, things having nothing in common save that they were felt to be troublesome?

Is love of liberty ever anything more than a desire to be liberated from some special restriction? And when it is got rid of does the desire for liberty die down until something else feels intolerable? Again, how does the desire for freedom compare in intensity with the desire to feel equal with others, especially with those who have previously been called superiors? How do the fruits of liberty compare with the enjoyments that spring from a feeling of union, of solidarity, with others? Will men surrender their liberties if they believe that by so doing they will obtain the satisfaction that comes from a sense of fusion with others, and that respect by others which is the product of the strength furnished by solidarity?

The present state of the world is putting questions like these to citizens of all democratic countries. It is putting them with special force to us in a country where democratic institutions have been bound up with a certain tradition, the "ideology" of which the Declaration of Independence is the classic expression. This tradition has taught us that attainment of freedom is the goal of political history; that self-government is the inherent right of free men and is that which, when it is achieved, men prize above all else. Yet as we look at the world we see supposedly free institutions in many countries not so much overthrown as abandoned willingly, apparently with enthusiasm. We may infer that what has happened is proof they never existed in reality but only in name. Or we may console ourselves with a belief that unusual conditions, such as national frustration and humiliation, have led men to welcome any kind of government that promised to restore national self-respect. But conditions in our country, as well as the eclipse of democracy in other countries, compel us to ask questions about the career and fate of free societies, even our own.

There perhaps was a time when the questions asked would have seemed to be mainly or exclusively political. Now we know better. For we know that a large part of the causes which have produced the conditions that are expressed in the questions is the dependence of politics upon other forces, notably the economic. The problem of the constitution of human nature is involved, since it is part of our tradition that love of freedom is inherent in its make-up. Is the popular psychology of democracy a myth? The old doctrine about human nature was also tied up with the ethical belief that political democracy is a moral right and that the laws upon which it is based are fundamental moral laws which every form of social organization should obey. If belief in natural rights and natural laws as the foundation of free government is surrendered, does the latter have any other moral basis? For while it would be foolish to believe that the American Colonies fought the battles that secured their independence and that they built their government consciously and deliberately upon a foundation of psychological and moral theories, yet the democratic tradition, call it dream or call it penetrating vision, was so closely allied with beliefs about human nature and about the moral ends which political institutions should serve, that a rude shock occurs when these affiliations break down. Is there anything to take their place, anything that will give the kind of support they once gave?

The problems behind the questions asked, the forces which give the questions their urgency, go beyond the particular beliefs which formed the early psychological and moral foundations of democracy. After retiring from public office, Thomas Jefferson in his old age carried on a friendly philosophical correspondence with John Adams. In one of his letters he made a statement about existing American conditions and expressed a hope about their future estate: "The advance of liberalism encourages a hope that the human mind will some day get back to the freedom it enjoyed two thousand years ago. This country, which has given to the world the example of physical liberty, owes to it that of moral emancipation also; for as yet it is but nominal with us. The inquisition of public opinion overwhelms in practice the freedom asserted by the laws in theory." The situation that has developed since his time may well lead us to reverse the ideas he expressed, and inquire whether political freedom can be maintained without that freedom of culture which he expected to be the final result of political freedom. It is no longer easy to entertain the hope that given political freedom as the one thing necessary all other things will in time be added to it—and so to us. For we now know that the relations which exist between persons, outside of political institutions, relations of industry, of communication, of science, art, and religion, affect daily associations, and thereby deeply affect the attitudes and habits expressed in government and rules of law. If it is true that the political and legal react to shape the other things, it is even more true that political institutions are an effect, not a cause.

It is this knowledge that sets the theme to be discussed. For this complex of conditions which taxes the terms upon which human beings associate and live together is summed up in the word "culture." The problem is to know what kind of culture is so free in itself that it conceives and begets political freedom as its accompaniment and consequence. What about the state of science and knowledge; of the arts, fine and technological; of friendships and family life; of business and finance; of the attitudes and dispositions created in the give and take of ordinary day-by-day associations? No matter what is the native make-up of human nature, its working activities, those which respond to institutions and rules and which finally shape the pattern of the latter, are created by the whole body of occupations, interests, skills, beliefs, that constitute a given culture. As the latter changes, especially as it grows complex and intricate in the way in which American life has changed since our political organization took shape, new problems take the place of those governing the earlier formation and distribution of political powers. The view that love of freedom is so inherent in man that, if it only has a chance given it by abolition of oppressions exercised by Church and State, it will produce and maintain free institutions is no longer adequate. The idea naturally arose when settlers in a new country felt that the distance they had put between themselves and the forces that oppressed them effectively symbolized everything that stood between them and permanent achievement of freedom. We are now forced to see that positive conditions, forming the prevailing state of culture, are required. Release from oppressions and repressions which previously existed marked a necessary transition; but transitions are but bridges to something different.

Early republicans were obliged even in their own time to note that general conditions, such as are summed up under the name of culture, had a good deal to do with political institutions. For they held that oppressions of State and Church had exercised a corrupting influence upon human nature, so that the orginal impulse to liberty had either been lost or warped out of shape. This was a virtual admission that surrounding conditions may be stronger than native tendencies. It proved a degree of plasticity in human nature that required exercise of continual solicitude. The Founding Fathers were aware that love of power is a trait of human nature, so strong a one that definite barriers had to be erected to keep persons who get into positions of official authority from encroachments that undermine free institutions. Admission that men may be brought by long habit to hug their chains implies a belief that second or acquired nature is stronger than original nature.

Jefferson at least went further than this. For his fear of the growth of manufacturing and trade, and his preference for agrarian pursuits, amounted to acceptance of the idea that interests bred by certain pursuits may fundamentally alter original human nature and the institutions that are congenial to it. That the development Jefferson dreaded has come about, and to a much greater degree than he could have anticipated, is an obvious fact. We face to-day the consequences of the fact that an agricultural and rural people has become an urban industrial population.

Proof is decisive that economic factors are an intrinsic part of the culture that determines the actual turn taken by political measures and rules, no matter what verbal beliefs are held. Although it later became the fashion to blur the connection which exists between economics and politics, and even to reprove those who called attention to it, Madison as well as Jefferson was quite aware of the connection and of its bearing upon democracy. Knowledge that the connection demanded a general distribution of property and the prevention of rise of the extremely poor and the extremely rich was however different from explicit recognition of a relation between culture and nature so intimate that the former may shape the patterns of thought and action.

Economic relations and habits cannot be set apart in isolation any more than political institutions can be. The state of knowledge of nature, that is, of physical science, is a phase of culture upon which industry and commerce, the production and distribution of goods and the regulation of services, directly depend.

Unless we take into account the rise of the new science of nature in the seventeenth century and its growth to its present state, our economic agencies of production and distribution and, ultimately of consumption, cannot be understood. The connection of the events of the industrial revolution with those of the advancing scientific revolution is an incontrovertible witness.

It has not been customary to include the arts, the fine arts, as an important part of the social conditions that bear upon democratic institutions and personal freedom. Even after the influence of the state of industry and of natural science has been admitted, we still tend to draw the line at the idea that literature, music, painting, the drama, architecture, have any intimate connection with the cultural bases of democracy. Even those who call themselves good democrats are often content to look upon the fruits of these arts as adornments of culture rather than as things in whose enjoyment all should partake, if democracy is to be a reality. The state of things in totalitarian countries may induce us to revise this opinion. For it proves that no matter what may be the case with the impulses and powers that lead the creative artist to do his work, works of art, once brought into existence, are the most compelling of the means of communication by which emotions are stirred and opinions formed. The theatre, the movie and music hall, even the picture gallery, eloquence, popular parades, common sports, and recreative agencies, have all been brought under regulation as part of the propaganda agencies by which dictatorship is kept in power without being regarded by the masses as oppressive. We are beginning to realize that emotions and imagination are more potent in shaping public sentiment and opinion than information and reason.

Indeed, long before the present crisis came into being, there was a saying that if one could control the songs of a nation, one need not care who made its laws. And historical study shows that primitive religions owe their power in determining belief and action to their ability to reach emotions and imagination by rites and ceremonies by legend and folklore, all clothed with the traits that mark works of art. The Church that has had by far the greatest influence in the modern world took over their agencies of aesthetic appeal and incorporated them into its own structure, after adapting them to its own purpose, in winning and holding the allegiance of the masses.

A totalitarian regime is committed to control of the whole life of all its subjects by its hold over feelings, desires, emotions, as well as opinions. This indeed is a mere truism, since a totalitarian State has to be total. But save as we take it into account we shall not appreciate the intensity of the revival of the warfare between State and Church that exists in Germany and Russia. The conflict is not the expression of the whim of a leader. It is inherent in any regime that demands the *total* allegiance of all its subjects. It must first of all, and most enduringly of all, if it is to be permanent, command the imagination, with all the impulses and motives we have been accustomed to call "inner." Religious organizations are those which rule by use of these means, and for that reason are an inherent competitor with any political state that sets out on the totalitarian road. Thus it is that the very things that seem to us in democratic countries the most obnoxious features of the totalitarian State are the very things for which its advocates recommend it. They are the things for whose absence they denounce democratic countries. For they say that failure to enlist the whole make-up of citizens, emotional as well as ideological, condemns democratic states to employ merely external and mechanical devices to hold the loyal support of its citizens. We may regard all this as a symptom of a collective hallucination, such as at times seems to have captured whole populations. But even so, we must recognize the influence of this factor if we are ourselves to escape collective delusion—that totalitarianism rests upon external coercion alone.

Finally, the moral factor is an intrinsic part of the complex of social forces called culture. For no matter whether or not one shares the view, now held on different grounds by different groups, that there is no scientific ground or warrant for moral conviction and judgments, it is certain that human beings hold some things dearer than they do others, and that they struggle for the things they prize, spending time and energy in their behalf: doing so indeed to such an extent that the best measure

G

we have of what is valued is the effort spent in its behalf. Not only so, but for a number of persons to form anything that can be called a community in its pregnant sense there must be values prized in common. Without them, any so-called social group, class, people, nation, tends to fall apart into molecules having but mechanically enforced connections with one another. For the present, at least, we do not have to ask whether values are moral, having a kind of life and potency of their own, or are but by-products of the working of other conditions, bio-logical, economic, or whatever.

The qualification will indeed seem quite superfluous to most; so habituated have most persons become to believing, at least nominally, that moral forces are the ultimate determinants of the rise and fall of all human societies—while religion has taught many to believe that cosmic as well as social forces are regulated in behalf of moral ends. The qualification is intro-duced, nevertheless, because of the existence of a school of philosophy holding that opinions about the values which move conduct are lacking in any scientific standing, since—according to them—the only things that can be *known* are physical events. The denial that values have any influence, in the long run, on the course of events is also characteristic of the Marxist belief that forces of production ultimately control every human rela-tionship. The idea of the impossibility of intellectual regulation of ideas and judgments about values is shared by a number of intellectuals who have been dazzled by the success of mathe-matical and physical science. These last remarks suggest that there is at least one other factor in culture which needs some attention: namely, the existence of schools of social philosophy, of competing ideologies.

The intent of the previous discussion should be obvious. The problem of freedom and of democratic institutions is tied up with the question of what kind of culture exists; with the neces-sity of free culture for free political institutions. The import of this conclusion extends far beyond its contrast with the simpler faith of those who formulated the democratic tradition. The question of human psychology, of the make-up of human nature in its original state, is involved. It is involved not just in a general way but with respect to its special constituents and their significance in their relations to one another. For every social and political philosophy currently professed will be found upon examination to involve a certain view about the constitution of human nature: in itself and in its relation to physical nature. What is true of this factor is true of every factor in culture, so that they need not here be listed again, although it is necessary to bear them all in mind if we are to appreciate the variety of factors involved in the problem of human freedom.

Running through the problem of the relation of this and that constituent of culture to social institutions in general, and political democracy in particular, is a question rarely asked. Yet it so underlies any critical consideration of the principles of each of them that some conclusion on the matter ultimately decides the position taken on each special issue. The question is whether any one of the factors is so predominant that it is *the* causal force, so that other factors are secondary and derived effects. Some kind of answer in what philosophers call a *monistic* direction has been usually given. The most obvious present example is the belief that economic conditions are ultimately the controlling forces in human relationships. It is perhaps significant that this view is comparatively recent. At the height of the eighteenth century, Enlightenment, the prevailing view, gave final supremacy to reason, to the advance of science and to education. Even during the last century, a view was held which is expressed in the motto of a certain school of historians: "History is past politics and politics is present history."

Because of the present fashion of economic explanation, this political view may now seem to have been the crotchet of a particular set of historical scholars. But, after all, it only formulated an idea consistently acted upon during the period of the formation of national States. It is possible to regard the present emphasis upon economic factors as a sort of intellectual revenge taken upon its earlier all but total neglect. The very word "political economy" suggests how completely economic considerations were once subordinated to political. The book that was influential in putting an end to this subjection, Adam

Smith's *Wealth of Nations*, continued in its title, though not its contents, the older tradition. In the Greek period, we find that Aristotle makes the political factor so controlling that all normal economic activities are relegated to the household, so that all morally justifiable economic practice is literally domestic economy. And in spite of the recent vogue of the Marxist theory, Oppenheim has produced a considerable body of evidence in support of the thesis that political states are the result of military conquests in which defeated people have become subjects of their conquerors, who, by assuming rule over the conquered, begot the first political States.

The rise of totalitarian States cannot, because of the bare fact of their totalitarianism, be regarded as mere reversions to the earlier theory of supremacy of the political institutional factor. Yet as compared with theories that had subordinated the political to the economic, whether in the Marxist form or in that of the British classical school, it marks reversion to ideas, and still more to practices, which it was supposed had disappeared for ever from the conduct of any modern State. And the practices have been revived and extended with the benefit of scientific technique of control of industry, finance, and commerce in ways which show the earlier governmental officials who adopted "mercantile" economics in the interest of government were the veriest bunglers at their professed job.

The idea that morals ought to be, even if they are not, the supreme regulator of social affairs is not so widely entertained as it once was, and there are circumstances which support the conclusion that when moral forces were as influential as they were supposed to be it was because morals were identical with customs which happened in fact to regulate the relations of human beings with one another. However, the idea is still advanced by sermons from the pulpit and editorials from the press that adoption of, say, the Golden Rule would speedily do away with all social discord and trouble; and as I write the newspapers report the progress of a campaign for something called "moral rearmament." Upon a deeper level, the point made about the alleged identity of ethics with established customs raises the question whether the effect of the disintegration of customs that for a long time held men together in social groups can be overcome save by development of new generally accepted traditions and customs. This development, upon this view, would be equivalent to the creation of a new ethics.

However, such questions are here brought up for the sake of the emphasis they place upon the question already raised: Is there any one factor or phase of culture which is dominant, or which tends to produce and regulate others, or are economics, morals, art, science, and so on only so many aspects of the interaction of a number of factors, each of which acts upon and is acted upon by the others? In the professional language of philosophy: shall our point of view be monistic or pluralistic? The same question recurs moreover about each one of the factors listed—about economics, about politics, about science, about art. I shall here illustrate the point by reference, not to any of these things but to theories that have at various times been influential about the make-up of human nature. For these psychological theories have been marked by serious attempts to make some one constituent of human nature *the* source of motivation of action: or at least to reduce all conduct to the action of a small number of alleged native "forces." A comparatively recent example was the adoption by the classic school, of economic theory of self-interest as the main motivating force of human behaviour; an idea linked up on its technical side with the notion that pleasure and pain are the causes and the ends in view of all conscious human conduct, in desire to obtain one and avoid the other. Then there was a view that self-interest and sympathy are the two components of human nature, as opposed and balanced centrifugal and centripetal tendencies are the moving forces of celestial nature.

Just now the favourite ideological psychological candidate for control of human activity is love of power. Reasons for its selection are not far to seek. Success of search for economic profit turned out to be largely conditioned in fact upon possession of superior power, while success reacted to increase power. Then the rise of national States has been attended by such vast and flagrant organization of military and naval force that politics have become more and more markedly power politics, leading to the conclusion that there is not any other kind, although in the past the power element has been more decently and decorously covered up. One interpretation of the Darwinian struggle for existence and survival of the fittest was used as ideological support; and some writers, notably Nietzsche— though not in the crude form often alleged—proposed an ethics of power in opposition to the supposed Christian ethics of sacrifice.

Because human nature is the factor which, in one way or another, is always interacting with environing conditions in production of culture, the theme receives special attention elsewhere. But the shift that has occurred from time to time in theories that have gained currency about the "ruling motive" in human nature suggests a question which is seldom asked. It is the question whether these psychologies have not in fact taken the cart to be the horse. Have they not gathered their notion as to the ruling element in human nature from observation of tendencies that are marked in contemporary collective life, and then bunched these tendencies together in some alleged psychological "force" as their cause? It is significant that human nature was taken to be strongly moved by an inherent love of freedom at the time when there was a struggle for representative government; that the motive of self-interest appeared when conditions in England enlarged the rôle of money, because of new methods of industrial production; that the growth of organized philanthropic activities brought sympathy into the psychological picture; and that events to-day are readily converted into love of power as the mainspring of human action.

In any case, the idea of culture that has been made familiar by the work of anthropological students, points to the conclusion that whatever are the native constituents of human nature, the culture of a period and group is the determining influence in their arrangement; it is that which determines the patterns of behaviour that mark out the activities of any group, family, clan, people, sect, faction, class. It is at least as true that the state of culture determines the order and arrangement of native tendencies as that human nature produces any particular set or system of social phenomena so as to obtain satisfaction for itself. The problem is to find out the way in which the elements of a culture interact with each other and the way in which the elements of human nature are caused to interact with one another under conditions set by their interaction with the existing environment. For example, if our American culture is largely a pecuniary culture, it is not because the original or innate structure of human nature tends of itself to obtaining pecuniary profit. It is rather that a certain complex culture stimulates, promotes, and consolidates native tendencies so as to produce a certain pattern of desires and purposes. If we take all the communities, peoples, classes, tribes, and nations that ever existed, we may be sure that since human nature in its native constitution is the relative constant, it cannot be appealed to, in isolation, to account for the multitude of diversities presented by different forms of association.

Primitive peoples, for reasons that are now pretty evident, attribute magical qualities to blood. Popular beliefs about race and inherent race differences have virtually perpetuated the older superstitions. Anthropologists are practically all agreed that the differences we find in different "races" are not due to anything in inherent physiological structure but to the effects exercised upon members of various groups by the cultural conditions under which they are reared; conditions that act upon raw or original human nature unremittingly from the very moment of birth. It has always been known that infants, born without ability in any language, come to speak the language, whatever it may be, of the community in which they were born. Like most uniform phenomena the fact aroused no curiosity and led to no generalization about the influence of cultural conditions. It was taken for granted; as a matter of course it was so "natural" as to appear inevitable. Only since the rise of systematic inquiries carried on by anthropological students has it been noted that the conditions of culture which bring about the common language of a given group produce other traits they have in common—traits which like the mother-tongue differentiate one group or society from others.

Culture as a complex body of customs tends to maintain itself. It can reproduce itself only through effecting certain differential changes in the original or native constitutions of its members. Each culture has its own pattern, its own characteristic arrangement of its constituent energies. By the mere force of its existence as well as by deliberately adopted methods systematically pursued, it perpetuates itself through transformation of the raw or original human nature of those born immature.

These statements do not signify that biological heredity and native individual differences are of no importance. They signify that as they operate within a given social form, they are shaped and take effect *within* that particular form. They are not indigenous traits that mark off one people, one group, one class, from another, but mark differences in every group. Whatever the "white man's burden," it was not imposed by heredity.

We have travelled a seemingly long way from the questions with which we set out, so that it may appear that they had been forgotten on the journey. But the journey was undertaken for the sake of finding out something about the nature of the problem that is expressed in the questions asked. The maintenance of democratic institutions is not such a simple matter as was supposed by some of the Founding Fathers, although the wiser among them realized how immensely the new political experiment was favoured by external circumstances—like the ocean that separated settlers from the governments that had an interest in using the colonists for their own purposes; the fact that feudal institutions had been left behind; the fact that so many of the settlers had come here to escape restrictions upon religious beliefs and form of worship; and especially the existence of a vast territory with free land and immense unappropriated natural resources.

The function of culture in determining what elements of human nature are dominant, and their pattern or arrangement in connection with one another, goes beyond any special point to which attention is called. It affects the very idea of individuality. The idea that human nature is inherently and exclusively individual is itself a product of a cultural individualistic movement. The idea that mind and consciousness are intrinsically individual did not even occur to anyone for much the greater part of human history. It would have been rejected as the inevitable source of disorder and chaos if it had occurred to anyone to suggest it—not that their ideas of human nature on that account were any better than later ones, but that they also were functions of culture. All that we can safely say is that human nature, like other forms of life, tends to differentiation, and this moves in the direction of the distinctively individual, and that it also tends toward combination, association. In the lower animals, physical-biological factors determine which tendency is dominant in a given animal or plant species and the ratio existing between the two factors—whether, for example, insects are what students call "solitary" or "social." With human beings, cultural conditions replace strictly physical ones. In the earlier periods of human history they acted almost like physiological conditions as far as deliberate intention was concerned. They were taken to be "natural" and change in them to be unnatural. At a later period the cultural conditions were seen to be subject in some degree to deliberate formation. For a time radicals then identified their policies with the belief that if only artificial social conditions could be got rid of human nature would produce, almost automatically, a certain kind of social arrangement, those which would give it free scope in its supposed exclusively individual character.

Tendencies toward sociality, such as sympathy, were admitted. But they were taken to be traits of an individual isolated by nature, quite as much as, say, a tendency to combine with others in order to get protection against something threatening one's own private self. Whether complete identification of human nature with individuality would be desirable or undesirable if it existed is an idle academic question. For it does not exist. Some cultural conditions develop the psychological constituents that lead toward differentiation; others stimulate those which lead in the direction of the solidarity of the beehive or anthill. The human problem is that of securing the development of each constituent so that it serves to release and mature the other. Co-operation—called fraternity in the classic French formula—is as much a part of the democratic ideal as is personal initiative. That cultural conditions were allowed to develop (markedly so in the economic phase) which subordinated co-operativeness to liberty and equality serves to explain the decline in the two latter. Indirectly, this decline is responsible for the present tendency to give a bad name to the very word individualism and to make sociality a term of moral honour beyond criticism. But that association of nullities on even the largest scale would constitute a realization of human nature is as absurd as to suppose that the latter can take place in beings whose only relations to one another are those entered into in behalf of exclusive private advantage.

The problem of freedom of co-operative individualities is then a problem to be viewed in the context of culture. The state of culture is a state of interaction of many factors, the chief of which are law and politics, industry and commerce, science and technology, the arts of expression and communication, and of morals, or the values men prize and the ways in which they evaluate them; and finally, though indirectly, the system of general ideas used by men to justify and to criticize the fundamental conditions under which they live, their social philosophy. We are concerned with the problem of freedom rather than with solutions, in the conviction that solutions are idle until the problem has been placed in the context of the elements that constitute culture as they interact with elements of native human nature. The fundamental postulate of the discussion is that isolation of any one factor, no matter how strong its workings at a given time, is fatal to understanding and to intelligent action. Isolations have abounded, both on the side of taking some one thing in human nature to be a supreme "motive" and in taking some one form of social activity to be supreme. Since the problem is here thought of as that of the ways in which a great number of factors within and without human nature interact, our task is to ask concerning the reciprocal connections raw human nature and culture bear to one another.

Albert Einstein

*Professor of Theoretical Physics and Member of the Institute
for Advanced Study, Princeton, New Jersey*

FREEDOM AND SCIENCE[1]

I

AT first glance it seems that freedom and science do not
have much relation to one another. In any case freedom may well exist without science, that is, to the
extent that man can live without science, man in whom the impulse of inquiry is innate. But what of science without freedom?

Above all a man of science requires inward freedom, for he
must needs endeavour to free himself from prejudices and must
constantly convince himself anew, when new facts emerge, that
what has been established, however authoritatively, is still
valid. Intellectual independence is thus a primary necessity for
the scientific inquirer. But political liberty is also extraordinarily
important for his work. He must be able to utter what seems
true to him without concern about, or danger to, his life and
livelihood. This is apparent in historical investigations, but it is
a vital precondition for all scientific activity however remote from
politics. If certain books are condemned and made inaccessible
in so far as their author is not acceptable to the government
on account of his political orientation or race, as is largely
the case to-day, the inquirer cannot attain an adequate basis
on which to build. And how can the building stand if it lacks
a secure foundation?

[1] Translated from the German by James Gutmann, Professor of Philosophy,
Columbia University.

It is self-evident that absolute freedom is an ideal which cannot be realized in our social and political life. But all men of good-will should seek to guard mankind's effort to realize this ideal in ever increasing measure.

II

I know that it is a hopeless undertaking to debate about fundamental value judgments. For instance if someone approves, as a goal, the extirpation of the human race from the earth, one cannot refute such a viewpoint on rational grounds. But if there is agreement on certain goals and values, one can argue rationally about the means by which these objectives may be attained. Let us, then, indicate two goals which may well be agreed upon by nearly all who read these lines.

1. Those instrumental goods which should serve to maintain the life and health of all human beings should be produced by the least possible labour of all.

2. The satisfaction of physical needs is indeed the indispensable precondition of a satisfactory existence, but in itself it is not enough. In order to be content, men must also have the possibility of developing their intellectual and artistic powers to whatever extent accords with their personal characteristics and abilities.

The first of these two goals requires the promotion of all knowledge relating to the laws of nature and the laws of social processes, that is, the promotion of all scientific endeavour. For scientific endeavour is a natural whole, the parts of which mutually support one another in a way which, to be sure, no one can anticipate. However, the progress of science presupposes the possibility of unrestricted communication of all results and judgments—freedom of expression and instruction in all realms of intellectual endeavour. By freedom I understand social conditions of such a kind that the expression of opinions and assertions about general and particular matters of knowledge will not involve dangers or serious disadvantages for him who expresses them. This freedom of communication is indispensable for the development and extension of scientific knowledge, a consideration of much practical import. In the first instance it must be guaranteed by law. But laws alone cannot secure freedom of expression; in order that every man may present his views without penalty there must be a spirit of tolerance in the entire population. Such an ideal of external liberty can never be fully attained but must be sought unremittingly if scientific thought, and philosophical and creative thinking in general, are to be advanced as far as possible.

If the second goal, that is, the possibility of the spiritual development of all individuals, is to be secured, a second kind of outward freedom is necessary. Man should not have to work for the achievement of the necessities of life to such an extent that he has neither time nor strength for personal activities. Without this second kind of outward liberty, freedom of expression is useless for him. Advances in technology would provide the possibility of this kind of freedom if the problem of a reasonable division of labour were solved.

The development of science and of the creative activities of the spirit in general requires still another kind of freedom, which may be characterized as inward freedom. It is this freedom of the spirit which consists in the independence of thought from the restrictions of authoritarian and social prejudices as well as from unphilosophical routinizing and habit in general. This inward freedom is an infrequent gift of nature and a worthy objective for the individual. Yet the community can do much to further this achievement, too, at least by not interfering with its development. Thus schools may interfere with the development of inward freedom through authoritarian influences, and through imposing on young people excessive spiritual burdens; on the other hand schools may favour such freedom by encouraging independent thought. Only if outward and inner freedom are constantly and consciously pursued is there a possibility of spiritual development and perfection and thus of improving man's outward and inner life.

J. B. S. Haldane

Professor of Genetics, University of London

A COMPARATIVE STUDY OF FREEDOM

THE first essential in any scientific study is a possibility of comparison. The measuring-rod, the stop-watch, and the balance are at the very roots of science. If our study of freedom is to have any practical results, we must try to tackle the question, Is A freer than B? A may be a bus-driver in New York, and B a bus-driver in Belgrade. Or B may be a corporation vice-president, a poet, or A's wife in New York. In almost every case we find the question unanswerable. A has more freedom than B in some directions, but less in others. And the different kinds of freedom are incommensurable. A can, if he wants to, read the works of Marx, and can afford to go to the movies every night, which B cannot. But B can have a drink after 10 p.m. and can afford a garden where his children can play, which A cannot. Who is to decide which is freer? Our best plan will be to specify different possible fields of freedom, so that we may be able to carry out comparisons within these fields. The overall summary will inevitably be subjective, but we can at least say that in some particular respect A is more free or less free than B.

Besides asking whether A is freer than B, we can ask the very important question whether A is becoming more free or less free in a given respect as the years go by. I would personally prefer to live in a country where freedom was increasing from a rather low level to one where it was declining from a high level. This again is perhaps a matter of one's own philosophy. But certainly such trends cannot be neglected.

Our classification of the fields of freedom will inevitably be somewhat arbitrary, and different classifications will overlap. Thus let us see what is meant by religious freedom, which most people in the United States honestly believe that they enjoy. It means legal freedom to believe any of a fair variety of doctrines and to persuade others of their truth. There is also legal freedom to attack the religious doctrines of others up to a point. But you will find yourself in jail if you walk into a Catholic church and denounce the worshippers as idolaters, or into a Protestant church and brand them as heretics. You may practise religious rites if they are not indecent or dangerous to life. But if you think you enjoy full religious freedom, try practising the Hindu Laya Yoga in New York and see how long the vice squad will leave you alone. Or bring over a crate of rattlesnakes and try the Hopi snake dance, and see how many laws you are breaking. As for the religion of the Latter-Day Saints, which turned the salt deserts of Utah into a garden, one of its main practices, polygamy, has been prohibited by the Congress of the United States. The plain fact is that in any society there has at most been freedom for a group of religions which enjoin fairly similar standards of moral conduct. So it will be logical to divide up religious freedom under freedom to communicate ideas, freedom in sexual relations, various kinds of economic freedom, freedom of children, and so on.

Besides this horizontal classification, so to speak, there is a vertical classification of freedoms at different levels. The most fundamental level is the technical level. This may be Marxism, but it is also common sense. There could be no freedom of the press before printing was invented, because there was no press to be free or unfree. Thus a technical advance makes possible a new kind of freedom and a new kind of bondage. Given the technical possibility, there must in general be some legal restrictions. In no country is the press so free that incitements to murder the rulers of a state may be printed within it. Most people will support this restriction. Besides legal restrictions there are customary restrictions. Law permits me, but custom refuses me the right to walk about the streets of London in—

> "A scarlet tunic with sunflowers decked,
> And a peacock hat with the tail erect,
> Which might have had a more marked effect."

In primitive societies there is no division between legal and customary restrictions, and in England, too gross a breach of custom may turn out to be the crime of "insulting behaviour."

Economic restrictions on freedom are of primary importance. A vast number of technical possibilities are only open to a small minority. Very few people can own a steam yacht. Somewhat more can own a grand piano or an automobile. The all-important liberty of communicating ideas is enormously restricted by the fact that very few people are rich enough to own a daily newspaper. Further, the development of technique tends to increase economic restrictions on liberty, simply because modern technical inventions embody a great deal more labour-time than most of those of the past. Augustus Caesar could have more clothes and a larger house than an ordinary well-to-do Roman. But, unless he had wanted to have a pyramid built for him, he had few or no kinds of qualitative freedom, beyond his special political freedom as Emperor, which many other Roman citizens did not enjoy. Communists, who are often regarded as enemies of freedom, lay great stress on the fact that in practice many kinds of freedom, though not legally or customarily restricted, are economically restricted, so that they are the privileges of a small minority. "Liberty," they claim, "is such a precious thing that it must be rationed." Under socialism, as practised in the Soviet Union, certain liberties, for example the liberty to print or to voyage in a yacht, can only be practised by groups.

Finally we must consider internal restrictions on freedom. These may be at a variety of levels which in practice we rather arbitrarily divide into physiological and psychological, though every doctor realizes that the distinction is seldom quite sharp. Clearly a paralytic has less freedom than a man with full power over his muscles. But most people would regard a man with a wooden leg as freer than a cocaine addict or a victim of an obsessional psychosis which compels him to wash his hands twenty times a day. Beyond this it is harder to go! We all know people whose idea of "true freedom" is the following of some very narrow path. We can hardly define psychological freedom without venturing into philosophy. Freedom is something more than being able to do what one desires so far as the laws of nature permit. The drug addict with unlimited supplies of his drug is at least relatively unfree. His actions are controlled by a single motive, and lead to madness and death. A rich man who oscillates in a narrow orbit of office, bed, golf-course, and annual holiday in the same resort, is controlled by a narrow set of motives. He is relatively unfree because he has been so effectively conditioned by society that he has no will of his own. We need not however go to the other extreme and hold up as an example of complete freedom the man who never keeps an appointment or is faithful to one woman for a month on end. The so-called Bohemian can be described as the slave of his own caprices, and psycho-analysis would probably show that he is dominated by irrational motives of which he is unconscious.

As a geneticist, I see the problem in this way: Every human being, apart from monozygotic twins, has a unique genotype. For example, my own genotype determines in me a subnormal capacity for music and a supernormal capacity for mathematics. Every genotype can be placed in many different environments. In some the individual will develop its powers and act freely; in others this will not be so. If I had been born into a musical family and had had no opportunity of learning mathematics, I should have been less free than I am. Some genotypes, such as those which determine idiocy, can never attain to much freedom. A few, perhaps, can only find their realization in anti-social activity, though this is doubtful. But in any modern society a vast number of different activities are open. In so far as the choice between these activities is based on genotypes we can say that the society is free. Or to put it in another way, that society is freest in which each individual is pursuing those activities which give most scope to his or her innate abilities. I am perfectly aware that Aristotle defined happiness as "unimpeded activity." It may be said that I am speaking of happiness rather than freedom. The framers of the American Constitution realized that they were closely connected, though I suspect that happiness arises rather as a by-product from other activities than from its own deliberate pursuit.

But we cannot leave the matter on this merely biological level. I agree with Spinoza, Hegel, Engels, and Caudwell, to whose analysis of freedom in *Illusion and Reality* I am profoundly indebted, in defining freedom as the recognition of necessity. This is obviously true in the technical field. As long as men thought in terms of magic carpets, seven-league boots, and angels who carried a house from Palestine to Italy, they could not begin to investigate the necessities embodied in the laws of physics. And until they did this they could not build railways or automobiles. It is also true in the social and political fields. A free man willingly obeys laws which he recognizes as just, that is to say, necessary in the existing social context. And it is true in the psychological field. Here one is free so far as one understands one's own motives. In order to do this one must not merely examine one's own consciousness and so far as possible one's unconscious, but also the social system by which one has been conditioned. A man who accepts his mother's moral teaching as the voice of conscience is no more free than one who believes his sex hormones when they tell him that the last pretty girl he has met is the most wonderful woman in the world. The difference between a man and an animal is largely a matter of consciousness, and the difference between a psychologically free and unfree man is also largely a matter of consciousness.

FREEDOM OF MOVEMENT

Imprisonment is the very negation of freedom. And freedom to go where one wants to is a very important kind of freedom, if only because one can escape from many kinds of bondage provided emigration to a freer country is possible. In the nineteenth century freedom of movement meant political freedom for many millions of Europeans who crossed the Atlantic to the United States. To-day this is no longer so.

Freedom of movement depends in the most obvious way on technical inventions, such as roads, the riding of animals, wheels, harness, ships, railroads, automobiles, and aeroplanes. But this .technical progress has had two effects. It has made legal restrictions on freedom of movement necessary, and it has led to economic inequalities. Bullock-cart drivers on country roads in India do not seem to worry much about the rule of the road. A collision between two vehicles moving at three miles per hour does not greatly matter. But somewhere about ten miles an hour a rule of the road becomes necessary. At twenty miles an hour the energy liberated in a head-on crash is increased fourfold, and the rule becomes a matter of life and death. With higher speeds an elaborate road code, and special police to enforce it, are needed. That is to say, some legal restrictions on freedom are the inevitable result of technological gains in freedom. In actual fact many of these legal restrictions result in real gains of freedom. I can drive much faster because drivers are restricted to one side of the road than I could if both were legal. And being a rational man I recognize the necessity for this restriction and gain in freedom by doing so.

I gain from other restrictions. The anarchist's ideal would, I suppose, be that anyone should be free to go anywhere. But I am actually freer because this is not so, and no one has a legal right to enter my house except with my permission or with a warrant from the State. I should be still freer if I possessed a small private garden. But privacy can be carried too far, and it is carried too far when one man can enclose a hundred square miles of mountains for the purpose of shooting, and keep the public off them. In this case, as in many others, a considerable measure of equality is a requisite for freedom.

In practice, however, restrictions due to private property in land are less serious than other economic restrictions. Most people in Britain cannot move about as they would like to for one of two reasons. Either they have a job, get only very brief holidays, and, though they may have saved a good deal of money, dare not leave their job for fear of losing it. Or they are out of work and cannot afford to travel. It is extremely difficult to arrive at any data, but I am inclined to think that the average man has a greater freedom of movement in the United States than anywhere else, and that this freedom is increasing most rapidly in the Soviet Union, where it is already fairly high. This, if correct, is due to the great development of transport and the high real wage in the U.S.A., and the system of holidays with pay and workers' holiday resorts in the U.S.S.R., together with the fact that as there is no unemployment there, workers tend to move very freely from one job to another.

It is also due to the large size of these two States. It is extremely difficult to leave one's country in search of work. And in an increasing number of States one cannot take any large sum of money out of it, so that in practice one can only travel abroad on State business or business approved of by the State. The difficulties of foreign travel have been increasing for the average man since 1900. A rich man, or a man with political influence, can fly half round the world in a week. But I can remember when I could travel to most European states without a passport, whereas now I must often waste days in getting the necessary visas. Freedom in this respect is declining rapidly. The restrictions are certainly mainly due to economic causes. If, as seems likely, capitalism works progressively worse as the years pass, they will increase. And it will become increasingly desirable to be a citizen of a State covering a large area. For this purpose, by the way, the British Empire is not a State. One needs a passport or permit to travel to Ireland or Canada from Britain.

As for the internal or psychological aspects of freedom of movement, we are slaves of custom to a most surprising degree. I spent three days this winter going up the principal mountains of Wales in January, when they are covered with snow. I met exactly two other parties, though the Alps were crawling with Englishmen a year ago. And in certain types of society there is a strong ideological objection to travel. It is instructive to read the words which Dante puts into the mouth of Ulysses in hell. In one of the greatest passages in literature he describes a voyage of exploration to South Africa. And he repents it. Dante thought it was wicked to sail outside the Straits of Gibraltar.

Very few people are explorers. A ban on exploration is no infringement of the liberty of the vast majority of people. Yet it may have a decisive effect on the history of a nation. The present expansionist drive in Japan is largely a belated attempt to overcome the handicap produced by the prohibition of foreign travel from 1636 to 1860. A blow to the liberty of a very small minority may be a blow to a whole people.

FREEDOM AS A CONSUMER

Every human being is a consumer, even if not a producer. Every improvement in the technique of manufacture means a potential increase in freedom of consumption. So does every increase in real wages. Hence a comparison of the real wages in different countries tells us a good deal about the amount of this kind of freedom. Given the possibility of buying something beyond essential food, clothing, and shelter, freedom depends on the choice of commodities or services which is available and the way in which the choice is actually made.

Legal restrictions may be few, as in the United States. (Some people think that lethal weapons are too easily bought there.) They may be very serious, as in Britain during war, when many foreign-made goods are unobtainable owing to import restrictions. Over large sections of the world freedom of consumption has been drastically curtailed in recent years in order to promote national economic self-sufficiency, or autarchy. Apart from the question of books, which will be considered later, the most interesting problem is that of alcohol and drugs. Heroin is an unrivalled cough cure. I have several times taken large amounts of it for a considerable period without developing the faintest craving. Probably many others—perhaps a majority— would be none the worse if they could buy it freely whenever they had a cough. But there are enough potential addicts to justify its prohibition. Many people would prohibit alcoholic beverages because when they are sold freely some people abuse them. The attempt was a failure in the United States, but may succeed in India. No prohibition of this kind should be regarded as desirable in itself. In fact, even if we agree that narcotics should not now be sold freely, we may hope that our descendants will one day achieve sufficient psychological freedom to make free sale possible.

Custom, as well as law, plays a very big part in limiting freedom of consumption. There may be a standardized type of expenditure for a given class or profession. Thus, until recently in England, the ritual killing of foxes, grouse, salmon, and so on, at appropriate times of the year, was the hallmark of respectability. At an earlier period a gentleman was expected to form a library. In the present age of transition England is probably unusually free in this respect, freer than the United States or France. On the other hand, as we shall see later, England is one of the least free countries in the world as regards discussion of the merits of consumable goods.

I think it probable that, owing to the high average real wage, the United States heads the list as regards freedom of consumption. This was almost certainly so during the epoch immediately preceding the Eighteenth Amendment and the economic collapse of 1929. To-day there are so many families with no margin for buying beyond the barest necessities that it is not so certain. The most rapid increase, though from a low level, is occurring in the Soviet Union.

FREEDOM AS A PRODUCER

I personally enjoy nearly maximal freedom as to how I earn my living. I am paid to devote myself to a certain branch of science. I give a few lectures and conduct research on problems which interest me. I have no fixed hours of work, and I could take three months' holiday a year if I wished. Besides this I earn some money by writing. But I do not have to support opinions of which I disapprove in order to earn my living. In fact I combine a decent remuneration with free choice. A few other intellectual workers are equally fortunate, but this number is rapidly diminishing, at least in western Europe. How few paid manual or administrative workers enjoy this kind of freedom is shown by the universal demand for recreation, i.e., an alternative to work and purely cultural activities, such as listening to good music, and by the fact that many people actually look forward to retiring from their work.

On the technological level freedom of production is being rapidly strangled by the abuse of patent laws by monopolists. In many industries the small firm is hopelessly handicapped for this reason, quite apart from underselling and other activities of trusts.

Freedom as a producer means, in particular, freedom to choose your occupation, freedom to regulate its details, and unless the occupation is pleasurable, short hours of work and long holidays. Where there is widespread unemployment there can be no freedom of choice. A man with a job holds it like a bulldog, and does not try a number until he gets one to his liking. Under capitalism the workers have little opportunity of controlling their conditions of labour, though trade unions can accomplish something, and as a voter the worker may be able to help himself in a very indirect way. Where, as in Germany, neither method is available, illegal strike action may still have some effect. But direct control, as on a Soviet collective farm, or to a less extent in a Soviet factory, is only possible under socialism. Since hours and holidays are satisfactory in the Soviet Union, and unemployment does not exist, it appears that man is freer as a producer there than elsewhere. Since in all capitalist countries the independent producer is being more and more completely eliminated, the prospects of freedom for producers under capitalism do not seem to be bright.

FREEDOM AS A CAPITALIST

In Dante's hell the sins of Sodom and Cahors were punished by a shower of slowly falling flames. But while the former class of sinners could escape them to some extent by running, the latter, who were usurers, or as we should say, financiers, were not allowed this privilege. However, usury is now permitted throughout Christendom, and this freedom has been an essential condition of the immense technical advances made under capitalism. These advances are slowing down because finance, which formerly served industry, is now strangling it.

In the Soviet Union the sin of Cahors is punished in this world, and so are other activities by which one man appropriates what, according to Marxist economics, is the value created by the labour of others. These activities include not only usury, but private trade and the employment of others for profit. The extreme form of the latter kind of exploitation, namely, slavery, is of course almost universally illegal. The anti-socialist claims that a very vital kind of freedom has been suppressed. The socialist retorts that this kind of freedom, like freedom to drive on the wrong side of the road, is incompatible with the fullest technical progress, and that those natural powers which are developed in the capitalist can be used under socialism in administrative posts. Outside the Soviet Union freedom of trade and investment is at present being effectively strangled in most belligerent and some neutral countries, except for those very large corporations which to a considerable extent control the States. It is hard to say where the capitalist is freest. I should hazard a guess that Argentina stood somewhere near the opposite pole from the Soviet Union.

SEXUAL FREEDOM

The minimum amount of freedom compatible with the reproduction of the race was enjoyed in Paraguay, where the Jesuits married off their Indian subjects without allowing a choice of spouses. Marriage between different groups of the population may be illegal, as in Germany and South Africa; it may lead to loss of employment, as when officers in the British Guards "marry beneath them;" or it may merely meet with social disapproval. Divorce and re-marriage are permitted in most countries, though not, for example, in Italy.

Extra-marital intercourse is rarely a crime, provided the parties are of a certain age. However, adultery is liable to severe punishment in India. And prostitution is criminal in many countries, though only in the Soviet Union is the man concerned punished more severely than the woman. Intercourse between two males is generally criminal (though not in Denmark), while that of women is rarely so. There is an equally bewildering variety in the customary limitations to sexual activity. In some circles within the same country monogamy is rigid, in others people normally "live in sin."

Almost everyone will agree that complete sexual freedom (which I suppose would include freedom of rape) is undesirable. Dante and I (to mention no others) would say the same of economic freedom. As regards legal sexual freedom Denmark probably heads the list of civilized states, while Ireland ranks very low both as regards legal and customary freedom. The high cultural level and the rarity of prostitution in Denmark seem to show that such freedom may be harmless.

The main economic bars to sexual freedom are unemployment and gross disparity of income. Both of these may lead a woman to cohabit (whether in or out of wedlock) with a man whom she does not love, but whose income is more secure or larger than her own would be were she independent. It may similarly, but more rarely, induce a man to marry a woman for her money, or to live with her. This kind of check on freedom is probably most pronounced in the "Latin" nations and least so in the Soviet Union.

A discussion of psychological checks awaits the development of a comparative analytical psychology.

FREEDOM TO COMMUNICATE IDEAS AND STATEMENTS

This field of freedom includes freedom of speech, of the post, and of the press. Technologically it depends on the inventions of writing, printing, telegraphy, radio, and so on, and on the development of arts such as poetry, drama, and cinematography. Incitements to certain crimes and grossly indecent speech, writing, and art are everywhere illegal. Further, one or more of the technical means of communication may be a monopoly of the State or of big business. Thus radio is directly controlled by the State almost everywhere in Europe, but not in the United States. On the other hand the United States film industry is probably more trustified than those of some European nations.

The legal restraints may be by civil or criminal law. State prosecutions of men for speeches and writings are rather rare in England, though a Mr. Gott has several times been imprisoned for rude remarks about God, and ten years ago communist speakers and writers were constantly being imprisoned. If Britain follows the example of France, this condition is likely to recur. But as compared with many countries Englishmen have a wide liberty of propaganda on general matters. For example, in France the State forbids public statements in favour of the Third International; in the Soviet Union, against it. In England both are permitted, but favourable statements must be cautiously framed.

In law there is extremely little freedom of political discussion in England. Sedition is defined as a word, deed, or writing calculated to disturb the tranquillity of the State, and lead ignorant persons to subvert the government and laws. In actual practice you can say a great deal in ordinary times, and print a great deal if you can get a printer. But in times of political tension the law may be enforced against the opponents of the government. Not of course against the opponents of the king. In 1936 the *Daily Worker*, the communist party organ, was alone among daily papers in suggesting that Edward VIII might consult his own wishes regarding his marriage. The undoubtedly seditious and possibly treasonable activities of the leaders of the Conservative party and the Church of England which led to that monarch's abdication were not, of course, interfered with.

In the Soviet Union the position is the opposite. Legally there is fairly complete freedom of speech. And actually there is a good deal. I have heard a man say that he could not see much difference between Stalin and Nicholas. A member of an important Soviet merely replied that there was quite a big difference. But on the whole, custom is more stringent than law; so that there is somewhat less verbal political criticism than in England, though much more than in Germany or

Italy, and perhaps more than in France. On the other hand the press has in practice little freedom in political matters. In fact in Europe a press consistently opposing the government is only found in Britain, Switzerland (and before Hitler's invasion), in Belgium, Holland, and the Scandinavian countries. In Switzerland, Holland, and Belgium, this liberty was largely restricted. Thus among European nations, Britain enjoys considerable press freedom in political matters.

On the other hand English civil law makes any statement which could affect the financial interests of a well-to-do man very dangerous. For example, a firm recently circulated a leaflet to the effect that I habitually used a medicine which they sell. I have never even seen it. I was told that the statement was not a libel on me. I attempted to deny it in the press and even to suggest that the firm had in some measure departed from the strictest canons of morality in using my name. This suggestion was held to be probably libellous, and no journal would publish it for fear of an action. Finally one journal has consented to publish a bare denial without any comment.

Similarly it is extremely dangerous to make any attack on the character of a rich man in public life. In consequence there is an entirely erroneous impression in many quarters that British politics are less corrupt than those of France or the United States. Attempts have been made to start consumers' research in Britain, as in the United States. But the law of libel prevents this. Hence there has been a considerable deterioration in the quality of some British manufactured goods in recent years from the high standards of the nineteenth century.

To my mind the correct law would be fairly simple. Either statements of a general character about commodities made without any evidence being adduced in their support, such as "Guinness[1] is good for you," should be illegal; or, better, it should be legal to make such statements and also equally unsupported statements, such as "Bass[1] is bad for you, and Worthington[1] is worse." At present, in commercial matters one can only praise, and not blame. Given the further fact that

[1] These are names of beers widely sold in England.

advertisers exercise a very strong influence over the policy of newspapers, so that in practice numbers of advertisements appear in the news columns, it will be seen that there is very little freedom of criticism in commercial matters.

This kind of criticism appears to be highly developed in the Soviet Union, particularly in such journals as *Krokodil* and *Vechernaya Moskva*. And indeed it is a necessity if socialism is to be successful, since such criticism is a possible alternative to competition for sales between different firms, as a means for keeping up the quality of goods.

The freedom of the press is both legally and economically limited. In most countries libel, whether seditious or not, is more severely punished than slander. Everywhere technological progress is tending to improve the position of the big daily newspaper with a circulation covering a radius of 250 miles or so from its press, as against the small paper. Hence large capital is needed to start a daily newspaper, and wholesale distributive organizations can be used, and are used in England, to boycott any newspaper which criticizes the government too severely. In practice this method, and the influence of advertisers, means that in capitalist countries the circulation of socialist journals is very small compared with the number of socialists, even where such journals are legal. In the Soviet Union any attempt to start an opposition journal would probably be prevented by practical rather than legal difficulties.

The position as regards publication of books is roughly parallel to that of the press. In Britain the law of libel is the main check. I have personally been prevented from criticizing fraudulent claims made for foods and drugs, from suggesting that certain doctors were incompetent, and from exposing pro-Nazi activities of British Conservative politicians and writers. The ban on indecency makes a scientific discussion of certain branches of human physiology rather difficult. But it is not a serious difficulty. On the other hand it is extremely severe in Ireland and used with great effect. Books published in Britain which are politically offensive to the government have long been prevented from entering certain parts of the Empire, and since the war their export to neutral countries has also been stopped. However, as regards book publication Britain is incomparably freer than most European states.

Other methods of disseminating opinion, such as the drama, are often subject to censorship. This is so in Britain. At the present moment for example, the censor, though be allows a measure of anti-war propaganda on the stage, forbids all reference to the help rendered to Hitler by members of the British government in the years before the present war. On the other hand the censorship of indecent passages has been greatly relaxed of recent years, and almost all portions of the female body are now legally visible on the London stage. This is doubtless a gain for liberty for spectators, but hardly for girls who lose their jobs if they try to exercise the liberty to keep their clothes on. There is also a censorship of films in most countries. These forms of censorship are strongly supported by the Catholic Church, although of late years this body has probably disseminated more indecent (and untrue) stories than any other organization, mainly in connection with the Spanish war. As a matter of fact the Republican government was rather puritanical. The film censorship is everywhere strongly political.

The radio is generally a State monopoly. At one time the British radio sponsored discussions on political, social, and religious topics, but these were always censored to some extent and were finally discontinued. It is now purely an organ of government propaganda. The United States radios are very much freer, though like the press their general political policy is controlled by that of the advertisers. However, British listeners are certainly freer than those of many other countries. They are permitted to listen to the German radio (a freedom of which I have not myself taken advantage for some months), while Germans who listen to the British radio are imprisoned.

We see then that the liberty of the press which was gained during the nineteenth century has now been lost in most countries, partly by direct government action, partly by the use of the civil law, and partly by technological advances which have favoured centralization, and therefore control by big business. On the other hand the radio and cinema have never achieved so great a freedom as the press.

It is probable that the highest degree of freedom of communication of ideas exists in Denmark and in certain parts of
the United States, notably in New York State, while the lowest
degree is to be found in Germany and Italy. This kind of freedom is a very important one, but intellectuals are apt to speak
and write as if it were the only kind. Actually an intelligent
but reactionary government will allow a large measure of freedom of press and speech, being well aware of the fact that
discontented people can "blow off steam" by this means .with-
out causing any serious disturbance, particularly in countries
such as Britain with a long tradition of fairly free discussion.
This is all the more the case if they can control the radio, the
films, and the more widely circulated newspapers. For this
reason freedom of speech and press, though correlated with
political freedom, is not synonymous with it.

I have not mentioned the internal barriers to freedom of
expression. And yet they are of profound importance. Some
of us are no doubt congenitally incapable of original expression
in words, music, photography, or any other art form. But most
psychologists, and most ordinary people who have had sym-
pathetic dealings with children, believe that the majority of
human beings could make some real contribution to culture if
they were put in the right environment. For some reason or
other

> "Shades of the prison-house begin to close
> Upon the growing boy."

This may be due to economic causes. In the case of many
a mute inglorious Milton, the poet says that

> "Chill penury repress's their noble rage,
> And froze the genial current of the soul."

But as the rich and the moderately well-to-do are almost as
dumb as the poor, this is not the whole story. Probably most
people could express themselves best in some communal activity
such as symphonic music, drama, or dance. "Civilized" society
is well organized for mass production of commodities and for
mass consumption of standardized cultural commodities such

as cinema films and phonograph records. But it is far less organized than most primitive societies for collective artistic activity. Possibly the Soviet Union may be leading the way here. My own opinion is that the prospects for artistic activity are probably brightest in China, where art has never been thoroughly commercialized, and if peace and security are restored the natural artistic ability of the people will find a new scope. And the genuine respect of the Chinese for intellectual activity may make China in the future, as it has more than once been in the past, the intellectual's paradise.

POLITICAL FREEDOM

On no aspect of freedom is there more confusion than on that of political freedom. At one time it is taken to mean government by natives of one's own country, rather than by foreigners. Yet there is more political freedom (though not very much) in a province of British India such as Bengal than in a "native state" with an absolute ruler, such as Hyderabad or Nepal. It is also regarded as synonymous with democracy, and the latter with parliamentary government, though the Greeks who invented the word democracy (which meant government of the people, by the people, for the people, which did not, however, include women or slaves) had no parliaments. Finally it is taken to mean the right of stating opinions on political matters.

Nowhere in the world do these conditions exist in their entirety. The first type is only possible in practice for powerful nations. The members of smaller nations may easily find themselves in the position of citizens of Iraq, Estonia, or Cuba, and this possibility increases with the development of transport. Actually they are better off as members of a larger aggregate in which they enjoy a measure of cultural autonomy and equality of citizenship. It is useless for Welshmen or Georgians to say that they are oppressed by English or Russians, when Lloyd George, a Welshman, was chosen (and may conceivably be chosen again) to rule England in a critical hour; while Stalin, a Georgian, is the most important man in Russia. It may be that Welshmen would be freer if Wales enjoyed as much autonomy as Georgia, but actually the Welsh nationalist movement is not very strong. Where there is not equality of this kind, nationalist movements certainly make for increased freedom. This was, I think, the case in Ireland, and is in India. On the other hand the nationalist movement of the Sudeten Germans, which brought them under Hitler, diminished their freedom.

The second type of political freedom is claimed for all kinds of political systems. Even the Nazis claim that they enjoy "true" freedom, because Hitler expresses the political ideals of every true German. If so there must be a lot of untrue Germans. Now in the past there have been two main types of democratic government, namely, the Greco-Roman and American types. In the former all citizens met together frequently, listened to orators, and voted for or against laws. In the latter they elect representatives at rare intervals, and these latter legislate. I call this system American rather than English, because when America became a democracy, the English Parliament was still elected on a very restricted franchise.

The obvious advantage of the first system is that the citizens decide matters directly concerning them, and of which they have immediate knowledge. Its disadvantages are, firstly, that voting is public and intimidation therefore possible, and that while well adapted for the government of a small city, it is impracticable for a State, let alone an Empire. It was largely for the latter reason that it broke down when Rome acquired an Empire.

The American or representative type is adapted for a large State, but has the disadvantage that representatives can and do break their election pledges, that the people can only vote at rare intervals, and that in practice they have a choice only between representatives of a few organizations (e.g., the two great American parties), whose policies are framed in secret by a small number of men. In the Soviet Union an attempt has been made to combine these two types of democratic mechanism. The village Soviet has the advantages and disadvantages of a Greek Assembly, whilst the supreme Soviet corresponds to the American Congress.

In theory this is an ideal system, but it is claimed that in practice all power is in the hands of the Communist party and its sympathizers. In practice, however, parliaments are also controlled from outside. In 1921, when Mr. Lloyd George then Prime Minister of Britain, was displaying a certain radicalism in his financial policy, the *Financial Times* asked, "Does he and do his colleagues realize that half a dozen men at the top of the big five banks could upset the whole fabric of government finance by refraining from renewing Treasury Bills?" Certainly the Labour party realized this ten years later. "Upsetting the whole fabric of government finance" is, of course, not sedition!

In practice, then, the political liberty in a parliamentary democracy is largely at the mercy of big business. But not wholly so. Enough parliaments have annoyed big business to render it necessary to suppress parliamentary government over much of Europe. And not only in Europe. Newfoundland was unable to pay its debts to Britain. In consequence "the mother of parliaments" began to eat her children, and Newfoundland is now governed by British officials. It will be remembered that when Britain refused to pay its debts to America the British Parliament was replaced by an American Governor-General!

The plain fact is that over most of the world such parliaments as survive are as subservient to big business as is the supreme Soviet in Moscow to the Communist party. And even the most violent opponents of Communism will hardly claim that big business is democratic. Nowhere in the world is there political liberty as Jefferson conceived it, and as it actually existed in the days before monopoly capitalism developed. There is still a fair amount in parts of north-western Europe, the Soviet Union, the United States, the British Dominions, and some Latin American republics. On the whole it seems to be on the upgrade in the Soviet Union, China, and (with intermissions) in India, but stationary or on the down grade elsewhere.

So long as the present class struggle goes on we cannot look for any great measure of political freedom even in the intervals between wars. Only a classless society which does not feel itself menaced either from within or without is likely to develop a

off

true political freedom in which discussion is both legally and economically free, and constitutionally elected governments are not overthrown by the violence or economic pressure of minorities. We may look forward to such a day, but we must not deceive ourselves into believing that comparative freedom of discussion, pleasant as it may be for intellectuals like myself, is synonymous with full political freedom. If the newspapers, radio, and other means of large-scale propaganda are mainly controlled directly or indirectly by big business, there is only rarely need for the forcible suppression of opposition. But the possibility of such suppression is always in the background. Under the Emergency Powers Act of 1939 any British citizen can be imprisoned without trial for an indefinite period. It will be very surprising indeed if this act is not used to strangle constitutional opposition. In England to-day political freedom has *de jure* no existence at all, even if *de facto* a good deal remains.

But if speech is still theoretically free, as indeed it is in the Soviet Union, this is because speech is an obsolete method of propaganda compared with radio and the press, and if our oligarchs control the latter they can afford to allow a rather moderate liberty of the former.

RELIGIOUS LIBERTY

We saw at an earlier stage that religious liberty embraces a very wide field. In the sense of freedom to propagate religious and irreligious opinions and to perform rites which are not held to be cruel or indecent, it is fairly widespread. However, it is rarely complete. For example, a conscript in Britain must register as a member of some Christian sect or as a Jew, for the purpose of burial. Being neither a Christian nor a Jew, I exploited the liberty available to me as a soldier in 1914-18 by registering as an adherent of several different branches of Christianity, and of Judaism, on different occasions. Adults are not compelled to attend religious ceremonies, though they are hard to avoid in the army. But children can be and are compelled to do so in most countries, whilst in the Soviet Union I understand that organized religious instruction of children is forbidden. Thus in practice religious liberty is often like that of Germany after the Reformation, when each petty ruler was free to persecute his subjects if they disagreed with his theological opinions. Every British father is a princeling who can beat his children if they do not go to the church of which he approves, or go to one of which he does not.

Religious freedom is seriously compromised where religion involves ritual, food or rest. It is very difficult for an orthodox Jew to rest on Saturday in England, or for an orthodox Christian to rest on Sunday in Russia. In fact full religious freedom is impossible in an integrated community, simply because many religions can only be practised in their entirety when the vast majority of a people hold them.

The minimum of religious freedom is found in some Mohammedan countries such as Afghanistan, Persia, and parts of Arabia, and in Spain. It is rather low where there has recently been a violent reaction against religious intolerance, as in Mexico. It is below the maximum where any form of religion or irreligion is associated with the State, as in Britain, Italy, Sweden, and the Soviet Union. It may also be lowered where a religion is associated with foreign influence, as is Christianity in China. Here the Chinese, who are on the whole very tolerant in religious matters, have forbidden missionaries to attempt conversions to Christianity because such activity is thought likely to break up the national unity.

The highest degree of religious freedom is probably found in the United States, where the State is formally neutral in religious matters. But complete religious liberty is impossible, simply because all religious bodies are somewhat intolerant when their supporters control the government. They may be very intolerant like the Catholic Church, or very slightly so, like the Society of Friends, but they cannot, from their nature, be completely tolerant.

FREEDOM OF WOMEN AND CHILDREN

The freedom of women has very little to do with the freedom of sexual relations. It is minimal in Mohammedan countries such as Arabia, Persia, and Afghanistan, where all women are veiled and those of the well-to-do classes are imprisoned. The impossibility of romantic love in such countries is compensated by homo-sexuality. It is maximal in countries such as the United States and the Soviet Union whose women not only enjoy legal equality with men but are actually appointed to responsible positions such as that of ambassador. Indeed in the United States women's rights are perhaps over-developed in connection with alimony for divorced wives, which enables a number of women to live an idle life at the expense of men. The same type of male subjection is found in a less developed form in England. Complete liberty and equality in this matter can only be achieved where work is available for every able-bodied adult.

Children enjoy little liberty where the family is patriarchal and their corporal punishment is commonly practised. State education generally makes for greater liberty for children, who often obtain a valuable political education by playing off their parents against their teachers. In Britain the children of the poor are far freer than those of the rich. A rich boy can be birched on his bare back at Eton up to the age of nineteen, and is then sent to a university where he is locked up every night until he is twenty-three or so. In fact, ruling classes the world over, are cruel to their own children. They have to be moulded into efficient members of the class, and must suffer in consequence. The Hitler *Jugend* appears to be an attempt to inflict the English public school spirit on all the children of an unfortunate nation.

Complete freedom for children is impossible, but children can, in practice, be given freedom at a very early age if their training is directed to teaching them the recognition of necessity. This means that they must be allowed to see and feel the consequences of their own actions, which will inevitably include some broken limbs and other injuries. If they are neither bullied nor pampered they develop human personalities at a very early age, and may be responsible citizens at the age of seventeen.

It is particularly difficult to compare different countries as regards the freedom of children. Child labour for long hours at monotonous work is no doubt a negation of freedom. But a boy doing interesting paid work for short hours is far freer than one in a school learning dull and often useless lessons.

CONCLUSION

We have ranged over a number of fields in each of which a greater or less degree of freedom is possible. Nowhere have we found the problem simple. This is partly because one man's freedom limits that of another, so that most kinds of freedom demand a measure of equality. If six bankers can control a State, it is time that the bankers had less freedom. In fact freedom in a Class State means mainly freedom for one class, and that generally turns out to be a poor sort of freedom. In particular, if a ruling class is to be efficient, its members must be severely conditioned in youth. On the other hand the overthrow of the class state has meant in the Soviet Union a period of "dictatorship of the proletariat" with considerable restrictions on freedom, and would probably do so elsewhere.

Three facts must be kept in mind. Even the freest of men has been so conditioned that he does not notice the lack of some freedom which a man born in another place or time would regard as essential. This is why we are honestly apt to regard our own country as "the land of the free and the home of the brave," when we see the restrictions to which foreigners submit without a murmur. Curiously enough the foreigners often think the same when they visit our country. An intellectual who is making a fairly good living often regards himself as almost absolutely free. He is freer than many of his fellows. But he is only free because his product, whether in science, art, or literature, happens to find a market. When the market changes he finds that his freedom may be freedom to starve. However, the market is not a natural phenomenon, like the weather. It can be controlled, and although this involves some restriction of freedom, more and more people are coming to think that it results in a considerable increase of freedom on the whole.

Secondly, freedom is positive as well as negative. Man is a

social animal, and human freedom can only be freedom in society, that is to say, freedom to act as a social being. This is a hard saying, because it means that certain kinds of freedom, for example the freedom of a landlord to keep the public off a hundred square miles of mountains or the freedom of a few bankers to overthrow a government are anti-social. But it turns out that they are anti-social just because they restrict the freedom of others. The Greeks had a word for the man who used his freedom to turn his back on society. The word was "ἰδιώτης", in English: "idiot."

Thirdly, freedom is not static. It is always finding new fields. For example we are beginning to recognize the right of animals to freedom. It is now thought wrong to chain up a dog for life, though the anthropomorphism of our ideas on this matter can be illustrated by the case of an eagle which recently returned to its cage in the London Zoo after two days of miserable liberty. Like everything that grows, freedom negates itself. The individual lover of freedom may join an organization which limits his own choice. Moreover, he is more likely to find himself in prison than the man who always takes his cue from the majority.

And the same is true on a larger scale. A war or revolution fought for freedom means the temporary loss of a good deal of freedom. In the long run the loss is generally more than made good. But a social change, like a technological advance, always means a loss of some former liberty. We must realize that the freedom of one man may be the bondage of another, that the charter of liberty of one generation may form the chains of its successor.

I believe that a comparative study of freedom on the lines which I have indicated would do a great deal to increase the respect between different nations, many of which, if far from ideal, have at least something to teach others in this important matter. It would enable us to see the beam in our own eye before crusading to remove our neighbour's mote. And a historical study would show us the way in which freedom has actually developed, and help all lovers of freedom to strive for a real increase of that great good. The position of freedom in the modern world is so precarious that its preservation and extension require not only good will, but all the thought which we can devote to it. The problem of freedom is not a simple problem. Now as never before in history *Notre salut dépend de notre intelligence.*

Lancelot Hogben

THE CONTEMPORARY CHALLENGE
TO FREEDOM OF THOUGHT[1]

AGITATION for the removal of religious tests in the
English universities coincided with a vigorous episcopal
crusade against the evolutionary doctrine. This circumstance is chiefly responsible for the growth of a movement to
check the influence of the Churches on English educational
policy and public discussion of such matters as the age of the
earth, the spiritual value of venereal disease, and the personal
convenience of anæsthetics. It attracted leaders of scientific
thought who wanted to be free to discuss their discoveries,
manufacturers who wanted to promote technical instruction,
social pioneers who were exasperated with clerical landlordism
or episcopal opposition to reforms, and neopagan æsthetes
who recognized scope for a new priestcraft without the tire-
some taboos of the old order.

This ragbag of liberal rationalism and free thought as the
terms were used in the opening years of the present century.
You were a free thinker if, like T. H. Huxley or Sir Arthur
Keith, you did not believe in table turning and asserted the
need for biological knowledge as a foundation for rational
citizenship. You are also a free thinker if, like Aldous Huxley,
you believe in spirits, or if, like Bernard Shaw, you would
incarcerate biologists for torturing dumb animals. You were

[1]An address delivered to the Conference of the World Union of Free Thinkers
in London, September, 1938.

a free thinker if you thought, as did Herbert Spencer, that cut-throat competition is a necessary basis of production. You are likewise a free thinker if you think, as Karl Marx thought, that capitalism is burglary sanctified by superstition. You were a free thinker, if you wanted to retreat with Mr. Lowes Dickinson into a parochial anachronism called the Greek Way of Life. So also are those who wish to hurry forward to the antiseptic World-State of Mr. Wells.

Such an alliance could hold together only while the signatories to the pact had good reason to fear the power which the Churches could exercise against them, or had no reason to fear more powerful antagonism from other quarters. If more powerful impediments do indeed exist, those of us who are scientific workers are forced to re-examine the meaning we confer on rationalism and free thought, when we identify them with our own convictions.

It is then clear that many people who are not scientific workers do not use them in the same sense as we do. When some people talk about rational argument they mean confidence in a logical edifice built on a foundation of self-evident principles. The scientific worker distrusts the exercise of man's reasoning powers except in so far as they are continually disciplined by factual verification and search for new data. Those who identify rationalism with an undue respect for verbal logic generally identify freedom of thought with permission to persist in discussing age-old conundrums without guidance of new information or intention to arrive at a definite conclusion which might influence human conduct. Scientific workers need have no interest in this pastime and no special sympathy for creating or preserving opportunities for exercising it.

It is plain humbug for a teacher of chemistry to say that he aims at giving his student an open mind about the atomic weights of the elements. His aim is to lead the student to definite conclusions which can be used as recipes for chemical manufacture, and the freedom which he demands is the freedom to test their usefulness in the domain of action. The job of the scientific worker is to find out what the world is like, and to communicate his discoveries about it. As a citizen it is also his responsibility to discuss their social relevance with other citizens. Among scientific workers intellectual freedom therefore means the removal of social obstacles to discovery, communication, or public interpretation of new facts. So how to preserve it raises the question: What impediments to scientific enquiry exist in contemporary society?

It is obvious that organized Christianity was an impediment to scientific enquiry in the Italy of Galileo, in the France of Descartes, in the Germany of Haeckel, and in the England of Darwin. Because somewhat similar conditions exist in other countries to-day, it is a privilege and a duty to express the international unity of the scientific outlook through the World Union of Free Thinkers. On the other hand it is not obvious that the Churches now constitute a powerful obstacle to scientific enquiry in Protestant countries such as Britain, Sweden, or Iceland, and it is not obvious that a liberal form of Christianity such as Quakerism need be hostile to the growth of science and its applications in man's social life.

§ 2

A fruitful discussion of intellectual freedom from the standpoint of the scientific worker must begin with a study of social forces which impel and impede scientific progress. The conventional and idealistic view is that scientific discovery owes its impetus to curiosity, and that the principal obstacle to its fulfilment is superstition. Given the facts that man is (a) curious and (b) superstitious, we can still ask in what circumstances his behaviour is more curious or more superstitious. The common-sense view to which we are led by study of the history of science is that material necessity is the mother of invention. Curiosity predominates when social conditions conspire to force new and urgent problems on the attention of a sufficiently extensive personnel. Contrariwise, discovery does not flourish when social conditions provide cheap substitutes for ingenuity.

Cheap labour and cheap valuation of human life act as a

check on discovery. The Attic Greek culture which drew material inspiration from the surplus wealth created by slave labour in the silver mines was scientifically sterile, because it was the culture of a leisured class divorced from contact with the instruments of production. In the history of science few social circumstances have been as important as those which led to the disappearance of chattel slavery. This view, well supported by Professor Farrington's recent book on Greek civilization, is repeatedly illustrated in *Science for the Citizen*. If we accept it, we are able to approach the conflicts between Christianity and science from a new viewpoint. For our present purpose we must distinguish two parallel and opposing currents in Christian syncretism. One may be called the Spartacist ethic derived from its *Essene* background. The other was the Platonic metaphysics for the reception of which the Pauline teaching prepared the way.

Inspired by the former, monks founded hospitals to which the progress of science owes far more than most free thinkers are willing to admit. Christian medicine opened the doors to the Jewish missionaries of Moorish science, and it can scarcely be doubted that the influence of the early Church encouraged the decline of chattel slavery. The overthrow of the pagan schools of Alexandria was the partial destruction of a culture which had long since fossilized and could no longer provide guidance for fresh human achievements. Unhappily the cosmogony of the Timaeus, already enshrined in Christian theology, outlived the sound navigational science which was salvaged by the Moors. Progressively, the official metaphysic of Christianity approximated to a Platonism which accepted the necessity of servile labour and, as a corollary, exalted ratiocination out of contact with the mundane realities from which science draws its sustenance.

As Platonism supplanted Essenism, the Platonic ingredients of Aristotle's ethics and Aristotle's physics had long since displaced the temper of the *Natural History*, when the Parliament of Paris passed the well-known law of 1624, prescribing that chemists of the Sorbonne must conform to the teachings of Aristotle on pain of death or confiscation of goods. Each

department of knowledge which is recognized as a science in
the modern sense of the word has felt the same paralysing grip.
The dead hand of Christian Platonism which checked the
progress of Astronomy, of Chemistry, of Physics, and of
Biology guided the pen of Gladstone in his luckless onslaught
on the evolutionists. In the year after the publication of
Darwin's book Gladstone expressed the official view of the
English governing classes in a memorandum for Lord Lyttelton
with reference to the Public Schools Commission.[1]

> Why, after all, is the classical training paramount . . . ? Is it
> because we find it established, because it improves memory and
> taste or gives precision or develops the faculty of speech? All
> these are but . . . narrow glimpses of a great and comprehensive
> truth. . . . The modern European civilization . . . is the com-
> pound of two great factors, the Christian religion for the spirit
> of man and the Greek, and in a secondary degree the Roman,
> discipline for his mind and intellect. St. Paul is the apostle of the
> Gentiles and in his own person a symbol of this great wedding
> —the place of Aristotle and Plato in Christian education is not
> arbitrary nor in principle mutable.

Much water has passed under the bridges since Gladstone
told Parliament that "after all science is but a small part of
education."[2] The Universities Test Acts have been repealed.
Natural Science and the humanities are now co-partners in
university property and according to the more or less explicit
articles of partnership there are two sorts of knowledge:
useful or scientific, and humane or gentlemanly. Useful knowledge leads you to definite conclusions, and (like 1066) this is
a good thing because it gives us motor cars promoting travel
whereby gentlemen can come to no conclusions about more
topics. The mission of humane knowledge is to prevent you
from coming to definite conclusions by propounding the unanswerable. This is also a good thing. When curiosity might
tempt them to conclusions which prompt ungentlemanly effort
or disloyalty to the property rights of other gentlemen, it takes
gentlemen out of danger.

[1] Morley, Appendix, p. 445, 1911 edition, ref. to Vol. ii, p. 326.
[2] Morley, Book III, Chap. VIII.

In short the social function of the new compromise is to protect the study of human society from what is called empiricism (of approved topics) and muck-raking (when the subject is a forbidden one). To those of us who live in Britain evolution is no longer a forbidden topic. The perennial eclecticism of Protestant Christianity has in turn assimilated evolution, the higher criticism and birth control, if undertaken in a prayerful spirit. To some extent it retains its hold on people because its more vocal spokesmen include many men of humane and generous outlook anxious to redress remediable social grievances. In Britain an organized movement to assert the claims of free scientific inquiry in *higher* education would be scarcely necessary, if we had to reckon with no serious opposition from other bodies.

None the less the birth-throes of a new science are still painful. Although we do not confine a man to a Bishop's palace with the use of books when he looks up a telescope and announces a new truth about the satellites of Jupiter, penalties for inquiry into forbidden topics are scarcely less discouraging than in former times. If he pries into the balance sheet of a great financial corporation and publishes the truth about it, we send him to hard labour without writing materials. We no longer call it heresy. Our secular theologians call it criminal libel.

To-day active opposition to realistic research is mainly directed against attempts to study how man can enlist the new powers which science has placed at his disposal for the satisfaction of common social needs and the prolongation of human life. This opposition takes different forms in different countries. In some it is honestly anti-rationalistic. In our own it is professedly "rational." An example of the former is Fascist propaganda which exploits fear of unknown contingencies and sentiments of frustration which fasten on the foreigner in our midst as the convenient symbol of inconvenient innovations. In Britain the main obstruction to scientific humanism is the old enemy of science. No longer the ritual Platonism of the Churches, it is now the secular Platonism of the universities.

Two features of a culture which has its social basis in servile labour are exemplified by Platonism. Both are hostile to the scientific outlook and both were recognized as such by the pioneers of the English Royal Society, when the foundations of English empirical tradition were established. One is a pernicious belief in the all-sufficiency of formal reasoning unchecked by search for new information. The two Bacons in succession led the revolt against it. Sprat, episcopal author of the first history of the Royal Society, and Joseph Glanville, the contemporary free thinker, who wrote about the hallowed pastime of witch burning, afterwards called it the "notional" or "disputatious" way. The other hallmark of a leisure-class culture is ostentatious insistence upon sheer uselessness. In contradistinction to this conception of gentlemanly erudition Robert Boyle urged that the Invisible College value only "such knowledge as hath a tendency to use."

For topical illustrations of the "disputatious" or "notional" way no comparison between anatomy or astronomy in the medieval universities and the teaching of economics in the universities of Britain at the present day could be more damaging than the remarks of Sir William Beveridge in his recent farewell address to the London School of Economics. The futility of contemporary social studies in Britain is directly traceable to the dominant Platonism of the humanistic teaching in the older universities, especially Oxford. A course of Greats (ancient or modern) accompanied by practical exploits in the Union debating society provide the chief method of preparing students for research and teaching in economics and sociology. The results might be anticipated, if only because the research mentality is negatively correlated with great facility in *oral* discourse.

Uncontaminated exaltation of uselessless in its most benign form is best studied among teachers of languages. They are as peace-loving as most of us. They are more alert than the average citizen to the linguistic misunderstandings which armament manufacturers and dictators are swift to exploit. Above all they are in a position to realize how much the furtherance of an enduring world peace is bound up with promoting a world language; and they have the raw materials at their finger tips.

So we naturally expect to find them foremost in making a constructive contribution to the problem of linguistic minorities. Alas, the truth is far otherwise! To endow human life with *new* powers and inventions, as Bacon defined the goal of naturalistic studies, is not the aim of humanistic teaching in British universities. In Great Britain the only important research undertaken to promote the development of an international language is that of Mr. C. K. Ogden in the Orthological Institute. Like the Royal Institution where Davy and Faraday laboured, it has no connection with a university.

There is still a third way in which the influence of Platonism in English university policy can obstruct the rational recognition of the new constructive powers which science has placed at our disposal. Such an educational reformation must begin with a new outlook on the teaching of science. Science has been introduced for vocational reasons without regard to its social background, its social impact, or its social potentialities. A reformation of this kind could be carried through speedily if the departments of education in our universities were willing to give the lead. In junior positions we have some excellent young men and women with a vision of what education might and should be. A big obstacle to the success of their efforts is the fact that a degree in classical philosophy at a medieval university is an almost indispensable preliminary for promotion to professorial reponsibility.

The supposititious merit of the humanistic teaching which British universities provide is that it encourages tolerance. When a deep understanding of the social forces moulding contemporary society is needed a broad mind is a high price to pay for an empty head or—what comes to the same in the end—a head filled with no information relevant to the specific peculiarities of our own civilization. This dichotomy between humanistic studies which bask in the enjoyment of a refined uselessness and natural science which endows human life with new powers and inventions is surely a key to the outstanding paradox of modern rationalism. We are witnessing two concurrent processes. For the time being confidence in the exercise of man's reasoning powers applied to the manufacture of substitutes, the production of power, the control of diseases and the discovery of new means for communication and transport is growing. Meanwhile confidence in the use of reason for adopting our social institutions to the new task of exploiting new found knowledge for the satisfaction of common human needs is losing ground on all sides. So the kingdom of reason suffereth violence, and the violent take it by force. The apparent growth of rationalism in the domain of external nature may soon be arrested, and even if science and civilization do not perish together in a general conflagration, both will suffer a heavy set-back for years to come.

§ 3

We live in a community in which all branches of natural science are to some extent subsidized by the State. There is no longer any vigorous opposition to the teaching of science from the Christian Churches, and a totalitarian Government which might impose the teaching of a particular biological or other doctrine has not yet established itself in this country. It is more likely that a Totalitarian movement will attain than that the Christian Churches will *regain* the power to restrict scientific inquiry. So we need be far less interested in philosophical differences which separate us from liberal Christians who share similar social views than we might have been fifteen years ago. What concerns us more is how those who share the scientific outlook should meet the challenge of Totalitarianism.

On a long view those who believe that the challenge of Totalitarian movements calls for a united intellectual front "to defend our social heritage" invite defeat. Such makeshifts claim rational assent in so far as we are convinced about two things. One is that there is immediate danger of the rapid spread of Totalitarian doctrines in Britain. The other is that there is much likelihood of early collapse of the dictator cult. The prospect of a protracted conflict of ideologies admits no easy solution. It calls for candid admission of the shortcomings of a social culture which is not training a personnel competent to give constructive leadership in a democratic society. The present task of rationalism is to take the initiative in exposing the defects of our existing educational system and in providing proper remedies.

Totalitarianism of the German type is in part a response to the hopeless monotony of life in the beehive city of modern industrialism. To that extent reason can offer but one antidote to its allurements. Our task should be to awaken a lively sense of the social possibilities of the new powers which science confers. The real obstacles to freedom of thought to-day are obstacles to the co-ordinated realistic study of social institutions from this standpoint. In Britain those obstacles come chiefly from the humanistic teaching of the universities, where Platonism remains more firmly rooted, because no longer the handmaid of theology. Secular Platonism has a seductive serenity which permits its votaries to believe they are rational when they are merely suspending violent effort. The pleasant aspect which this confers leads persons of all persuasions to seek them as allies in circumstances when quality is less important than quantity.

It is enough that those who attack are united by the common aim of crushing the enemy. Such is the common denominator of rationalism when an established Church has forfeited its capacity to make converts without relinquishing its intention to control education. Allies in defence must be united by the more substantial ties of common loyalty to the institution they are defending. Hence the plea for a united intellectual front to protect liberal culture against the onslaught of a world movement with the fanatical vitality of sixth-century Islam derives no justification from the successful alliance of evolutionists and Oxford Liberals in the struggle against ecclesiastical control of the English universities. A defensive alliance against Fascism can too easily become an undertaking to whitewash the patent defects of a social culture which has ceased to inspire reverence. It becomes a Conservative rally to retain the culture of a privileged class with the defects inherent in a culture based on social privilege. It thus surrenders the divine fire of rebellion to the perpetual custody of its opponents.

K

The Mediterranean civilization is on its death-bed. A vigorous rationalism prescribes Caesarean section. Genteel bulletins announcing that the patient is progressing favourably will not diminish the sales of fake medicines. In Britain the time has passed when men can be profitably united by the common tie of mere scepticism. The challenge of Fascism must be answered by a creed as positive as Fascism itself. There may yet be time to salvage what is best in European culture, as we know it, if we ourselves take the initiative of proclaiming our own shortcomings, the shoddiness of much we have inherited from the slave civilizations of the Mediterranean world, and the need for a great educational reformation to prepare a man for the new Age of Plenty which lies at hand. This must be the *positive* minimum of a united front to meet the challenge of Fascism.

Frank Kingdon

President of Newark University

FREEDOM FOR EDUCATION

THE whole process of evolution has been marked by casualties as organisms developed at certain stages have not been able to adjust themselves to environmental changes. In other words, the mere existence of a certain species is no guarantee of its survival. There has to be maintained an equilibrium in the rhythm of adjustment or an inhospitable change in the environment destroys the organism. When species lose their capacity for modification they are destroyed. When they are slower at change than their environment, they either begin to degenerate or have to take a lower place in the organic hierarchy or pass away. An organism that does not keep pace in itself with environmental change is lost.

Left to its own devices, nature has produced at every stage of the universe's history those organisms which were adapted to each stage. The process of rejection has been a ruthless one, but at any given moment, the whole picture has been harmonious. The forms of life that fit the world as it is are the ones that exist in the world as it is.

I

The emergence of man precipitates a new factor into the situation. He does not leave nature to itself. By the intervention of his intelligence he changes his own environment. He speeds up the processes of change in the world to which he must adjust himself. This means that he creates a new hazard for his own survival. If he himself does not change at a pace that keeps him within hailing distance of the changes he is making in his world, his own success in mastering that world will destroy him.

Education is an instrument of survival. It is man's attempt to keep individuals up to date with their world, to make individuals adequate to living in and dealing with their environment. It is society at any stage engaged in moulding individuals to fit the current social forms.

One difficulty is that, while the intelligence initiates social changes, it cannot comprehensively forecast their effects. They have their own momentum and work almost as impersonally and as independently as natural forces. The intelligence gives the impetus, but it sets in motion forces that then work out their own nature and take their own heads to achieve their own results. Man finds himself confronted by a dual task, that of understanding and controlling the social complex which he, himself has created as his own environment. At the moment the second control is even more difficult than the first, because we have not yet been able to devise an intellectual method for reducing social dynamics to scientific formulas. We know that social forces work by their own laws, but we cannot yet define those laws. We have not reached the point where we can accurately and comprehensively predict the social effects of any given invention, of any political policy, or of any major social event. This makes both social decision and education essentially opportunistic.

An important factor that complicates social interpretation is the potentially powerful one of individuality. It is true that every man is a social product, but it is also true that each is unique, and while the area of uniqueness in all men may be a restricted one, in some it is large enough so that their distinctively unique individualities become powerful agents of change. It may be possible to show that every genius is a combination and expression of ideas and tendencies prevalent in his time, but it still remains a fact that they were precipitated in him at just the time and place they were because he was

the individual he was and not another. We have no way
of knowing when this kind of individual will appear, or
where. Nature and society are continually surprising us by
presenting us with unexpected human talents from unlikely
places.

Another difficulty is that between periods of major social
crisis our social forms become organized into institutions that
are comparatively rigid in practice and dogma, and that accu-
mulate to themselves extraordinarily powerful prestiges. They
represent both tradition and vested interests. Powerful and
selfish men have a stake in their continuance, many people
have an emotional attachment to them, and all the strength of
our natural apathy tends to maintain them. Consequently,
when a period of major social reconstruction comes, they gather
all their resources to resist it. The forces of change cannot be
stopped, however, and so a period of intense struggle ensues,
in the course of which institutions are either modified or
smashed. As the rate of social change is accelerated, it becomes
more and more difficult for more and more institutions to
adjust themselves to it. Consequently, in a society growing
steadily more complex we have wars and revolutions on consistently greater scales. The increasing magnitudes of events of
violence are symptoms of the more comprehensive extensions
of social dynamics.

This is an important comment because it indicates one fact
that is clearly characteristic of our current social trends. They
are making our social units, in terms of which we have to think
consistently, more inclusive. Every fresh experience pushes out
the boundaries of our common interests. For five thousand years
our key institutions have been enlarging. The family has merged
into the tribe and the city; the tribe and the city have grown
into states and principalities; states and principalities have been
combined into nations; and nations have expanded into
federations and empires. These enlarged units have been not
merely political contrivances, but vital foci of cultural
development.

More and more inclusive units of society, however, demand
more and more expansive individuals to operate them. Men

cannot stop with tribal loyalties and yet keep a nation going, for the larger unit will split on rivalries among the lesser units. Individuals must extend their intelligences and imaginations to identify themselves with the expanding borders of their social unities.

Such an extension on the part of men does not come naturally. Each of us is essentially provincial. It has always required an effort to lift men out of their local loyalties into wider ones. A man can always be interested in himself. He can identify himself with his family, but even here he does not maintain the same intensity or consistency of interest that he does in his own personal affairs. Beyond the family, his identification is spasmodic. Its intensity is proportionate to his feeling of emergency. He will rally to his city and his nation if he feels that they are in danger or on the threshold of glory, but for the rest of the time he is comparatively indifferent, and even critical and restive. Our emotional reserves seem to be limited, and therefore to be exhausted by our immediate preoccupations. We are left with the question whether men can go beyond a certain provincialism of outlook, but we at least have the encouragement of knowing that when they are convinced that their interests demand their identification with a group as large as a modern nation they have been able to achieve it.

The achievement of extension also runs into the obstacle of man's natural apathy. Something in us resists change. We are sufficiently of the physical world so that its tendency to inertia is characteristic of us. There are always those who anticipate what is coming and seek to prepare men for it; but the mass of humanity does not move until events leave no alternative. Consequently, we go along on a series of sharply distinguished plateaus instead of a steady rise of change. We maintain a level of life as long as we can, and then we have to go through some sort of crisis of effort to establish a new one. At each level we pitch our tents and act as though we had found our final establishment. No easy answer can be given to the question whether men can throw off their natural apathy, become intelligently aware of their changing environment, and act consistently to modify their own outlooks and their institutions to meet the demands of change.

II

In our contemporary world man has made the whole planet one unified environment. Communications have erased boundary lines from our non-political experience. We actually live our days and do our thinking against the wide perspective of the whole round earth. Nothing happens anywhere that is not at once reported to us. The widening circles of social relationships that have carried us from family to tribe to nation to empire now embrace the whole company of mankind and present us with the fact that every child now born has the whole world for his stage. As a fact in experience, we are citizens of one city of planetary dimensions knit together in a web of transportation and communication that makes any movement anywhere felt throughout the entire social structure even to the ends of the earth.

To illustrate what this means let us think of the cultural forces that have been most powerful in our American life over the period of the past twenty-five years. I think that a strong thesis could be maintained on the proposition that the most influential stimulants of our creative thinking have been not native but foreign in their origins. Such names as Kagawa of Japan, Sun Yat Sen of China, Lenin of Russia, Marx of Germany, Croce of Italy, Bergson and Stendhal and Proust of France, Gandhi of India, Shaw and Wells and Barrie of Britain, Joyce and Yeats and Moore of Ireland, immediately come to mind as active ferments in our thinking. Men like Stalin and Chiang Kai-shek, Mussolini and Hitler, are so much a part of our experiences that even their gray shadows flickering on a screen in a dark theatre divide a crowd into cheering and hissing partisans. Men and ideas are no longer remote because they are foreign. They are emotional symbols quick in the blood of the actual world in which we choose our friends and select our parties. The planet is our field of force.

Meanwhile, however, our institutions remain parochial. They

were established in the days when boundaries actually shut men in by keeping strangers out. Economically, educationally, religiously, and militarily we are organized on provincial lines. Our currencies are national. Our business organizations are "American companies" or "British" or "French" or "German" firms. Our schools are organized around specific nationalistic traditions. Churches are shaped to the national societies that they serve. Armies and navies are almost by definition weapons of provincial groups. The powerful institutional patterns, including, be it noted, the effective learned societies, of our social behaviour are all moulded into the forms of those divided group interests that come to us out of the days before the world had become one community.

As we have indicated, the most commanding of all our institutions is the Sovereign National State. It puts its stamp upon practically every one of our activities. So great is its prestige that it has become virtually sacred, demanding undivided allegiance from its citizens, and thundering anathemas upon any who question its dogmas. It seems so normal to us for the world to be organized into nations that we may wonder why anyone should even raise a question about it. This simply emphasizes the almost incalculable strength that this comparatively young institution has acquired. Men have in the past thought about the Emperor, the Church, or the City, as we now think about the Nation. It is at this moment the most strongly entrenched social unit, carrying over into our cosmopolitan environment all the emotional and institutional investment it stored up in a more provincial era.

Here, then, is the basic tension of our times. In actual experience we are world-citizens but the institutions by which we live are provincial. We are like children growing up in a home that speaks a language foreign to that of the surrounding community. Within our institutions we use the tongue of our restricted group, but when we cross their thresholds we find ourselves facing conditions for which our provincial speech has no meaning. Either we shall have to adjust our traditional organizations to the new dimensions of experience or else the course of events will smash them.

An excellent parable of what this means is the story of Japan. For centuries this island empire lived its exclusive life in a world divided into neighbourhoods having restricted dealings one with another. In the middle of the last century, however, boats driven by steam turned the oceans into convenient highways, and the restricted neighbourhood known as Japan found its waters invaded by continually increasing numbers of visitors. It could not shut them out. They were emissaries of a new age that automatically suspended traditional relationships. The proud nationalism of Japan, rooted in religious concepts and absolute in its assumptions of superiority, had to come to terms with the world-community. The Son of Heaven could no longer enjoy his disdainful isolation. What has happened so obviously to Japan has actually happened to the whole institution of nationalism, even though we have not seen it so clearly. Just as the world of the Renaissance moved in upon the medieval Church and shook it to its foundations, so the international community has advanced upon nationalism in our day, forcing us to a new orientation of all our institutions in the light of our new experiences. The origin of our contemporary chaos is the fact that our traditional patterns of social organization are incapable of solving our problems on the scale of our new frames of social experience. They carry over provincial imperatives into a community of planetary dimensions. Either they will be re-fashioned by intelligent planning or else they will be destroyed by revolution.

The difficulty with planning institutional change is that institutions are habits and vested interests as well as social tools, and so they gather to themselves the almost imponderable support of apathy. When change threatens, men rally to the support of the traditional. This is happening now. In a period when we are obviously becoming more cosmopolitan we are seeing a resurgence of almost fanatical nationalism. At first glance, this may seem paradoxical. It really is not. It is a phenomenon as elemental as the clustering of sheep in their fold when a thunderstorm threatens. We naturally retreat from the novel into the familiar because the novel is a threat and the familiar is assurance of security. Trained to provincial thinking we literally do not know what to do with a unified world. In our bewilderment we seek refuge in exalting old patterns of life. Institutions menaced by unprecedented forces mobilize to perpetuate themselves. Nationalism is now doing just this. Facism is nationalism making its last desperate stand against the tide of events. In its emergency it gets the support of businessmen, of the military, of the majority of churchmen, and of most educators, because all these live by activities themselves rooted in nationalism. Scenting the approaching storm the sheep herd in the fold. They are grateful to the shepherd who speaks the bold and encouraging word, and they follow him without question whithersoever he leads them.

Ours is the generation that is consummating the end of the era of exclusive nationalism. Our whole society is in the throes of giving birth to a world order. The beginning of the end of the old epoch came with the outbreak of the Great War, significantly called the World War, in 1914. November, 1918, produced what has been truly called the Armistice, for it was no cessation of hostilities; these have been continuing in scattered areas of the earth through the intervening twenty years and are now apparently gaining force for another concentrated struggle involving all nations. Dimly the spirit of the new day shadowed itself forth in the League of Nations, but the incubus of old forms was too heavy for it to carry, so that it broke down under the strain of rival national claims. We have already had a war for twenty-five years, sporadic and scattered but continuous. Every sign indicates that, as in past crises, our world reorganization will require a thirty years' war. All that this means is that it takes thirty years for an old generation wedded to traditional forms to pass away, and a new generation to rise in its place facing its own environment in its own terms.

Thus our struggle is more profound than most of us realize. We have upset the historic equilibrium of countries, races, and continents. Ours is more than a contest between traditional democracy and fascism or communism. It is the death of an old order and the birth of a new. The Hitlers, the Mussolinis, and the Stalins are symbols of a vanishing day, resolutely and ruthlessly using all its accumulated reserves of material and

emotion to fight off the annihilation it bitterly fears. They are
incidents, and events are more than they are. Society is on the
march toward a new stage of comprehensive organization, a
stage as definite as the emergence of tribe from family, of nation
from tribe, or empire from nation. We are on the threshold of
a federation of the world. Our institutions are persistent but
out-dated, and their vigour in resisting change is the measure
of the intensity of our struggle.

III

Two questions clearly emerge from our analysis. Are individual men capable of identifying themselves with the whole
race of mankind in the common quest for life? Is mankind able
to develop institutions capable of supporting the new world
structure of experience? Neither can be answered simply.

As individuals we are not fully contemporaneous with our
own world. We have not caught up with our technical achievements. Man has learned how to change his environment but
not himself, so that we have no modern men to match the
modern world. Perhaps we can put it in another way. The
characteristic of our technical advance has been extension, the
inclusion of wider and wider areas within interdependent
units, but the chief trait of individual men is still preoccupation
with egocentric interests, the exaltation of the premise of the
provincial. In an environment that is continually approximating
an organic pattern of mutually dependent cells, individual men
are still thinking and acting as though they, the cell units, were
independent entities sufficient unto themselves and answerable
to no law save that of self-interest narrowly defined. We have
not learned to include the fact of mutual dependence and the
desirable virtue of mutual aid as effective motives in our
behaviour. Man impoverishes man, class exploits and hates
class, nation rises against nation, race persecutes race. In
human relationships we perpetuate, and even exacerbate, our
divisions while every technical advance draws us physically
closer together in a shrinking world. We are not emotionally
prepared for our new proximities. The lion and the lamb are

being forced to lie down together before the lion has learned to eat straw like the ox.

In a sense, we are not even contemporaneous with ourselves. On the technical side we are twentieth-century men and from a strictly rational point of view we can perceive the implications of our new devices. We are not exclusively rational beings, however, and in the recesses of our complex inheritances move impulses of the long past. Nineteenth-century ideas are obviously powerful in each of us, and few can deny the active presence of medieval superstitions in certain kinds of decisions. We are not fully up-to-date with ourselves, for part of each of us is still untamed. Our highly technical success, as a matter of fact, has made this extraordinarily clear to us. The work of a man like Freud, for example, is an expression of the way in which the continuing savage in man has been thrown into bold relief by the demands of an increasingly complex society. An essentially primitive man can use the radio, the automobile, the aeroplane, with a skill at least equal to that of a man of culture, but none of them will add one cubit to his spiritual stature. There is a realm of technical achievement and there is one of cultural insight, but there is little evidence that progress in one means advance in the other. This truth has its own poignancy at this moment when we see civilization exercising an unprecedented power over the physical world, and yet reverting to virtual barbarism in the group relations within its own structure.

Having said this, however, we have to balance it by remembering that men have shown the capacity to enlarge their loyalties effectively enough to give periodic stability to broadening social units. The citizen of San Francisco feels himself one with the citizen of New York in the bonds of a common country. The man of Toronto identifies himself with the whole British Commonwealth of Nations. These mark unpredictable advances beyond the family loyalties of early men. I have occasionally met Christians deeply conscious of the spiritual ties that unite them to all "members of the Body of Christ"; and I know individuals who identify themselves completely with the world-wide proletariat. These may seem delusions to such as do not understand them, but they show that human beings are capable of finding satisfactions in human fellowships convincing to them, even though founded upon almost nebulous areas of common interest.

Our answer, then, to the question of man's ability to identify himself with mankind is that there are obvious inherent obstacles but that his power of emotional extension has already been proved to be so great that we are not justified in believing that it has been exhausted. I should sum up my conclusions in the matter in two statements and a comment. First, the mere success of techniques will not automatically produce men morally capable of handling them; the two kinds of success are distinct. Second, this being so, we must face the problem of producing comprehensive men as an essential one upon the solution of which depends our whole social success; we might go so far as to say that the necessity of the case demands that the next field of knowledge to be explored shall be man's knowledge of himself, and that we cannot claim to be genuinely scientific until the science of humanity is brought to the level of our knowledge of the physical world. The comment I should like to make is that a critical social emergency may make it so clear to, us that the mutual advantage of all is the personal advantage of each—though the realization is more likely to come as a general disaster plainly a threat against personal security—that we shall be shocked out of our provincialism and find personal interest allied with collective good so plainly that we shall be forced to stand together. Where slow persuasion fails an emotional panic may succeed.

The possibility of re-fashioning institutions depends somewhat, but not altogether, on what we have just discussed. Men must think of themselves as world-citizens before they will give attention to designing the machinery of a World-State, but our social organizations have their own vitalities and rhythms of metamorphosis. At certain points they act like entities in their own natures, and at some stages they mould men more effectively than men affect them; Frankenstein may be a caricature but he is not a myth.

The aboriginal tribalist in all of us dies uneasily, so that there is a tendency in every articulated group to take to itself the ancient prerogatives of the tribe. Each has its totem, its vows, its peculiar patois, and its formula for its own justification. Given any length of life the tradition of any group lends it an aura of sanctity, which means a command of the emotional investments of its members. This produces powerful resistance to criticism and rejection of proposals for change as though they were utterances of blasphemy. This emotional tenacity of institutions is the source of their social lag. They continue until they become slums of the spirit in a transformed society, and even then all housing projects that would displace them are rejected by their inhabitants, who cannot bear to see the old premises dismantled.

Intellectually, it is not too difficult to draw the blueprints of an orderly world community. Here are two thousand million people living on one of the lesser planets of a comparatively undistinguished stellar system. At their command are certain computable resources which, with their labour and knowledge, they could exploit to assure food, clothing, shelter, and a degree of comfort for all. The technics of production and communication are already here. A federation of States within a code of law is not only imaginable but clearly definable. A fellowship of faiths can be conscientiously designed. Education as a world-wide partnership of eager minds is theoretically plausible.

When plans for such a federation of the world are so engaging, why do we not proceed at once to put them into effect? Because the past is so entangled in our emotions and our moral judgments that we cannot bring free minds to our task. And our institutions are the skeleton of the past on which we have to hand the life of the present. They must grow as the bones of a child grow or our civilization will be crippled and in pain. They must submit to the disciplines of extension in a day when social experiences are increasingly inclusive.

In the past men have modified institutional forms either through compromise or catastrophe. Compromise is evidence of flexibility. Catastrophe is the breaking point of rigidity. There is no reason to believe that these alternatives have been suspended.

We are not living in the twilight of civilization. We are at the end of one of its phases. But that is another way of saying that we are on the threshold of a new phase. The story of progress from epoch to epoch has been like the myth of the phoenix; society has passed through the fires of war and revolution periodically, and institutions grown old have been destroyed, but it has risen from the flames renewed in youth and with institutions modified to new conditions but still essentially valid for the unchanging characteristics of human life. We are passing through the flames. The inevitable workings of change will refashion our social forms. It is perhaps not too late even now to do what no generation has ever yet been able to do, to mould the shape of a new epoch through intelligent compromise rather than through social catastrophe. It is banal to say that a new era comes not to destroy the old but to fulfil it; yet this very statement emphasizes the fact that we cannot think of such fulfilment without an echo of destruction sounding in our minds. The paradox of progress is the paradox of birth: fresh life emerging from the threatening shadow of death.

IV

When we try to define the place of education in the processes of experience through which we are passing, we realize that what we mean by such a definition is what we are going to do about the mind. Education is an activity as engineering or manufacturing are activities. It is the application of methods to raw materials to produce planned results. We believe that certain types of individuals are desirable and that human beings can be moulded into these types by certain kinds of training, one of which is the specifically educational, the inculcation of the right ideas in the right combinations.

The moment we say the "right" ideas, however, we indicate the predicament of education. People differ about what is "right." And a difference about what is "right," unlike some other differences, is almost incapable of compromise, for what is not "right" is "wrong," and when discussion moves in such antitheses obstinacy of opinion is called conviction, and that is a fighting word. Education naturally becomes the battleground of conflicting convictions.

The school occupies an unusually sensitive place in our society. It is a community enterprise, subject to public control and necessarily responsive to public opinion; this characteristic inevitably makes all school administrators jealous of public approval, an attitude that tends toward timidity, an over-cautious safeguarding against easily misunderstood experimentation. On its other side, the school touches the home with unique intimacy: it is personalized for every parent in terms of what it is doing to beloved sons and daughters; thus it becomes emotionalized, and discussion of its work takes on a tone of intensity that no other public activity has to meet on so general a scale. Moreover, practically everybody has been to school and so feels that he knows about education; this means that the professional educator is not conceded the acknowledgment of expertness that is given to those who work in more mysterious fields—a citizen who would not think of questioning a treatment prescribed by a doctor has no hesitation in passing final judgment on school methods and curricula. Again, every individual or group that has an idea to propagate or an interest to defend turns to the school as a convenient tool for its propaganda, so that educators are being continually bombarded with requests to include this or that course of training in their programmes; on the one hand voices denounce the schools for neglecting the essentials, and on the other they condemn them for not including particular pet nostrums. All this means that every social conflict reports contentiously in educational institutions. In a day like ours, when fundamental social adjustments are in the making, education is naturally a focus of our bewildering uncertainty.

This reflects itself in the differences among educators. There are, for example, those who maintain the traditional attitude that the business of school and college is to teach certain approved subjects in a factual way, and no more; while there are others who insist that the school must reproduce in itself the environment of the society into which the young people will later enter, and that it has failed if it does not train them in effective social attitudes. On another front, there are some who believe that it is the school's business to present the local philosophies of government and to ignore all others; while some others hold the idea that conflicting political and social theories of all kinds must be expounded fairly if the school is to keep faith with expectant minds. There is probably no field where the experts are indulging in such severe self-examination as in education. This is a sign of health. It is also an indication, however, of how energetically our current confusion is registering in the whole educational enterprise.

Confusion, however, is no adequate ground for inaction. We are like Athens sending its yearly tribute of young men and maidens into the labyrinth to lose their way and be devoured by the Minotaur; nevertheless, like it, we must seek our Theseus, who, with the thread of Ariadne and his own sword, can make his way through the maze and slay the monster. Education cannot relinquish its obligation to emancipate growing minds.

However hampered by community pressures and administrative timidity, educators must define and work toward their goal of liberating human minds and equipping them for new dimensions of experience. They must consciously sharpen the intelligence as an instrument of adjustment. The majority of people still think of education as a routine for teaching young persons to read and count. The idea of teaching them to think has an uneasy suggestion of the subversive about it. Even higher education is popularly looked upon as either a vocational advantage or a pleasant reverie over the provincial and dead cultures of the past. We hardly dare to talk aloud about an educational programme geared to the machines of modern communication and planned as a guide to the general mental operations of the entire world community. We certainly have no international fellowship of educators devoted to reconditioning the mental life of mankind to match our cosmopolitan relationships.

The result is that education has fallen victim to the aggressive provincialism of our traditional social groups. Resurgent German nationalism has seized the universities and turned them into mechanical sounding boards for state propaganda, overtly

L

enslaving them, dictating their teaching, emasculating their originality, and exiling their nonconformists. Not as openly, but relatively as effectively, politico-economic units elsewhere are forcing schools and colleges to espouse the *status quo*. Frightened parochialism in all lands is concentrating on checking educational experimentation.

Educators—administrators and teachers by their own respective methods—must resist such pressure. The necessity arises neither from pride in eccentricity nor any sense of intellectual superiority, but from the reasonable assurance that the free mind is a social asset. Society is an expression of intelligent co-operation. Because it is made up of human beings it is dynamic, that is to say, it carries the forces of change within itself; one of its unchanging characteristics is that it is always changing. The mind recognizes and interprets these changes, and devises new machineries for new emergencies. If the mind is fettered by old forms it cannot exercise its inherent elasticity to compass new needs, and so the whole process of orderly adjustment breaks down. The only guarantee of adequate rational flexibility is intellectual freedom controlled by social responsibility.

We have to recognize that such freedom will produce manifestations of unsound criticism. Even the best minds have their aberrations. We cannot help that. The nature of the intellect is what it is. Whatever its weaknesses, it is the most skillful equipment for adjustment that we have, and it works most effectively in an atmosphere of free exchange. Indeed, this is its safeguard. The play of mind on mind checks and purges individual eccentricity. No one's thinking is fully convincing to another. Therefore the most assured way to average conclusions, which are obviously not always brilliant ones, is through the free expression of the opinions of all. Inarticulate people are apt to doubt this because of their almost instinctive distrust of the articulate, and the articulate are apt to be impatient of it because of their unwillingness to credit the inarticulate, but in the end each has his authority and both the pace and content of decisions are benefited by their interaction.

In a critical period like ours, when all philosophies are being subjected to searching scrutiny and all institutions tested for essential stability, it is natural for every impulse to caution among us to assert itself. So we have a strong tendency to feel that we must be careful what we say, and to resent the free utterance of others to the point where we are ready to agree that actual restriction must be imposed. Yet it is in precisely such a time that we need all the light we can get, and the only way we can get light is through shared thinking. This means frank utterance, frank criticism, and courageous debate. It is the method of social wisdom in a decisive hour.

In the light of man's needs and of unfolding events, we are justified in declaring that education must mould its forms to serve four clear ends. It must train minds to think in cosmopolitan terms that will enable them to see local cultures against the corrective perspective of world experience and so fit them for the creative emergence of a comprehensive culture of mankind. It must maintain an active international fellowship of free minds meeting and sharing each other's research and discoveries in the assurance that facts and their implications know no boundaries of parish or nation or race. It must courageously act upon its own premise that reason is man's most expert instrument for mastering the physical world and organizing his own society, and when the processes of thought are threatened by the restrictive dogmatisms of any political forms it must at any cost refuse to surrender the independence of the mind. It must recognize that its full task consists not only in training people in freedom but also in preparing them for freedom, which means for control of themselves as well as of their world, and includes educating them consciously for change and, at the same time, for responsibility.

Harold J. Laski

Professor of Political Science University of London

NATIONALISM AND THE
FUTURE OF CIVILISATION

I

NO Englishman who cares for freedom has ever been able to watch without emotion the struggle of an oppressed people for self-expression. The famous phrase of John Stuart Mill that "it is in general a necessary condition of free institutions that the boundaries of governments should coincide in the main with those of nationalities" is only a sober way of stating that which Byron and Swinburne, Meredith and Browning, hymned in passionate song. As a people, we have rarely failed to sympathize with the effort of any nation to secure in terms of statehood the principle which Mill laid down. Greece, Italy, the republics of South America, all owe not a little to English pilgrims of the spirit to whom a failure in this realm would have meant unendurable bitterness. Mr. H. N. Brailsford is not the last of those to whom the call of national freedom was the kind of sacred appeal which could not go unheard.

I do not deny the strength of the national claim; the evidence is too fiercely strong on every side of us. I admit, gladly and willingly, that a people charged with the care of its own destiny achieves thereby a spaciousness not otherwise capable of being attained. Self-respect, exhilaration, creativeness—all these seem to be the definite outcome of self-government. The suppression of the yearning to be free always poisons the well-springs of the body politic. Austro-Hungary, Ireland, the old Turkish empire, India, stand as irrefutable evidence of that truth. In so far as we can give to each nation the power to express itself as a state it seems to me clear that we liberate a spiritual energy which, beyond discussion, adds to the happiness of mankind.

But it is one thing to admit the title of statehood to a nation; it is another thing, and a very different thing, to admit that statehood can safely imply all that it has been taken to mean in the course of the last hundred years. It is easy to see that, whatever the loss in administrative efficiency, a nation that is deprived of the right to determine its own way of life suffers an abridgment of personality which, sooner or later, issues in violence. We should gain nothing—and we should lose much —by the forcible suppression of the Welsh language in schools. We should gain nothing, and again we should lose much, by denying to Soviet Russia the right to conduct her own vast experiment on lines far different from the historic experience of Western Europe. To the degree that we refuse to India what is essential in statehood for her national freedom we impoverish the spiritual well-being of the world.

It is, however, idle to deny that there is an egoism in the national State which bodes ill for mankind. A wide cultural freedom, local self-government, geographical unity—these are all intelligible, even admissible claims. But the demands that we encounter do not end there. The nation-state, having come to be, yearns to be strong. It adopts policies the impact of which upon other nation-states must cause any observer misgivings of which I cannot exaggerate the gravity. It seeks security from attack; and there comes the problem of armaments and strategic frontiers. It seeks an outlet for its surplus population; and there are restless experiments in colonization. Its merchants reveal anxiety about their markets; and we are plunged into imperialist and mercantilist adventures about which the spirit of nationality throws a dangerous glamour. Immigration, religious unity, the attitude to colour, are merely illustrations of the way in which the exclusiveness which is of the essence of nationality gives rise to issues which do not admit of any simple solution. National minorities within an alien state—in Poland, for example—create problems which menace the peace of the world. Seventy years ago Mazzini's lyric enthusiasm for the nation-state seemed to almost every generous mind in Europe—Lord Acton is the only notable exception I know—a gesture of emancipation. I doubt whether any body of generous-minded men would display that certitude now.

What has happened? The science of the nineteenth century industrialized civilization; it annihilated the distances of the world. Continents ceased to be separated from one another; Buenos Aires became neighbour to London. Economic exploitation proceeded upon a scale which required whole continents for its satisfaction. The new industrialism demanded ever more raw materials, and then ever more markets in which to dispose of the finished product. Civilization came to depend upon mechanisms so delicate and so inter-related that a boom on the Stock Exchange of New York might alter the habits of life of a Balkan peasant. The power in the hands of the industrialist and the financier shaped the remotest places of the earth to his pleasure. China could no longer sleep beneath her mighty wall; the African jungle gave place to the road and the railway. And behind the men who planned these immense conquests, these dramatic, if only half-visible, crusades, was the newest power of all—the organized authority of national States. It is their entrance upon the scene of action which has given to the claims of nationality a perspective so different from what we could have even dreamed fifty or sixty years agoi

For what has happened is the harnessing of the national spirit to this vast search for economic power. It may have its imperial phase: Mannesmann in Morocco, Rhodes in Africa, an oil company in Mexico bring to their aid all the passionate intensity of faith that it embodies. It may be of a local character: the manufacturer of Australia or Czechoslovakia seeks to protect his market from the invasion of a foreign rival. We get the pectacle of nations armed to the teeth and using their weapons to compel the acquisition of wealth. Sometimes, as in Persia, they agree to divide the spoils. Sometimes, again, as in Northern Africa, their inability to agree brings them into the circle of contingent conflict. The zest for expansion is so great that human ingenuity is exhausted in its service. Its contempt for alternative ways of life is so profound that not the least of its results is the way in which the Ancient East has been quickened into challenge of Western Europe. It is Asia to-day which resents our dominance. Will it be Africa -to-morrow?

A world of competing nation-states, each of which is a law unto itself, produces a civilization incapable of survival. For the law between those states is the law of the jungle. It is instinct, at every point, with hate and fear and insecurity. To the measure of its power, each nation-state seeks to realize its destiny without regard to the effect upon its rivals. You can see that in the relations between France and Germany, or between Japan and China. But the temper is not confined to the great nation-states alone. Poland and Lithuania, Hungary and Rumania, are suffused with a similar spirit. Because each is the sovereign master of its own will, its power alone is the measure of its possible achievement. And, thinking in terms of power, it must equip itself with the instruments by which power realizes its ends. It becomes the victim of that meanest of all illusions in which bigness is mistaken for grandeur. It becomes deaf to the voices of Reason or Pity or Love. It is so anxious at all costs to affirm its own essence that it is careless of the price the world may pay for its affirmation.

The question into which I wish to inquire is the compatibility of this nationalism with civilization. Admitting as I have admitted, the right of each nation to live under the government of its choice, I want to discuss the extent of the powers that government should possess if nationhood is not to destroy the tradition of a civilized existence. I shall argue that the principle of self-determination is one to which distinct limits have to be set. I shall try to show that the inescapable interdependence of nations makes it impossible for any one nation-state finally to decide any question in which other nation-states have a serious concern. I shall urge upon you that the facts drive us to the envisagement of the nation-state not as a sovereign community, but as a mere province in the *civitas maxima* of mankind. Just as we spent the nineteenth century in thinking nationally, and in completing the pattern of the institutions of national self-government, so, I shall seek to show, we must spend the twentieth in learning to think in international terms, in building, as best we may, the organs of that international community every year of delay in whose coming brings us so much the nearer to disaster.

II

The nation-state is a sovereign state; it therefore knows no will higher than its own. It is the final judge of its own purposes; within the realm of law, it is answerable to no one for its acts. The tragic consequences of that power we saw in the War of 1914; we are seeing it again in the Sino-Japanese dispute. But war is the only final term in a series which poisons the atmosphere of peace. Armaments, strategic frontiers, tariffs, embargoes, limitations upon the transit of persons and of goods, all these are part, though only a part, of the technique by which the modern state seeks to accrete power unto itself. There is no limit to the things it can do save its own power to accomplish them. And behind that will are ranged the profound and irrational impulses of nationalism which supply it with an emotional force largely blind to ideals of right and wrong.

We had some measure of what that force implied in the late war. Each of the belligerent nation-states was completely convinced of its own purity, and just as completely convinced that its opponents had deliberately willed the war. Each stigmatized doubt or hesitation as unpatriotic. Each had no difficulty in enlisting on its side the influence of the different Churches, which, for the period of the War, reduced their deities to tribal emblems to be placated by special incantations. In the anxiety for victory there was no cruelty too horrible to perpetrate, no sacrifice too great to demand. Most of us, I suppose, now realize how shameful was the cruelty, how vain the sacrifice. But all the elements which were present in 1914 to occasion the outbreak are present among us in undiminished vigour. There is no one unaware that a recurrence of 1914 must mean the end of civilization. There is no one, therefore, but must admit that the power to will war cannot be left to the unfettered discretion of any nation-state. But there are few prepared to make the inferences necessary to the translation of that admission into fact.

Yet I suggest to you that the inferences are, in sober truth, clear enough. They are simply the international aspect of our constitutional maxim that what touches all must be decided by all. Exactly as in the national-state majority-rule has proved itself by its obvious conveniences, so in the international community the will of the single national-state must give way before the larger claim it encounters. It cannot fix its own armaments, because, in the great society, that is a claim to fix the armaments of all other nation-states. It cannot define its own frontiers, because that is a claim to fix the frontiers of other states. It cannot claim extra-territoriality for its legislation in other communities, because that is the demand for the power to control the habits and customs of other communities. Once, in a word, the action of one nation-state at all seriously affects the life of another, we have an obvious subject of cosmopolitan law-making. For that subject, the present discretion of a single nation-state must be replaced by the law of an international community organized for this purpose.

I see no escape from this conclusion; and I think it frankly means the end of the sovereignty of the state in international affairs. It compels us to think of the *civitas maxima* first, and of the nation-state as a mere province in that wider community. I do not desire to minimize the consequences of this conception. Frankly, it ends a tradition which has behind it the experience of four hundred years. It means difficult experiment with novelties neither the implications of which, nor the institutions for which, we yet fully know. It will alter the perspective of our thinking as profoundly as any change in human history. It will, not least, put our loyalty upon a plane different from any to which modern times have been accustomed. Yet the only alternative to its acceptance is disaster.

For think of the area international government must cover if it is to offer us the security we need. Currency, tariffs, armaments, treaties, frontiers, statistics as the necessary basis of all international legislation, the power to decide all disputes between existing nation-states, and to bind them to the acceptance of the decision, the control of the movements of peoples, the care and protection of the backward races—these, I think, are indispensable minima of international control. So long as any one of them is left to discretion instead of law, there is the danger of conflict; so long as there is the danger of conflict there exists a menace to the continuance of civilization. We cannot avoid the consequences of the environment we have created. Modern science means a world-market; a world-market means world-interdependence; world-interdependence means world-government. To act upon the consequences of that tremendous syllogism is the only pathway to our security. If we leave to the nation-state now the sovereignty it has enjoyed in the past, we leave it to exploit the rest of the world without regard to the latter's well-being. We harness to that exploitation all the impulses and emotions nationhood engenders. We put reason on one side for the sake of a power unallied to justice.

The transformation of the nation into the sovereign-state is, in a word, what Professor Gilbert Murray has aptly termed the flaw in the nineteenth-century system. Sovereignty in the international field was intelligible enough when difficulties of communication made the kind of interdependence we know almost unthinkable. The influence of science and mass-production was then wholly sporadic in character; Detroit and Nanking were as distant as two planets. All that has passed. Is it not, then, essential that we should effect an institutional recognition of its passing? Can a system of government which developed to fit the needs of a civilization hardly touched by scientific discovery really suffice for one which lives in and by its acceptance of what science achieves? Can a London which the aeroplane now makes a day's journey from New York afford to think on a scale inadequate enough, in all conscience, when New York was six weeks' voyage if the winds were favourable? Can an England which could not survive unless its food-supplies were brought almost hourly from the ends of the earth afford to think in terms suitable to its simple self-sufficiency of the seventeenth or eighteenth century? Can we look at wars which bring whole populations within the direct ambit of their ghastly outcome as though they were still matters which affected no more than a comparative handful of professional soldiery, or a score of men-of-war at sea?

We must learn to think internationally or we perish—that, I suggest, is the clear alternative before us. You cannot think of a decision made by a nation-state within the realm of those functions I described a moment ago which does not have far-reaching consequences upon the rest of the world. When we went off the gold-standard in September 1911, we altered in its essence the economic position of Scandinavia. The American tariff has had decisive ramifications upon the social history of Western Europe. A reckless credit policy by a small Austrian bank alters not only our power to maintain the standards of unemployment insurance, but the whole incidence, at least for a period, of the distribution of English political power. Where the dogma of national sovereignty implies results so momentous, is it not likely to lead to that helpless anarchy which is always the precursor of chaos?

We have become so accustomed to the dogma that we are, almost unconsciously, the prisoners of the emotions to which it gives rise. Great Britain as a sovereign-state means, we say, Great Britain as the mistress of her own destiny. Are we to surrender to foreigners, who neither understand our ways nor care as we care for our interests, the control of that destiny? Can we conceive ourselves as accepting decisions vital to our own way of life which go against us? Would America, for example, accept an order from a world authority to admit Japanese immigrants in unlimited numbers to the Pacific States? Should we refer a quarrel between ourselves and the Irish Free State to a tribunal we could not control? Should we alter our tariff at the behest of a world-authority if we knew that the steel manufacturers of France and Germany could then drive those of Great Britain from their own home-market? Do not the grim and inescapable psychological facts make the idea of world-government an empty, some would even add an ignoble, dream?

There is no habit more dangerous to our well-being than to confound the institutions we have inherited with the necessary institutions of society. Let us look, for a moment, at the internal functions of government. A century ago few save the most daring thinkers would have admitted that housing, health, and scientific research were, to take random illustrations only, a definite matter of governmental concern. Town-planning and the control of transport are becoming as naturally an accepted part of consciousness as the rule of the road. Just as the internal sphere of government moves to fit the pressure of our needs, so, I suggest the external sphere of its authority will move to fit it also.

More slowly, no doubt, and more unwillingly, because the emotional acceptance of the results is more difficult. National feeling is a sentiment tough and obstinate in the way that the religious sentiment is tough and obstinate. It will yield to no magic formula of diminution; only long experience will soften its intensity. But few people who are not professional students of the subject realize how wide is the already existing area of international organization, or how profound is the allegiance it is able to evoke. The very fact that the Council of the League was unable to avert the outbreak of hostilities at Shanghai was felt by literally millions of men and women to be a major disaster for the world. With all its imperfections, no observer aware of the facts can doubt that there has come into being a League-consciousness of which even the most national-minded statesmen have to take account. And any one, again, who studies what the League has accomplished in little more than a decade—who also compares its fortunes with the effort of the Holy Alliance a hundred years ago—cannot help concluding that it has become a pivotal part of our institutional life.

I do not, of course, minimize its defects. It is unlikely to succeed so long as it remains a League of sovereign-states; and it is bound to move too slowly for the facts so long as it depends upon the rule of unanimity. There have been grave failures —the Silesian plebiscite, the weakness before the problem of minorities, the painfully slow progress towards effective disarmament. The successes, alongside the problems, are definitely on a minor scale. The gaps in the Covenant are serious. The absence of Russia and America from membership does the most serious damage to its possible utility.[1] But state the case against the League at its very worst, it would be yet true, like the God of Voltaire, that if it did not exist we should have to invent it. To make it function in a full and continuous way is necessary to our survival as a civilization.

I recognize fully that it does not so function, and it is important to know the cause of that inadequacy. The critics who insist that it is because it cannot exorcise the demon of nationalism—that it is, so to say, in its very conception against human nature—seem to me to miss the point. For to urge that is to argue that nationalism is incapable of satisfaction except in terms of the full adventure of sovereignty. Such a view I hold to be a mistaken one. That full adventure does not, except in form, belong to Switzerland or to the Scandinavian countries; yet on its plane the nationalism of each is full and rich and contented. Effectively, it does not, either, belong to the British Dominions; I see no reason to suppose that their nationalism is stunted as a consequence. Nationalism, I believe, can be fully satisfied without flowing into the channels of sovereignty. What it seeks is freedom from an alien control like that of Austria over Italy, of Turkey over Bulgaria, or Russia over Poland. The sources of the search for sovereign powers must, on the evidence, be sought in different directions.

Here, perhaps, I may interpolate the remark that the attempt to make sovereignty in international law the fullblooded monster revealed, for instance, in Hegel and some of his disciples is a totally unnecessary effort. It arises from a series of historical causes I cannot now stay to examine, on one side, and, on the other, it is the sacrifice of life to logical formalism. For in the actual facts of international life sover-

[1] The reader will remember that this was written in 1932. League history since that date has had a grimmer content.

eignty and statehood are not convertible terms. Few lawyers now take Austin's rigorous view that international law is not law at all; its inescapably binding character, the responsibility of the state for its infraction, are becoming more and more widely recognized. There has grown up a veritable system of state servitudes—financial, judicial, administrative—which are not now regarded as derogatory to statehood. Whatever may be the demands of logic; in practice, the sovereignty of states must now be understood invariably in a relative and restrictive sense. Any other view introduces impossible difficulties and dubious fictions into the problem of explaining the facts which confront us.

In other words, non-sovereign statehood is a conception to-day which does no violence to reality. Why, then, do states insist that derogation from the majesty of sovereign power is an adventure upon which they are not prepared to embark? Why do we say, for instance, that there are some international disputes we are not prepared to submit to arbitration? Why do we sign the Kellogg Pact with the reservation that there is a region in the Middle East in which our interest is emphatic and special? What underlies the continual American insistence hat membership of the League would destroy its sovereignty? Is the search for sovereignty by the nation an adventure from which there is really no prospect of escape?

I agree that, if escape is impossible, the conception of a *civitas maxima* is an idle and an empty dream. If we cannot get a widespread and profound acceptance of the League spirit, and that in all its implications, the pursuit of perpetual peace is certainly a hopeless adventure. But is such pessimism justified by the facts? Are not the main causes of war rooted in facts with which we can deal, if we want to deal with them? Can it ever be said of whole peoples that there are ends they deem so precious that, whatever the cost, they are prepared to fight for those ends? Here, I think, we have to distinguish carefully. I can conceive without difficulty causes for which men will willingly die. A nation fighting for its freedom has, I make no doubt, a full sense that it is engaged in a holy adventure. But we are compelled to inquire whether most modern wars are in fact of this type. We are compelled, further, to decide whether nationalist sentiment is enlisted behind them until the actual moment of conflict comes. We are entitled to know, in a word, whether men lose hold of reason until its opportunity to decide disagreement has already been abandoned by the leaders of a nation-state. My own view is that, for the most part, the common people have no interest in, or passion for, the making of war until its coming is so inescapable that the instinct of pugnacity triumphs over common sense. Then reason becomes the slave of passion, and its power to bind men to its service is nullified until weariness or defeat decides the issue once again.

Take any of the great disputes which have led to or threatened war in these last generations. The conflict over Morocco, the scramble for Africa, the fight for the spoils of Manchuria, oil in Mexico and the Middle East, iron in Lorraine, Egypt as the gateway to the East—as we survey the issues, is it not vital that each one of them involves a search for economic power? It is never, be it remembered, a search by the nation-state. The policy is that of a group of *conquistadores*—now Rhodes, now the Mannesmann brothers, the *Comite des Forges*, Standard Oil. They see the opportunity for exceptional profit. They secure, by means into which it is rarely politic to inquire, concessions of economic value in some alien territory. They expend large sums in the development of those concessions. Then difficulties supervene. They are challenged by foreign competition. They lack security for their labours. The foreign state or native chief does not live up to his bargain. For some such cause as this, the adventurers come to their Foreign Office to demand the use of force for the protection of their investment. Is not that the history of African settlement, of the adventures of the United States in South America, of the occupation of Egypt, of Japan in Manchuria?

And when the adventurers go to their Foreign Offices and obtain their support is not the result the alliance between the search for profit and the sentiment of nationalism? We want our group to win rather than some group of foreign capitalists. The arts of propaganda are exhausted in the effort to persuade us that some particular search for profit is in fact a holy war. Are Englishmen, we are asked, to die unprotected in a foreign land? Are we to do nothing to protect the initiative, the enterprise, the capital, of men who have taken our flag to the uttermost ends of the earth? We can look back on the War of Jenkins' Ear and know it for the sordid commercial struggle that it was. But, in grim fact, are not most modern conflicts at bottom similarly commercial and sordid? Do we not wrap them up in the same fine cloak of idealism, and discover reasons to justify that which, in naked fact, reason would be unable to justify? We did that in the South African War. We surrounded a mean search for gold with every sort of noble motive—progress, the rights of British subjects, and the rest. We made the man in the street so bewildered by propaganda that he believed himself to be battling for a veritable army of the Lord by the time the first guns had been fired. Yet he was, in fact, simply lending the urgency of national sentiment to a struggle between a dubious group of financial adventurers and the farmers of the veldt for the right to dominate the economic future of South Africa.

I have used a British illustration; but the picture would be just as true if I spoke of French or German, American or Japanese, history. In every case nationalism becomes the servant of economic imperialism; it gives the latter its driving force, and the intensity of the adventures provoke war. For, as a general rule, the end of the adventurer in this realm is simply profit. Even where, as in India, he embarks on great constructive work, his economic penetration and his political control are alike meant to serve that end. He does what is demanded by the need of maximum security for his profit—but he does no more. In the subject-populations he breeds only dislike; in his rivals he breeds only covetousness and envy. And the protective armament in which he clothes himself is the power to appeal in his defence to nationalist sentiment. He counts upon his ability to fashion it to his purposes. So far, of course, he has been right in the assumption that he will succeed.

For study the public opinion of any nation, and one becomes terrified by the ease with which it is capable of perversion.

France, the historic enemy, becomes the natural friend overnight. We discover the soul of Russia in 1914 and insist upon
her natural barbarity in 1918 after the Bolsheviks had seized
power. We are lyrical about the United States until the
Armistice; we picture her as Shylock demanding her pound of
flesh when, in our troubled circumstances, she demands the
payment of the debt we have incurred. Nothing seems more
simple than to invent a criminal nation for the crowd. Nothing
is more easy than to make our ally the incarnation of all the
virtues. There was even a time, during the Crimean War, when
the Sultan of Turkey could be represented to the British people
as a kind of reincarnation of Alfred the Great.

The flag follows trade, and it gives to trade an emotional
penumbra from which the trader derives enormous advantage.
The rivalry of financiers to obtain concessions in mines and
railways in the Middle and Far East during the nineteenth
century is an illuminating commentary on the habits of
imperialism. It could, I think, be said with truth that the
partition of China among the European powers between 1850
and 1900 was prevented only by the inability of the protagonists to agree about the division of the spoils. And when you
examine the results of the relation it is always an effort to
protect the commercial and investing classes of the states
involved. They are the nation for the purpose served by the
state. The working classes share in the result only in a way so
indirect that it is doubtful if they can truly be said to have
benefited by its operations.

Upon all this I desire to make two observations. The first is
that the nationalism which issues in imperialist conflict has
been possible only through the ignorance of the common
people. That ignorance, moreover, is the outcome of the class
structure of our society. So long, as Lord Acton wrote, as a
single class retained in its hands "the making of the laws, the
management of the conditions, the keeping of the peace, the
administration of justice, the distribution of taxes, the control
of expenditure," it was inevitable that the masses should be
the servant of its purposes. It wanted profit; it regarded the
use of force simply as a means to making its profit secure. And

M

since in each nation-state this class had a similar outlook the end was inevitably conflict. The only way out was an educational system which gave the masses a full light upon the relationships in which it was involved, the ends for which its crude patriotism was exploited. But you could not get such an educational system so long as economic power was in the hands of the commercial and investing classes. It was not to their interest, since it would have revealed the character of their exploitation. That, put brutally, is why we have to spend more on armaments than we do on education. That, also, is why every state-system of education bends its energies to the intensification of nationalism. You can see that intensification in the history books we use. All the energy and enthusiasm are lavished on the men who gave the nation-state its present form and power. Our children learn amply of Nelson and Wellington, of Clive and Rhodes. Is there an equal effort to make plain to them the greatness of Jeremy Bentham, the noble protest of Bright against the Crimean War, the effort of Charles Bradlaugh to achieve genuine religious freedom? We do not have education for peace, simply because, under our system, that would destroy the foundation upon which the imperialist uses national sentiment for his purposes. We shall not get education for peace until we have ended a social system in which, as in our own, inequality makes the many the servants of the few.

My second point is, perhaps, of more immediate practical import. The nationalism of Western Europe sought to organize all Asia for its economic profit; and the result has been a widespread and conscious revolt of Asia against European domination. You can see that in the revival of Turkey and of Persia. You see it, again, in the nationalist intensity of India and China; you see it, in all its formidable strength, in the typically Western imperialism of Japan. Even Afghanistan sought, under Amanullah, such a reorganization as would enable it to resist encroachment from Western Europe. I do not myself see how the effort of Asia to win its independence can easily be attained without at least the prospect of grave disaster to the world. We have largely destroyed its historic character for our own selfish purposes; and we find that the standards we have imposed in its place carry with them an ideology which threatens our private interests there. You can see in Asia a conflict between civilizations which has bred chaos. That chaos involves our intervention to protect our commercial interests; and intervention, as it meets the renascent nationalism of the East, clearly means large-scale conflict. We cannot, I myself believe, keep India or China in perpetuity in semi-subjection. Yet how precisely we are to assist them to win their independence and integration when the latter spell the ending of imperialism is not, I think, clear. Once Asia is fully self-conscious and fully organized, it will end Western control. But if the road to that ending lies through the kind of vehement economic nationalism we ourselves know to-day in Western Europe, it is difficult not to feel that the outcome is dark indeed.

I have, of course, no magic formula to propose; you cannot heal so deep-seated a disease with an incantation. I am satisfied if I have persuaded you that nationalism breeds imperialism, and that the latter at long last breeds nationalism again in the peoples whom it subjects to its control. To-day it is Asia; will it be Africa to-morrow? Have we not, if we would escape the immense conflict that such a sequence portends, to think in different terms? Having tried the world of sovereign-states, each looking to its own interests, each unlimited in law in the will it may seek to operate, each competing with its rivals in terms of force, and force alone, as the ultimate arbiter between different wants, can we really be content with the results? Does not the mere selfishness of ensuring our own survival compel us to think in different terms?

If we do so the alternative is unmistakable. We have to think of the world-community, the *civitas maxima*, as the starting-point of the social adventure. No part of this community can have the right or the power to act as its own will deems best warranted, without regard to the will of other parts. That body of law which represents the needs of the whole must bind the will of each of its constituent members. Differences between their wills, adjustments of their relationships, cannot be a matter of the independent volition of any state. We need institutions which prevent the state from hindering the needs of the world-community from being realized. And that is to say that the world-community and the sovereign-state are incompatible terms. We must choose between the one and the other; we cannot have both. We must recognize that international law has a claim superior to municipal. We must admit that there are things a state is not entitled to will—fields of decision in which its choice is one term only in an equation of choices. Little by little there must grow in the League of Nations the authority to determine all questions, decisions upon which have more than an incidence in a single state. Nationalism emerging into statehood results, in a word, in an egoism we have discovered to be intolerable. Either we must curb its excesses—which means the end of the sovereign-state —or they will destroy civilization.

Do not think that I imagine that this can be done in a year or even a decade. No one who realizes how painfully the nation-state was born, how important were the needs it once served, can imagine that its hold upon the allegiance of men can be radically disturbed, as it were, overnight. But there is all the difference in the world between travelling over difficult territory with a conscious knowledge of one's goal and travelling with no clear sense of direction in which we propose to move. If we approach our problems, as they arrive, with the definite intention so to solve them that the solution in each instance, even at the cost of loss to ourselves, results in gain to the idea of a world-community, we shall strengthen its hold as part of the habit of our lives. If Japan had thought in that fashion during her dispute with China, the prestige of the League would have made the conquest of the next obstacle infinitely less difficult. If we had signed the Optional Clause without reservations, our faith in the pacific settlement of international disputes would have created a deeper and wider faith in others. If we had insisted from the outset upon the proper treatment of the minorities under the Peace Treaties of 1919, the evasion of clear obligations by nations like Poland would have been far less natural than it now seems. If, in a word, we really believe in the League and all it implies, we must prove our faith by constant service to it. And as we serve it, we shall find, or so I think, that its transformation into a genuine world-community, so far from being a challenge to our power, will, on the contrary, be its main security. For it will give us the assurance of peace; and only in peace can the virtues of a nation achieve their rightful reward.

III

There is an internal as well as an external side to the problem of nationalism; and my plea would be fatally incomplete if I did not consider its problems. Just as there is a struggle for power between nation-states, so there is a struggle for power within them. The conflict of classes has a direct bearing upon the problem of the international community. I am even tempted to say that a nation-state will treat other nation-states as it acts towards its own citizens. Where there is repression within there will be at least the straining toward violence without; we become to others what we have been content to be to each other.

In this aspect the Labour clauses of the Treaty and the work of the International Labour Office are of extraordinary interest. They show the interdependence of the nations with a clarity perhaps more revealing than any other documents of the modern time. National competition in things like the conditions of work, the effort to underbid your neighbour by lowering the standard of wages or lengthening the working-day, produces instant reactions all over the world. Unless we can secure effective and equal social conditions the conflict of business men for the possession of markets is bound to assume its present form; and inherent in that conflict is the dangerous economic nationalism to which I have already drawn your attention. You cannot maintain high tariff-barriers in a unified world-market; but you cannot avoid the clamour for protected markets if rivals are to undersell one another in terms of the inadequate conditions they can force upon Labour.

Nor is that all. We are members of nation-states in which, even though there sometimes be the formal aspect of democracy, its reality remains unachieved. The bias of state-action is always in favour of those who possess the levers of economic power; even where they make concessions they do so, not because they should, but because they must. And the consequence of that bias is that the will of the state means, in daily action, the will of those who possess the economic power of the community. The history of imperialism makes it clear that the Foreign Office and the Colonial Office are at their command. One ministry may resist; one statesman may denounce; in the end, all are driven to give way. I see no method of preventing the state from becoming the tool of those who invest abroad except by the international control of investment.[1] I cannot here attempt to outline what that implies in detail.[1] But it would, I suggest, prevent things like the domination of the South American republics by the United States, or our own conquests of India and Africa. International control can, if we so will, be made to mean the moralization of external policy. It can prevent the investor from exploiting nationalist sentiment for purposes which are too often innocent of ethical motivation.

But more than this is implied. Make the strongest case you can against democratic government, and it yet remains the only political system in which men are recognized to possess an equal claim upon the common stock of welfare. Alternative systems, however admirably they may begin, always end by protecting the interests of a few. Dictatorships become concerned for their own self-preservation; aristocracies, whether of birth or wealth or creed, sooner or later confound the public good with their private welfare. But if we choose democratic government we cannot be satisfied with its merely formal expression. However great may be the winning of political democracy, it is only a stage to the conquest of what democracy fully implies.

That full implication is, I suggest, equality in every aspect of life. Do not mistake me. I do not mean by equality identity of treatment. I recognize, and with gladness, the infinite variety of human personality; the need, accordingly, to give it the most diverse means of expression. But if you have a national

[1] Cf. my *Grammar of Politics*, pp. 611-14. (*George Allen & Unwin Ltd.*)

society in which, like ours, men live so differently, they are bound to think differently. They have an interest in the result of the social process so different that there is no common ideology binding them together. They do not share in a common ideal; they do not strive for a common ideal. They lack that fundamental unity of purpose which gives vigour and tenacity to the national life. No society can hope to be democratic that is divided into the two nations of rich and poor. That division, more than any other, I believe is responsible for imperialist adventure. For its true implication is to force upon the rich the choice between sacrifice and revolution. They are rarely prepared for the first; it alters too drastically their way of life. They so rarely realize the coming of the second that, almost invariably, they postpone concessions until they are too late. And to avoid the price of concession, the class which possesses economic power seeks an opportunity of investment abroad, where the return to capital offers the chance of maintaining that way of life to which it is accustomed. Capitalism becomes imperialism by the very logic of its being; and the necessary outcome of imperialism is always conflict.

It is, I think, no accident that the birth of British imperialism —the end, also, of the Free Trade epoch in this country— should have coincided with the challenge of Continental nations to our industrial supremacy. Nor is it accident that the closing of the West in the United States should have led that country into her South American extravagances on the one side, and her excessive mercantilism on the other. Japan, in my judgment, begins to think in similar terms; and you can see in her effort the same fatal implications. The internal struggle for economic power always leads to imperialism as the easiest way to avoiding the duty of economic justice. At the outset the path always seems a simple one. In the end it is always a *cul-de-sac.* It does not solve the problem; it merely postpones it. In England, as an internal issue, it resulted in the eclipse of Liberalism; but it only raised up the Socialist Party to make the struggle between rich and poor take on a more obvious and more dramatic intensity.

My own inference from this is the vital one, that economic equality is the effective condition of democratic government. On the experience of history, it is the only way known to me of preventing the conflict between rich and poor from issuing either into imperialism or into revolution; and neither of these seems to me compatible with the life of reason, since each has its being in the rule of force. In an economically equal society the incidence of the state ceases to be biased in one direction; its power can be genuinely used, as it cannot be otherwise used, for the common good in a sense that really has some meaning. In such a society, also, there is less danger than now that ignorance may be exploited by propaganda; for there is less interest in keeping the reality of education a virtual monopoly of the few. There is less chance of utilizing the power of organized religion to maintain a *status quo* the inherent injustice of which is seen as soon as it is examined; and the Churches do not, as a result, maintain themselves in the degree that they are the servants of reaction. Whatever may be our doubts of Bolshevism, let us at least admit that its leaders were right when they insisted that religion has been the opium of the people.

I plead, therefore, for an economically equal society as one of the essential ways of preventing the perversion of national sentiment to the maintenance in power of a wealthy class. It may help the status of the poor, at least in a material sense, to share in the spoils of the imperialism which is born of inequality; but the price is always paid by those who are exploited in the territory brought under imperialist control. The Mexican peon, the Chinese coolie, the Indian ryot, have been compelled to pay the price for the Anglo-American standard of living. More, I do not believe you can suppress freedom abroad without danger to its reality at home; and imperialism always means the suppression of the demand for freedom among the peoples subject to imperialist domination. It was not accidental that the Indian "nabobs" poisoned our eighteenth-century politics; that the American Revolution was followed by the grim oppression of the younger Pitt; and I cannot help seeing significance in the fact that two legal members of the Viceroy's Council in

India, Sir Henry Maine and Fitzjames Stephen, were both, after their experience of autocracy abroad, the passionate critics of democracy upon their return to England.

"Choose equality and flee greed" is, as Matthew Arnold insisted, the clear lesson of historic experience. But I am not so foolish as to suppose that we destroy the dangers of nationalism merely by creating an equal society. Such a state would still need markets and raw materials; it would doubtless fight for access to them if access were denied. It is even conceivable that a genuinely democratic society might be more fiercely nationalist than under the present system. For the erosion of inequality would give to the claims of the state a title to allegiance it does not now possess. Its citizens might easily come to feel a patriotism almost religious in its intensity. There is some interesting evidence that this is the case in Soviet Russia. The appeal made there by the idea of equality is obviously remarkable. And the French Revolution showed, in an important way, how the removal of deeply-felt oppression gives to the ideas which replace it a drive and an energy far greater than are possessed by those which deny to the mass of the nation their place in the sun. To safeguard the world-community from the dangers of democratic nationalism is not less important than the duty of denying to the capitalist state the power to enlist national sentiment in its service.

Again, as I think, the way out is the abrogation of national sovereignty. A world-community, properly organized, and with the right to control the activity of its constituent parts, could genuinely seek to meet the difficulties involved. I do not see that they can be met in any other way. Indeed, I should be almost tempted to argue that the abrogation of national sovereignty is the condition upon which alone peace is safe in a world of democratic states. For if economic penetration gives to such states the chance of improving upon a wide front their standard of life, the temptations to use their power for this end might well prove irresistible. I, at any rate, do not feel certain that such states would feel a special tenderness for Africans or for Asiatics, that they would not take advantage of the weakness or divisions among the less advanced peoples to exploit them for selfish purposes. Imperialism of this type might well divide the Western world into camps as fiercely hostile to each other as religious parties in the sixteenth century. It would not be easy to set limits to the consequences of such a disaster. It would breed a temper of persecution all over the world that would make havoc of those spiritual values which, in the long run, are the really precious qualities in civilization.

There is one other aspect of the national spirit which is shown when it proclaims itself as a sovereign-state to which I want to draw your attention. To establish the state as sovereign, it seeks always what Lord Acton called the abrogation of the intermediate powers in the community. It is so fiercely absorptive in temper that it will admit the right of no body which may be conceived as even a possible challenge to its will. The republic, one and indivisible, lives by the erosion of all competing loyalties. The allegiance of men to the state is regarded as necessarily prior to all alternative allegiances. That title is not founded on the conduct of the state. Its law does not permit the citizen, either as an individual or in association with other individuals, to judge its policy, to allow his mind freely to protest about its activities. The state is the armed conscience of the nation, and so it proclaims itself as being; and we differ from its views at our peril. It invokes on its behalf all the mysticism which nationality secretes within itself. Acceptance, and blind acceptance, of its purposes becomes in very truth a religion. Think of the difficulty attendant upon criticism of the nation-state in time of war. Realize how hard it is to attack a government which is able to conceal its limited and partisan purposes behind the label of nationalism. The destruction of intermediate powers in Italy and Russia leaves the individual a helpless unit before the demands of the state. His will is stricken into impotence. He can speak with safety only as he echoes or supports the policy of those who operate the engines of policy.

Once it is conceived that the claims of the state are *a priori* superior to all other claims, that they are entitled to acceptance just because they are the claims of the state, there is an end to all justice and freedom in society. No organization is entitled to our loyalty merely because it is a point, a source of reference, in a legal hierarchy; its title depends upon the ethical adequacy which pervades its exercise of its power. And of that exercise individuals must, in the last resort, be judges for the simple reason that upon any other condition they abdicate the duty of citizenship. It is not an easy task to let one's mind play freely about affairs of state. It is made infinitely harder when the state presents itself as sovereign; when, moreover, that sovereignty is suffused with all the mystic glamour which comes from its position as the political embodiment of the nation. Diversity is strangled; individual rights are sacrificed; centralization destroys that eager spirit of local and functional responsibility out of which creativeness in government is born.

The power, in short, to call the state to account is essential to freedom, and it cannot exist where the state is sovereign. That power, by dividing authority, compels restraint in its exercise. It promotes independence of mind, and it gives that independence opportunity of expression by providing it with the means of organization. In such an atmosphere problems can be answered not merely in the context of the power possessed by the state, but in terms of the ethical adequacy of the solutions which are suggested. To differ from the state does not, then, imply an absence of patriotism; and that possibility of making such difference effective is the main safeguard we have against servility in the society which the state controls. I know, or course, that it is no longer fashionable to praise freedom and tolerance as desirable things. Yet I venture still to cherish them as the sole conditions known to me whereby Reason has a chance of victory in human affairs. The alternative is to assume that the big battalions have the right to triumph merely because they are the big battalions. That way, I suggest, lies a slavery both intellectual and moral.

I wish I had the time to exact of your patience a review of all that this attitude implies in institutional terms. I should like, above all, to show you its connexion with the newer tendencies in international law, especially its relationship to the possibility of an international penal law, the operation of which cannot but benefit, as I venture to think, the wants of us all. So long as international law derived its sanction only from the assent of sovereign states it could not have an effective penal side. It was bound to rest content with the indication of certain very limited classes of acts as reprehensible, and trust to the good faith of states to give effect to that indication. Once we begin to think in terms of the world-community, the stage is set for an ampler progress. It is not only that we are moving towards the idea of aggressive war as such, as a crime against international order, and, therewith, towards the idea that the duty of a citizen whose state embarks upon such an adventure may come to mean the imperative obligation to disobey its orders. It is not improbable that we shall come to view certain types of state-action, or the failure of state-action, as susceptible of punishment by an international court. A failure, for instance, to take proper precautions to prevent civil riots against foreigners may one day become an international delict to be tried in the Permanent Court. And I do not believe it to be unthinkable that where, as in the Sacco-Vanzetti case, the justice of the state has plainly failed, we may develop an international writ of *habeas corpus* to remedy the deficiencies of local error.

But this is to give rein to the imagination I may not now indulge. It is sufficient if I can persuade you that the concept of the non-sovereign state offers possibilities of creative adventure of which it is difficult to exaggerate the importance. The need to attempt them is plain. Even if it be true that their making is fraught with danger, the answer surely is that the alternative to making them is fraught with death. Nationalism has enjoyed its midsummer of high credit in these latter years. I understand, I think, its attractions—the fascination it has exercised over men who, like Mill and Mazzini, were the indubitable servants of high ideals. I have argued that the conditions under which those ideals seemed imperative have decisively changed. As soon as nationalism invoked the sovereign state as the means for its expression it endangered the very foundations of international security. The needs to which it was a response have largely passed. The concepts upon which it was based must give way before a new ideology more suited to the wants that we confront. We have to think of cosmopolitan law-making; it certainly cannot be made effective if the sovereignty of the state blocks the way to its construction. We need a new Grotius to outline the ground-plan of a new civilization.

IV

Two final remarks and I have done. The ideal for which I have been pleading is not a new one in history; great names stand high in the list of its advocates. We tend, I think, a little to forget how new in history is the conception of the state as freed from the shackles of law. To the eminent thinkers who founded the modern science of international law in the sixteenth century such a conception would have been unthinkable. They had, hardly less clearly than the most urgent internationalists of to-day, the dream of a world-community whose life was governed in terms of inescapable principle. You have only to read the works of men like Franciscus e Victoria, like Soto, like Grotius himself, to realize how sternly they would have repudiated the notion that the power of a nation is the measure of its rights. Signs are not wanting of a return to this attitude. It was said by Hall, a great English international lawyer whom no one would accuse of idealism, that the repudiation of international law during a period of conflict would be followed by an era in which men sought above all things the refreshment of its authority. That prophecy is rapidly becoming true. The search, all over the world, for means whereby the power of its principles may be widened and deepened is one of the most hopeful portents of our time. I will not trouble you with names. I suggest only that the decline of the positivist school of international law, the frontal attack now being made everywhere on the sovereignty of the state, give us reasons to hope that in this realm we are entering upon a great epoch of institutional creativeness.[1] If we have the will and the faith to welcome its coming, we may well make of our times one of the seminal epochs in the history of humanity.

[1] Cf. my *Introduction to Politics*, chap. iv, and Lauterpacht, *Private Law Analogies in International Law*, chap. ii.

Nor are we asking for the destruction of all that is so fine and distinctive in national life. We are protesting only that one of the forms it has assumed breeds anarchy by its nature, and we seek a safeguard against its dangers. I am not asking that the life of any nation shall be dominated by the power of another. On the contrary, I am seeking the enlargement of its freedom by removing the fear and insecurity that now haunt its frontiers. I seek to replace the rule of force by the rule of law. I seek to make the habits of nationalism fit the patent needs of mankind. At present our world is in perpetual danger of chaos because it is in perpetual danger of conflict. We are not entitled to optimism in face of the dangers we confront. But those very dangers ought to make us urgent about the task of reconstruction. "All things were together," said the old Greek philosopher, "until Thought came and arranged them." If we recognize, in our present situation, the obligation to think out our problems we may yet evade the relentless decree of fate. For fate bids us build an ordered world as the price we must pay for our survival. Do not let the difficulties of that task blind us to the splendour of its achievement.

APPENDIX

I leave this essay as it was originally written in 1932. The seven years that have passed since then have, I think, only reinforced the conclusions I have ventured there to emphasize. We have now been drawn into a momentous war which can only be justified by a peace which ends the possibility of aggression in the future by any nation-state. The technical pivot upon which our power to end aggression turns is the abolition of sovereignty. That must involve the rebuilding of a new world-order in which the nation-state is no longer sovereign. It therefore requires us to grapple with the conditions which led to the retention of sovereignty in 1919. This new world-order must be able directly to control all those functions, social, economic, political, in which power-politics are inherent. But it can only control them as there is, *pari passu* with its organization, thoroughgoing reconstruction of the internal order of each state towards the kind of equality of which this essay speaks.

We have to destroy "Hitlerism." But, to destroy it, we have to remove its causes. That will not be achieved merely by victory in the field. Vital as victory is, the far more important question is what we do with the victory when it is ours. The chance is given to us to learn from the history of the last generation that a world of sovereign national-states means inevitable disaster. We need, therefore, the conditions under which that sovereignty can go, and the institutions through which a new world order can operate. The key to our problems is the organization of an equal interest in peace; and that will not come merely by defeating Hitler. It will come only when we recognize that the boundaries between nation-states cannot be permitted, as they are now permitted, to interfere with the total well-being of the *civitas maxima*. That interference will continue so long as the contradiction between the forces of production and the relations of production persist in their present form. We have sought to project the idea of democracy on to the political plane; we have denied it access to the planes of economic and social life. Most of our national societies are, therefore, torn by internal dissensions which, as 1914 and 1939 make clear, cannot be resolved peacefully. We live in a world which faces the alternatives of internal revolution or external war as the only ways in which its pressures can be relieved. We need not live in that kind of world. The defeat of Hitlerism would, if we have the will and the courage, point the way out of it. But we must be prepared to pay the price, and there can be no doubt that the price means the replacement of privilege by equality in social relations. Without that replacement, there cannot be equality in international relations. Without that equality, war will continue (though it need not continue) to be rooted in the relations between men.

John Macmurray

Professor of Philosophy, University of London

FREEDOM IN THE PERSONAL NEXUS

THE traditional formulations of the problem of human freedom are so abstract that they have neither substance nor meaning. Or perhaps it would be more appropriate to say that they have substance and meaning only as it is lent to them by the personal interests and assumptions of individuals, so that they change from generation to generation, from country to country, from circumstance to circumstance. If the issue is to be put in the way of solution we must begin by determining what we are discussing when we discuss freedom. This cannot be done by any mere definition of terms, which would carry no further than the use of the word in the present context. We must determine the locus of the problem in universal human experience. We must discover the centre of disturbance. We must put our finger upon the concrete origin of the question, if it is to be real and not artificial; a problem of life and not of language.

The traditional dilemma of free will or determinism is entirely artificial, like most exclusive alternatives of a high order of abstraction. If a rigid determinism obtained in the field of human behaviour there could, of course, be no choice; and equally if a rigid freedom of will prevailed there could be no choice either, since both alternatives would be equally open. But it would be a waste of energy to pursue an abstract argument when it is easy to see by inspection that the debate is artificial. We need only suppose that we have accepted either alternative, and ask what difference it makes in concrete experience. If everything is determined, it still remains unquestionable that a man is freer out of prison than in it; freer in America at peace than in Germany at war; freer in health than in sickness, freer when he has money in his pocket than when he is penniless. If man possesses freedom of will equally these variations in freedom remain unaffected. The locus of the real problem lies in these variations of human freedom under varying conditions. The question is not, " Are we free?" but "How free are we?" It is not, "Have we freedom of will?" but "Under what conditions have we most freedom of will?"

Men have craved for freedom, demanded freedom, and fought for freedom. This proves that they have meant by "freedom" something that could be achieved by human effort; and not something that we either have or lack. If the free-will controversy were more than a scholastic wrangle, nothing could be done about freedom, whichever of the two alternatives were correct. This fact throws a curious light upon the metaphysical controversy itself. If we can increase freedom by taking the appropriate action, then freedom must be conditioned. It is only by altering its conditions that we can increase or diminish freedom. We can diminish a man's freedom of action by locking him in a room, and so changing the conditions of his action. To say that anything is conditioned is to say that it is determined. The conditions are its determinants. Thus what men have always meant by freedom is itself determined. In theory they have assumed that if everything is determined there can be no freedom. Yet what if freedom itself is determined? We tend to think too easily that men long for a freedom that is denied them by the forces of nature and history. Perhaps the opposite is nearer to the truth. Perhaps man is only too anxious to escape from a freedom which nature and history combine to thrust upon his timidity. Perhaps we are destined to be free whether we like it or not. To be free is to be responsible. To evade responsibility is to flee from freedom. If it is true that the inexorable laws of human development compel man to accept an ever increasing responsibility for his own destiny, then

N

freedom is determined at the metaphysical level, as an inevitable product of the laws of nature. In that event freedom and determinism are implicates, not contradictories.

There is also a subjective factor in the problem which demands preliminary attention. No one, I imagine, would consider that we are not free because there are many things that we are unable to do. A drowning determinist, clutching at straws, would hardly contend that we are not free because we cannot pay week-end visits to the moon. Freedom has clearly some relation to our desires, and our desires have their roots in the same nature of things that determines the possibilities of our action. No man can intend to do what he knows or believes to be beyond the bounds of possibility. It is doubtful whether we can even seriously desire, for any length of time, what we believe to be unobtainable. Freedom seems to lie in some *ratio* between our desires and our capacity to satisfy them; between what we can intend and what we can achieve. At least we may satisfy ourselves that men experience the lack of freedom only when their efforts are frustrated; only when they fail to achieve what they believe to be possible. The social function of the agitator, which has sometimes been of high importance in the history of freedom, is to persuade men to envisage, to desire, and to demand a freedom that they do not possess. His difficulty often lies in convincing the people that they are in bondage. His success depends upon convincing them that the new forms of life he proposes are really possible. The contented man is free, as the sages have always told us, because his powers are adequate to his desires. They have, perhaps, been too ready to assume that any man can be contented if he chooses. Even if he could, it is not at all clear that he ought to be. At any rate, it is important not to overlook this subjective factor in freedom. Men's desires vary. Their conceptions of what is possible are not fixed. Consequently, what is freedom for one man may be slavery for another, and the vision of a new possibility may turn freedom into bondage.

It would appear, then, that freedom, as we experience it, resides in the adequacy to our purposes of our powers, opportunities, and means. Its opposite is the experience of constraint, which varies when for any reason we must refrain from doing what we ourselves desire to do, or must do something other than we would. But this general formulation is too wide for our purpose. It covers checks to the spontaneity of our behaviour which appear as mere momentary vexations, no sooner felt than overcome; as well as those major and permanent frustrations that may make life not worth living. We have, as it were, drawn a circle round the field within which the problem is to be located. We must try to discover its centre. We have included all cases; we have to determine which are the crucial cases. The answer which I wish to suggest is that the centre of the problem of freedom lies in the nexus of personal relationships, and that all other types of constraint are derivative from the constraints of personal relationship, at least if they are real.

Before explaining this view, it will be well to consider the distinction between real and illusory freedom which I have introduced as a qualification. There is, we have seen, a subjective element in freedom, and it is, of course, on this account that freedom can be illusory. But the distinction between "subjective" and "objective" must be used in this context with extreme care. The ordinary distinction between the two is derived from the reflective field, in which we "stand over against" the world, in contemplation or in thought. In this attitude, whatever we consider is independent of the processes of consideration. It is "objective" in the sense that our activities of observing and thinking "make no difference" to it. But freedom is not objective in this sense; neither is it a property or character of anything objective. Freedom is a modality of action, and actions are not contemplated but performed. Here indeed lies the formal defect of the question, "Is the will free?" It postulates an objective entity called "the will," and inquires whether it possesses an objective property called "freedom." The phrase "my will" stands for "me acting," in contrast to "me observing and reflecting." Acting means realizing an intention, and an act cannot therefore be merely objective. Neither can it be merely subjective. It is a unit of experience which begins in the "subjective" and terminates in the "objective." It bridges the gap between "mind" and "matter," between the "self" and the "world," between "ideas" and "things," if indeed there is any gap to be bridged. Freedom, as a modality of this transition from subjective to objective, cannot be either merely subjective or merely objective. We must guard against the tendency to identify the illusory with the subjective and the real with the objective in this context. All freedom has both a subjective and an objective element in it, and these are not separable. They are rather aspects of one and the same thing. We are not necessarily free merely because we feel free; but on the other hand a constraint which is not felt is no real constraint. A contented slave is still a slave, though his slavery is no bondage for him; and when the poet writes that

> "Stone walls do not a prison make,
> Nor iron bars a cage"

we understand what he means, but refuse to take his statement *au pied de la lettre*. If freedom is to be real it must not be subject to destruction by a change of mood or an increase in knowledge. It must be rooted, as a subjective experience, in the objective nature of things. Otherwise it is illusory.

We may distinguish two types of illusory freedom, which we may call subjective and objective respectively. Freedom, we may say, is subjectively illusory, if the absence of any experience of constraint depends upon the absence of a desire to do what one would be prevented from doing. It is objectively illusory if the feeling of freedom depends upon a false belief in our power to achieve what we desire. The stoic ideal of a freedom to be achieved by getting rid of desire and "willing what happens" is the apotheosis of subjectively illusory freedom. Kant's effort to equate freedom with moral obligation falls into the same category. Desires which are suppressed do not cease to exist; they are at best inactive in consciousness. The objective type of illusory freedom is even more common. It exists wherever we over-estimate our capacities or our means; or are ignorant of the obstacles in circumstances to the achievement of our intentions. Corresponding to these illusory freedoms, there are illusory constraints. We are subject to illusions of weakness as well as of power; and we are afflicted with spurious desires, which lead us to demand impossible satisfactions that we do not really want, and which, if we were to achieve them, we should repudiate. The illusory character of such freedoms and constraints does not consist in their non-existence or their ineffectiveness. We are not dealing with ideas which have no counterpart in the real world. In action the subjective does not confront the objective as it does in reflection. Action passes *from* the subjective *to* the objective. It is a process in time, with an inherent reference to the future. The check to action which destroys our freedom in action may come at any point in the process. Illusory freedom is experienced as freedom. But it is incompatible with its own persistence, and is therefore self-defeating. We are not free to achieve the impossible. But we are often free *in* actions which must inevitably lead to frustration, because their objective, unknown to us, is in fact impossible. Such freedom is properly called illusory, since it depends upon illusions, and must lead to its own destruction.

With this distinction between real and illusory freedom in mind, we may return to the central issue. Real freedom depends upon the character of the nexus of personal relations in which we are involved. This is the thesis which I wish to expound. It can be expressed and understood best by drawing attention to the kind of experience of freedom and constraint which it makes the centre of the problem. If I am in the company of strangers whose good will is important to me, and cannot be depended on, my conversation with them and my behaviour towards them suffer from constraint. I cannot express myself spontaneously. I must think carefully before I speak, and seek to make a good impression. I must act a part; I cannot "be myself." If I leave this company and join a number of intimate friends whom I know and trust, this constraint disappears and is replaced by freedom. I can now allow my whole self to appear. I can say what comes into my mind. I can behave "naturally." I need not fear criticism, and so I can be spontaneous, speaking and acting without an eye upon effects. Here then is one familiar type of experience in which the contrast between "freedom" and "constraint" appears. My thesis is that this contrast is the central one; and that when we wish to go to the root of the problem of freedom, this is precisely the sort of case which we should accept as a type instance, and have in mind as an example. My reason for saying this is not that there are no other types of cases which are important, such as those which form the stock-in-trade of all discussions of political liberty. It is that the type of experience I have chosen involves, in principle, all the others; that if it is understood, then all the others are, in principle, understood; if it is solved, then all the others are soluble. The understanding of other types, on the other hand, is not possible, or at least cannot be complete, unless this type of case is understood; nor can the problem be solved in the other types of instances unless it is solved in this type. I believe, in other words, that the problem of freedom appears at different levels of experience, and that its solution at the upper levels depends upon its solution on the basic level. And I believe that if we consider the problem as it appears in the nexus of direct personal relationships, we are attacking it at ground level; we are laying bare its foundations. Only if we do this is it possible to envisage a radical solution. Even if such a radical solution is impracticable, it will still enable us to understand what partial solutions are possible and practicable at other levels, such as the political or the economic; and it will prevent us from expecting too much from reforms that do not go to the root of the trouble.

In our effort to determine the general field in which the real problem of freedom arises, we noticed that it was not the mere absence of power that created the problem, but the absence of power relative to a real desire. We noticed further that a real desire—the kind of desire that can give rise to deliberate action—depends upon a belief in the possibility of its satisfaction. This involved a curious paradox. It would seem that we can only experience a real loss of freedom in the presence of an impossible possibility. I do not mean by this that we must believe something to be possible which is in fact impossible; for this is the situation in which we enjoy a freedom which is objectively illusory. We must find ourselves in a situation in which a real possibility is actually impossible to realize; in which we believe, and believe rightly, that what we desire to achieve can be achieved and at the same time cannot be achieved. For it is only in such conditions that we can experience a real frustration of our will. It is only then that we feel, and rightly feel, that we are *prevented* from realizing our intentions, that we are *deprived* of our freedom.

How can such a situation arise? Surely any action that I propose is either possible or impossible. At most, it would seem, I may be mistaken in thinking it possible when it is impossible, or impossible when it is not. Surely it cannot both *be* possible and impossible at the same time. Logically, of course, it cannot. But logic does not have the last word.

For our logical judgments depend upon the distinction between subjective and objective, which holds in the field of reflection but not in the field of action. In reflection about the nature of the objective world we are guided by the postulate that all unreason falls into the subjective field; so that if any illogicality comes to light it must belong to the processes of thinking, and not to what is the object of our thought. But in action the unreason of the subjective field is carried over into the objective, and our mistakes are objectively revealed and have an objective embodiment. If two of us differ in our conclusions about an objective question, then the disagreement makes no difference to the fact; it merely shows that one of us at least is mistaken, and ought to change his mind. The error of another cannot here by its mere existence destroy the correctness of my own judgment. His inability to think logically does not interfere with the freedom of my own processes of thought. But when we pass from the sphere of thought to that of action this immunity is left behind. For in action the irrationality of others can frustrate the rationality of my intentions, and my irrationality can frustrate theirs. If our intentions contradict one another, they destroy each other's possibility. What is objectively possible becomes actually impossible. Wherever, indeed, the achievement of an intention depends upon co-operation, the simplest of objective possibilities may be made impossible by the unwillingness of those concerned to co-operate;

and this unwillingness may, on occasion, rest upon completely irrational and totally absurd grounds. The capacity of human beings to "cut off their noses to spite their faces" is very high, and it is not unusual to find a group of individuals who refuse to co-operate in the achievement of an objective which all of them desire, for reasons so irrational that they must conceal them even from themselves. This is the resolution of the paradox of the impossible possibility which lies at the root of the problem of freedom. It is the nexus of personal relationship that is responsible for the variation in human freedom. We can prevent one another from achieving our purposes, even when they are objectively possible, and so limit or destroy one another's freedom. Moreover, this is the only way in which real freedom can be limited; for only thus can what is objectively possible be rendered actually impossible. Only persons can limit the freedom of persons. Any limitation of freedom must have its source in us; in the character of our relationships, as personal agents, to one another.

It is the instinctive recognition of this truth that links the experience of a lack of freedom with the idea of oppression and tyranny. When men feel the loss of freedom they behave as though someone were responsible. They instinctively feel that some individual or class is wrongfully depriving them of a freedom which is theirs by natural right. The struggle for freedom is always a struggle against oppression. The oppressors have defended themselves on the plea that the freedom demanded was in the nature of things impossible; that the constraint complained of was in fact illusory. In this instinct there is a core of essential truth, however mistaken the accusation may be in any particular case. If men feel the loss of freedom they are always justified in looking for its source in the personal field. If men are not free, then they are oppressed. Their inability to do what they desire is not a mere lack of power, but a deprivation of power, for which the responsibility rests with their fellows. The fact that we often make mistakes in assigning the responsibility, that often indeed we are satisfied to wreak our vengeance on any available scapegoat, is no argument against this truth; any more than the fact that we often assign the wrong cause for an event suggests that it is causeless. We are therefore at liberty to lay down a principle of far-reaching importance. The solution of any problem of human freedom depends on the alteration of the relationships of persons. The importance of this principle lies in what it denies. It denies that any increase in power can solve the problem of freedom. Indeed, an increase in power which is not accompanied by a change in the nexus of personal relationships must inevitably diminish freedom. For it enlarges the field of objective possibility without altering the conditions of effective action, and so widens the gap between what can be intended and what can be achieved.

Consider two examples of this. The increase of scientific knowledge during the past century has immensely increased the range of human possibility. Much is really possible to-day that was objectively impossible a hundred years ago. As a result there has been a noticeable diminution of human freedom and an increase of oppression. There is nothing paradoxical about this. It is, in fact, just what must happen provided the character of the personal nexus remains, as it has remained, substantially unaltered. The increase in what is objectively possible cannot be equated with an increase in freedom. It increases the range and variety of the satisfactions that men can reasonably hope to attain. But if it leaves their forms of relationship adjusted to a narrower range of actual achievement only, then the effect is to diminish freedom. The subjective constituent of freedom must not be overlooked. Freedom does not consist in the objective existence of power, but in the possibility of using it for desired ends. If a century of scientific development has made it possible to raise the general standard of living by 20 per cent and it has actually risen only by 10 per cent then in this respect there has been a restriction of freedom by 10 per cent. (The figures, of course, are not to be taken seriously.)

Consider, in the second place, the increase in oppression which reveals itself in modern dictatorship. In olden times a despotic monarch, however arbitrary and cruel, could interfere with the freedom of his subjects only to a quite limited extent. In a modern society with the same type of relationship between ruler and ruled, the enormous increase in the range of human power involves a correspondingly enormous increase in the restriction of freedom. Not only is the tyrant's capacity to interfere with the activities of his subjects vastly increased, but the range of possible satisfactions which he can deny them is also greatly enlarged. Here again we see that an increase in objective possibility involves a decrease of freedom if the character of the personal nexus in society remains unaltered.

It might seem that this leads us to endorse the view, widely held at present, that freedom is a function of the structure of society. This is partly correct, but only partly. The more important corollary, which must be combined with this, is that the structure of society is itself a function of the personal nexus of relationship between its members. There is an ambiguity in our use of the term "society" which is apt to result in a dangerous confusion. In general, the term refers to that nexus of relationship which binds human individuals into a unity. The ultimate fact upon which all society rests is the fact that the behaviour of each of us conditions the behaviour of the others and is therefore a determinant of their freedom. But the resulting nexus of relationship contains two distinguishable elements in virtue of the types of motive which underlie the active relationships involved. It is of the first importance to recognize, and to bear in mind, that a subjective element necessarily enters into all human behaviour, and so into the constitution of all human relationships. The elementary type forms of these contrasted motivations are hunger and love. Hunger is a motive which gives rise to actions designed to appropriate something for one's own use. Love, in contrast, is the motive of actions in which we expend what is ours upon something or someone other than ourselves. Both these types of motive are *necessary* in the sense that they belong universally to the psychological constitution of human nature and are inescapable elements in the determination of human behaviour. Both give rise to a nexus of dynamic relationships which bind us together. The first type gives rise to functional co-operation in work, and its basic forms are economic. The second gives rise to the sharing of a common life. Since the term "society" has in our day come to be so closely bound up with discussions of the organized forms of political and economic relationship, we had better specialize it for this use, and distinguish the forms of relationship which spring from the impulse to share a common life by using the term "community" to refer to them. The contrast to which our attention is now directed becomes thus a contrast between society and community.

The exact difference between society and community and the proper relation between them are best recognized by reference to the intentions involved. The intention involved in society lies beyond the nexus of relation which it establishes. In community it does not. It follows that society is a means to an end, while community is an end in itself. This may be stated from another angle by pointing out that a society can always be defined in terms of a common purpose, while a community cannot. Let us look, by way of example, at the simplest possible type of case, in which only two persons are involved. Two men may be associated as partners in a publishing business. They may also be associated as friends. That these two forms of relationship are different, and at least relatively independent, is shown by the fact that they may dissolve the partnership and remain friends; or they may remain in partnership and cease to be friends. Their association as partners is constituted by a co-operation in the achievement of a common purpose. Its form is dictated by this purpose. It involves a plan of co-operation and a division of labour between them. In virtue of this plan each of the two has a function in the business, in performing which he contributes his share of work to the achievement of the common purpose. Success depends on the proper co-ordination of their functions; and if the plan achieves this and each performs his function efficiently, the partnership is a satisfactory association. The whole nature of their relationship as business partners is expressible in such functional terms with reference to the common end to which the association is the means.

Now consider their relationship as friends. We are not concerned here merely with their feelings, but with the kind of active relationship which is implied in their being friends. Notice in the first place that this association cannot be defined in terms of a common purpose. We cannot ask, "What is the purpose of their friendship?" without implying that they are not really friends, but only pretend to be friends from an ulterior motive. A relationship of this type has no purpose beyond itself. Consequently its form is not dictated by a purpose; it does not give rise of necessity to a functional division of labour. For the same reason it cannot be organized. Nevertheless it is not motiveless. Its motive is to be found in the need to share experience and to live a common life of mutual relationship, which is a fundamental constituent of human nature.

We can use the same simple instance to help us to understand the relationship of these two types of association. That they are at least partly independent of one another we have seen, since they may vary independently. But we must now notice that friendship, though it cannot be constituted by co-operation for a common purpose, necessarily generates such co-operation. A friendship which did not result in the formation of common purposes and in co-operation to realize them would be potential only. Indeed the underlying motive of love is precisely to do something for the satisfaction' of the other, and its mutuality inevitably leads to functional co-operation. But there are important differences to be noticed. Since the association is not *constituted* by a common purpose, it permits of a change of purposes. In a partnership, if the common purpose is dropped or becomes unrealizable, then the partnership is at an end. Not so with a friendship. If the two friends drop one common purpose for which they co-operate, it is only to find another. In the second place, the common ends which are worked for and the co-operation for their achievement are together means to maintaining and deepening the friendship. From this we must conclude that in the nexus of personal relationship community is capable of generating and containing society within itself, of making the co-operation for the achievement of common ends a means to itself and an expression of itself. Therefore it is clear that if the problem of community is solved the problem of society will be well on the way to solution.

It still remains true that within limits at least society can be independent of community. Our two men can be partners and co-operate in the work of running their business without being friends. The necessity of making a livelihood, the pressure of immediate self-interest, may be sufficient motives to maintain the association. But there are limits to this. In the first place, though their co-operation is theoretically possible in the absence of friendship between them, in practice the absence of friendship limits the possibilities of effective co-operation in many ways; while if strong personal antagonism enters in, it may easily render co-operation impossible. It may simplify the issue if we remember that we are using the term friendship to draw attention to the whole range of forms of relationship which depend upon other-regarding motives; that is to say, upon motives which give rise to actions intended to affect the lives and fortunes of others. Such motives range from murderous hate, through a theoretical point of pure indifference, to the love which is ready to sacrifice life itself for the profit of the loved one. If we keep this whole range of behaviour in mind it is much less clear that functional co-operation is quite independent of the more personal forms of relationship of which friendship is our example. The more positive the personal interest the easier, *ceteris paribus*, the co-operation must be. The stronger the personal animosities between co-operating individuals the more difficult and inefficient the co-operation is likely to prove. It is only at the theoretical point of complete personal indifference that the co-operation is freed from the influence of the more personal elements in the nexus of relationship. Such an indifference is psychologically impossible between people who are in direct contact with one another. But it is possible and natural in highly organized societies, where very few of the individuals co-operating can know one another personally at all.

In the second place, any social organization is liable to be hampered or even disrupted by the intrusion of personal animosities. The machinery of co-operation seems to work smoothly only if the personal relations of the individuals concerned are kept, as it were, at a level of low tension. The more each one concentrates on doing his own part in the common task the better. The more the relations between them are determined by the common objective and the functional necessities of the plan of co-operation, the more efficient their efforts are likely to be. In all forms of organized co-operation, therefore, there is a tendency to look upon the more personal forms of relationship as a source of possible danger to the unity of the group. There is a latent tension between the two aspects of relationship. Society demands from its members a devotion to a common end which transcends all "private" ends, and a loyalty which is ready to sacrifice both oneself and one's neighbour to accomplish it. But from the standpoint of community, such a demand is absurd and blasphemous. For its values lie within, not beyond, the nexus of relationship; and all co-operation is a means of expressing the common life. Persons, not purposes, are absolute.

It has been necessary to draw the contrast between those two forms of relationship in the personal nexus because it is vital to the problem of freedom.

Probably everyone to whom freedom is a practical issue would agree that it only becomes a real issue when there is oppression; when somebody is putting constraint upon someone else and so infringing his natural liberty. This is to recognize, of course, that the locus of the problem of freedom lies in the personal nexus. From this recognition it is a natural step to the view that the solution of the problem must lie in a reorganization of society which will order the relations of individuals in such a way that the tyranny of one man over another, of one group or class over another, is eliminated. All the great struggles for freedom have taken their stand upon this view. Yet when they have won their victories in the revolt against this tyranny and that and have established the new order for which they strove, the result has always proved a disappointment to the idealists. Freedom remained obstinately unachieved. Constraint and tyranny reappear in forms ever more complicated and more difficult to deal with. To-day, after centuries of struggle and effort, it is at least doubtful whether all the progress made has not left the majority of men less free than they were in the days of serfdom and slavery; with a wider gap than ever between their reasonable desires and the satisfactions they can actually attain. This is not to say that there has been no progress. Progress has been immense and in spite of the pessimists is increasing its speed every year. The measure of progress is the increase in the range and complexity of what is objectively possible for man. This has risen so high that it is not absurd to say that already we are in a position to eliminate poverty from the life of mankind. But freedom is measured by the ratio between what is objectively possible and what we can actually achieve. It looks as though that ratio is lower than it has ever been in the history of civilization. Two things seem to be true together in the strange period to which we belong: that man's power of achievement has grown vast beyond belief; and that his capacity to achieve any serious human purpose is diminishing at an alarming rate. It is an age at once of unparalleled effort and unparalleled frustration.

The reason for this paradox seems to me to lie in our failure to distinguish the two aspects of relationship in the personal nexus. Not only do we use the terms "society" and "community" more or less interchangeably, but we tend increasingly to think of the nexus of personal relationship as a nexus of organized co-operation. As a result we are bound to conceive the problem of freedom as a problem of social organization; and, since the central organ of social organization is the State, as a political problem, to be solved by political means. The effort to solve the problem politically can only have the result of producing the organization of tyranny in the totalitarian State.

For consider. If a man is primarily a function in an organized co-operation pursuing a "common" purpose, then he exists for the group, as a means to the achievement of the common purpose. This is equally true of all his fellows. He and they have no more fundamental unity which might determine or modify or in any way challenge the social purpose. It is this purpose which determines them, sets them their places and their functions. Only in virtue of this organizing purpose are they a group. One is inclined to reply at once that this is clearly nonsense; and indeed it is. But we must not locate the "nonsense" in the wrong stage of the argument. If human society were fundamentally a nexus of politico-economic co-operation, as so much of our modern thought and practice asserts or assumes, then any limitation of the claims of the group sovereignty upon the individual would be ridiculous, and any freedom for the individual would be accidental. The theory and practice of the totalitarian State are direct corollaries of this characteristic modern assumption. If, on the other hand, the individual has any ground of claim against the State; if it can treat him unjustly and deprive him of a freedom which is his by right of nature; then he is not primarily a functional element in an organized co-operation. He embodies in himself, as it were, an authority which limits and defines the merely political authority of the organized society. Moreover, it is not as a mere individual that he can claim such an authority; as a mere individual he cannot even exist. It can only be as a member of a more primary nexus of relationships than those of any organized society, and in which the ground of all organized society is to be found. This is the nexus of communal relationship, which we here distinguish from the social nexus. We have thus reached the point at which we can say that freedom can only be maintained in this nexus of human relationship by maintaining the primacy of the personal nexus of community over the functional nexus of organized society. If this is secured, then no doubt a well-organized society will provide greater freedom for its members than an ill-ordered society. But the most perfect organizing of society, if it involves the primacy of the State, as the authority of organized society, must result not in the extension but in the obliteration of freedom.

The problem of human freedom is then the problem of that nexus of human relationships of which friendship is the type. It belongs to the field of our direct personal relationships; not primarily to the world of our indirect, functional, or legal relationships. This was the one point which I set out to maintain. I may well conclude by showing that this means that the basis of freedom is personal equality.

The essence of any friendship consists in the achievement, in it, of a real sharing of life, of an effective mutuality of experience. This involves, of course, material co-operation, as we have seen. It is in this effort to achieve such a nexus of relationship between ourselves and others that we have our most direct experience of freedom and constraint. Freedom is the result in so far as we succeed. Constraint is the penalty, as it is the proof, of failure. Freedom is the product of right personal relations. Constraint in the personal nexus is evidence that there is something wrong with the relationships involved. This "rightness" in such relationships is in fact personal equality. If there is constraint in a personal relationship there is a failure to achieve and maintain equality. Unless people treat one another as equals they are not friends. If one treats the other as an inferior, then he is using him as a means, and the friendship ceases to be a friendship. Thus personal equality is the structural principle of relations which are communal in type, while the experience of freedom in relations is their characteristic expression. What throws the personal nexus out of gear, and so introduces constraint and limits or destroys freedom, is always a failure to achieve or maintain personal equality. In other words, what destroys freedom is the will to power. Where one man seeks power over others, where one class or nation seeks dominion over others, the denial of equality involved creates constraint and limits freedom. And there is no way in which freedom can be restored or increased except by overcoming the desire for power.

The conclusion is a negative one; and not particularly comforting. To all the plans for achieving or defending freedom by political or economic organization it comes as a serious and unwelcome warning. There can be no *technique* for achieving freedom. The field in which freedom has to be won or lost is not the field of economics or politics, of committees and rules. It is rather the field which has hitherto been the undisputed domain of religion. An age that has put religion aside without even recognizing the need to put something in its place has already lost the sense of freedom and is ripe for the organization of tyranny. On the other hand, the will to power, though it may affect an epoch like an epidemic, is still a disease. It is not natural. And it may help us back to health to recognize the disorder from which we suffer.

Thomas Mann

Lecturer in the Humanities, Princeton University

FREEDOM AND EQUALITY

MODERN democracy is historically nothing more than the form of sovereignty of the *bourgeoisie*, of the *tiers état*, which established its mercantile and industrial world-dominion upon the ruins of feudalism. It was achieved through revolution against the ancient forces of inequality and privilege, of spiritual as well as material oppression. It was achieved in alliance with the forces of enlightenment and reason, which were felt as divinely beneficent, the destruction alike of bondage and of prejudice. This world-dominion is one of freedom and at the same time one of peace, industry, usefulness, and prosperity. Benjamin Constant writes in the year 1813, toward the end of the Napoleonic era: "After the history-making epoch of war, we have arrived at the epoch of trade; the former is barbaric impulse, the latter is civilized calculation; the new nations aim only at tranquillity and in addition to this at wealth whose source is industry."

It is curious how clearly this utterance of the French novelist and political moralist reveals the sensitive function of the literary man to discern and to define the will of the times, the changes and transitions of the spiritual, ethical, and social life. He does this with a precision which is the result of acute powers of perception and of nervous reaction, and he registers these reactions even when outward circumstances, as in these days, make them difficult of recognition to less penetrating eyes. It was daring to declare, between Moscow and Waterloo, that the war period had been replaced by one of trade and of rational welfare; and yet the observation was, oh the whole, strictly accurate, especially since it was the function of the Napoleonic wars to spread the revolution and its bourgeois ideas throughout Europe.

Moreover, this particular author was not the only one to entertain such timely ideas. Another French social critic observed at the same time that money, cities, intellect, and trade were now taking the place of landed property, castles, and the honours of military life: he claimed that these changes defined the new social order which had already affected the Council of Monarchs and thereby reacted upon the people. The evolution from feudalism to *bourgeoisie* and democracy could not be more simply or more satisfactorily described. What was then a critical judgment based upon actual experience corresponds exactly to our own sentiments when we try historically to determine the new social spirit and the essence of democracy. The change was clearly felt everywhere and occupied every alert and observing mentality—whether in the form of a protest or of a hopeful agreement.

The attitude of Goethe toward the victorious democracy is of the highest personal and objective interest. Living, as he did, from the eighteenth century well into a decisive part of the nineteenth century, he was a deeply disturbed spectator of the governmental convulsions by which political forms spasmodically adjusted themselves to new moral and social conditions. His old age was troubled by the serious menace to the future of culture which would result from the period of rapid communication, of money and mass domination that he could see approaching. But stronger or at least just as strong were his sense of reality, his instinct to remain intensely alive, to absorb life, and to incorporate it within his gigantic life-work to his very last breath. Everybody knows the poetical tribute which he paid to the "New World"—an expression which he used in its double geographical and social meaning:

> America, your life is better
> Free from our old Europe's faults,
> You no ruined castles fetter
> And no basalts.

At the age of eighty his attention was directed especially toward America, as is proven by the last parts of *Wilhelm Meister*. The far-seeing and eager sympathy of the old man for Utopian plans and for great technical problems such as the Panama Canal was simply magnificent. He discusses the latter with a penetration and detailed knowledge as if it were more important to him than all the poetry in the world, and in the last analysis it actually was. The hopeful pleasure which he felt in the civilizing influence of technical progress and rapid methods of communication is not surprising in the author of *Faust*, whose highest experience, toward the end, is the realization of a utilitarian dream, the draining of a swamp—an idea that was peculiarly shocking to the narrow-minded, philosophical affectations of the German public at that time. The elderly poet delights in discussions of the possibilities of joining the Mexican Ocean with the Pacific and the incalculable results of such an undertaking. He advises the United States to undertake the idea and lets his imagination play with the vision of flourishing commercial cities which would gradually spring up along the Pacific Coast. He could scarcely wait for the realization of all this, as well as the union of the Danube with the Rhine, which, he conceded, would be an undertaking gigantic beyond one's fondest hopes. And there was a third idea—a really magnificent one; this time it was for the English—the Suez Canal. "Oh," he exclaims, "to see all this, it would certainly be worth while to preserve on earth for another fifty years." This tendency toward the useful, toward world-unity, was a tendency of the times, a democratic tendency. It finds additional expression in certain applications of liberal economic principles to the life of the mind, as, for example, when the aged Goethe speaks of a "free trade in ideas and feelings," or when he explains that national literature was no longer of great importance and that the day of universal literature had come.

It is impossible not to admire this ready acceptance of life under new conditions in a mentality that had matured to greatness in such a different world. But Goethe needed only to be touched by the new spirit in order to express it in words in which sensibility and sympathy can scarcely be distinguished.

It is hope that speaks in all these words, hope for the happiness and peace of humanity, hope that borders on the Utopian, and which constitutes a surprising concession to the spirit of the times on the part of an elderly poet who was fundamentally pessimistic about the cultural future. For hope, yes even Utopianism, is really a characteristic of this young democracy which combines in a most peculiar way industrialism with love of humanity and common sense with faith in the immanence of a golden age. In the French social prophecies of that time, we read: "The Golden Age which a blind tradition has hitherto placed in the past now lies before us." This faith is the spiritual fruit of sudden freedom from clericalism and feudalism, a rapid progress in the knowledge and control of nature, in technical skill and in wealth-producing business activity. This faith has decidedly moral and even religious associations; in spite of its materialism and utilitarianism, it reveals traces of spirituality. "Money, cities, spirit, and trade." "Spirit" is the "third word," and it plays no unimportant rôle in the total complex.

A general conviction prevails that after the disappearance of the old war atmosphere and of the institutions that depend upon the church, society must be based upon the two new forces, science and industry; also, that scholars and industrialists must henceforth divide the leadership of the world. Heine defends these beliefs enthusiastically in his book on *Conditions in France*, evidently under the social and religious influence of Saint-Simon who in 1825 had published his *Opinions, littéraires, philosophiques, et industrielles*. Another of Saint-Simon's books is called very characteristically *Nouveau Christianisme*. His pupil Dumoyer writes *De la morale et de l'industrie*, and this combination of industry and morality is more typical and more frequent than that of industry and science. Together with Auguste Comte, this same Dumoyer publishes *Le Producteur*, a periodical "which is to help the progress of humanity, in science, morality, and industry through the encouragement of the spirit of co-operation." The good-will and the confidence in humanity are almost overwhelmingly touching, and especially in this day may well put us to shame. It was a Utopianism of progress, practical-minded, to be sure, but basically very religious and oriented toward spirituality. It mingled the material and the sensual with the moral, and was dominated by ideas of peace, work, fraternity, welfare.

This did not imply an individual and egotistical welfare so much as a universal, social one. That precisely was the moral element. Morality and the social life are synonyms in this sphere; morality is the social spirit; scarcely anything but that. And imperceptibly, without a break, and as if it were taken for granted, we see here, in the first flowering of democratic thought, the transition of democracy into socialism. It is exceptionally noteworthy and instructive to observe in the work of Goethe's old age that a trend toward socialism is an apparent spiritual necessity in democratic morality. We find these sudden flashes of a collectivistic prophecy in the *Wanderjahre* where he deals, toward the end, with humanity's victory over its individualism and over its concept of individual culture, a concept which Goethe, himself, had primarily created and moulded. Here the ideal of the highest personal development, the highest cultivation and universality, are actually renounced, and a period of specialization is proclaimed. The inadequacy of the individual is revealed; only the sum total of humanity completes the human; the individual becomes a function; the concept of universality appears: the community.

Likewise in the system of Saint-Simon, the individual is of value only to the extent that he contributes to the improvement of the condition of the many, of the universality in which he must lose himself. There will always be inequalities, says Saint-Simon, but there must be none which God himself has not ordained. It is the right of inheritance which creates rich and poor, educated and ignorant, yes, good and bad individuals. Let it be eliminated, and chance can no longer put the tools of production into the hands of the lazy and the incapable. Everyone will be rewarded according to his capacities; every capacity according to its products; that is the formula of justice, maintains Saint-Simon, and the young socialists of 1830 are convinced that it corresponds to the original will of God. Saint-

Simon's thinking and willing are without doubt religiously determined, and are proclaimed by his contemporaries, themselves, as a religion, as *la religion Saint-Simonienne*. "Religion," declares Saint-Simon, "must lead society toward the great goal of the quickest possible improvement of the good of the greatest number." That statement expresses Christian feeling, but it is a developed Christianity, freed of dogma, and directed toward the earth and toward community life. It is a Christian humanism, that sees in humanity *la fille de dieu*, the daughter of God, and desires that her future be glorious. Man should consider and promote not only his physical life, according to heathen practice, nor only his spiritual life, as in ascetic Christianity, but both in combination. He is not merely a traveller and stranger here on earth, or a fallen angel who must keep his eyes fixed on the Beyond, but he has come upon earth with the vocation to complete the task of the gradual perfection of all things. The reorganization of the whole world-order is needed, but this must be achieved through efforts of the individual and left to the progress of time.

It would be impossible, even now, to define the idea of Christian socialism or of social humanism more precisely. Above all, a clear and exact appreciation is manifested of the independence of occidental Christian ethics from church and dogma, that is, of the capacity inherent in Christianity for spiritualization, which constitutes its great superiority over the religions of the classical world. In ancient Rome, says the literature of the period, the disintegration of state religion and pontifical office created moral anarchy, brought about a confusion of contradictory and unstable aspirations and philosophies which led to destruction. The ancient peoples and their states were destroyed because religion and politics were one and the same thing, and because religion was bound to a rigid priestly hierarchy. To Christian races, on the contrary, metamorphosis is vouchsafed instead of destruction; for in Christianity spiritualization is innate; Christianity is, itself, conducive to the spiritual life and therefore does not die with its dogmatic and pontifical forms, but remains the living spirit of the people; and while it purifies the public and cultural life, it, in turn, is stimulated through them toward transfiguration of itself.

It must be conceded that this insight into the immortality of Christianity, due to its capacity for spiritualization, is a meritorious discovery of the young socialism which was born of bourgeois democracy at the beginning of the nineteenth century. It is this power which enables Christianity to survive its churches and to remain, independent of them, the inspiration and the foundation of occidental civilization. It is a fact of greatest immediacy for us to-day, since it has become evident that Christianity will be swept into the crisis of democracy which we are experiencing. That is only logical, for democracy and Christianity are closely bound together. They are united to such an extent that democracy may be called the political expression of the Christian feeling for life; and in the name of Christianity we are defending nothing else than the ethical foundation of occidental life, the spiritual unity of our cultural solidarity. Though democracy itself, as a movement toward freedom, grew up in an emancipating struggle against oppressive clericalism, this did not prevent the new popular form of occidental society from retaining its roots in Christianity. Thus it is clear that democracy does not insist upon the preservation of the ecclesiastical-pontifical forms of Christianity if they prove to be outworn and obstructive. Democracy, itself, is an example and proof of the spiritualizing influence of Christianity and its power of sublimation, which make it possible for the post-classical social structures that Christianity has shaped to replace destruction with transformation. And we may conclude from the close relationship of democracy and Christianity not that they will disappear together but that they will survive together.

The early evolution of a religiously tinged socialism from early bourgeois democracy proves the close relationship of the two, and their common root. This root, this common ground, is Christianity. That there is also a contradiction and contrast between them is undeniable. The contrast between democracy and socialism is that of freedom and equality—a logical contradiction without doubt—for logically and absolutely considered, freedom and equality are mutually exclusive, just as the individual and society are mutually exclusive. Freedom is the creed of the individual, but equality is a social need, and social equality, obviously, limits the freedom of the individual. But logic has not a final nor the highest validity for life, and in human emotions, in human ethical requirements, freedom and equality are not a real contradiction. With a slight change of emphasis, democracy and socialism include both tendencies, for the contrast between them is resolved in that which transcends and relates both of them, in Christianity.

Christian humanity, moreover, has also combined the individual and social principle in a way that is emotionally unassailable and wholly natural. The value and dignity which it bestows upon the individual being, the human soul in its immediate relationship to God, are not contradicted by the equality of all before God. It is in the statute of human rights, this Christian heritage of the great bourgeois revolution, that both principles, the individualistic and the social, freedom and equality, are combined and mutually justify each other. In democracy, freedom predominates over equality. In socialism, equality prevails—in the name and for the purpose of freedom. But at the same time it cannot be denied that all socialism has a tendency to exaggerate the mechanization and regimentation of society and to sink the individual in the group, in a practical uniformity and in mass movements. But if we consider what high and final cultural and asthetic values are associated with individuality, it is easy to understand the alarm which mentalities like Goethe and Heine felt at the democratic transformation of the world and its socialistic consequences, which they were very quick to anticipate.

Goethe, the son of the eighteenth century, suffered so acutely under the convulsions of the French Revolution that it nearly cost him his talent and his productivity. For Heine, the social revolution seemed the direct outcome of the bourgeois revolution, and with visionary clarity, with mingled despair and consent, he saw the approach of communism—a world in which he expected Heinrich Heine's poetry would have no further use than to serve as wrapping paper for the sausages of the proletariat.

That the cultured person should fear the disappearance of

liberty and individual values in collectivity and socialistic equality is readily comprehensible. It is, so to speak, democracy's fear of itself—a fear that plays no small part in the distress and weakness from which the spiritual and moral position of democracy is suffering to-day. Democracy is being shamelessly exploited, exploited by the worst and lowest enemies of freedom —enemies that I need not name. They hope to make democracy "ripe for assault," to use their own language, by persuading it that it is the forerunner of Bolshevism. For this reason it may be the moment for a word of caution and defence.

Such fears would only be justified if freedom and equality constituted an insuperable and irreconcilable contrast. But for people of our feelings, determined as they are by our Christian influences, this is not true. These feelings accept as necessarily true that a human synthesis must be possible between limitation and justice, freedom and equality, individual and society, the person and the collectivity. Nor is this unreasonable. For reason tells us that pure individualism and absolute freedom are just as humanly impossible and contrary to culture as their liberty-destroying opposite. There would be no hope for humanity if it had a choice only between anarchy and that extreme socialization which destroys personality. But that is not the meaning of a socialism that feels democracy as its native soil, and demands an equalizing justice in the name of freedom; in other words, a social democracy. Socialism implies socialization. And this concept itself—the mere recognition of the fact that man is a social being—amounts to a definition and limitation of freedom and the individual. It means an appreciation which, to be sure, does not come easily to the individual proud of his special cultivation, that a purely individualistic, purely personal and spiritual humanity is incomplete and dangerous to culture. It means also that political and social activities are expressions of humanity; that it is not possible to separate them completely from spiritual and cultural activities. Nor is it possible to devote oneself to culture and declare that one is "not interested" in politics. In a word, culture together with politics denote the totality of the humane, which must be carefully distinguished from *totalitarian politics* in which one part, an ingredient or segment of the humane, swallows up the whole and destroys freedom. The just and reasonable division of emphasis between the individual and the social element in man, the limitation of the political and social to their natural and necessary share in humanity, culture, and life—that is freedom. When politics becomes absolute and establishes a total dictatorship over everything human, that is the end of freedom, and it is no less destructive of culture than anarchy. In the anti-human will toward this political absolutism, Fascism and Communism meet.

It is possible to find differences of opinion between these two, to make comparisons between their moral levels which will always be to the disadvantage of Fascism. The fact remains that there is no difference between them in their dictatorial negation of freedom; and as far as communism is concerned, its essential contrast to what we call social democracy, to responsible freedom, cannot be grasped too clearly nor emphasized too strongly. But if it is a lie to declare social democracy the first step toward Communism, deception reaches its pinnacle when Fascism—and especially German National Socialism—pretends to be a protection and a bulwark against communism. This is deceptive propaganda to which actually a considerable part of the middle classes have succumbed, at least for a while. I do not know how much progress the appreciation of the deceitful character of these claims has made—especially since certain very recent experiences. But it cannot be denied that the sympathy which Fascist dictatorship aroused among the possessing classes rested upon these claims, and that Fascism owes most of its successes, first in its own countries, then in the outside world, to the fiction that the choice lay between Fascism and Communism.

We were told that we must cling to Fascism, increase its power; and even if Fascism's unbridled thirst for power should endanger it, we must save it at every sacrifice in order to avoid Communism.

And yet the great body of middle-class citizens throughout the world should be warned, above everything else, of the horrible disappointment which awaits them if they succumb to this deceptive propaganda—a deep disappointment which the peoples that surrendered to Fascism have already tasted. It is entirely erroneous to assume that it is the function and intention of Fascism, or of German National Socialism, to protect private property and an individualistic economy. Especially in its economic policies, National Socialism is nothing but Bolshevism; they are hostile brothers of whom the younger has learned almost everything from the elder, Russian, brother. There is no doubt—all signs point to it—that the National Social Revolution which began as a radical movement to the right is developing, ever more rapidly, toward the left, that is, toward Bolshevism. Or rather, from right-wing Bolshevism it is on the point of becoming left-wing Bolshevism. Therefore it is absolutely certain that the expropriation of the Jews is only a prelude to more comprehensive acts of this sort which will be wholly free of any race ideology. And particularly if the concept of Bolshevism is understood in its popular mythical interpretation as the epitome of terror and raging destruction, no better picture of it can be imagined than that which was exhibited in the German pogroms.

There the world was given a clear illustration of what National Socialism really is: namely, the most radical, unrestrained, and destructive revolution which the world has ever seen, wholly unsuitable to serve as a rampart for middle-class conservatism or to be used by it for protective purposes. Indeed the word revolution is actually too honourable to define this phenomenon, for an invasion by the Huns would not be described as a revolution. Revolutions usually contain some relationship to the idea of humanity, a faith, a will—however confused—to progress and to bring about the improvement of human society. They have as a rule some passionate relationship to the Absolute and to the idea in the name of which they perpetrate their deeds and misdeeds. Because of this faith, this relationship and passion, and out of respect for them, humanity has always shown a tendency to forgive revolutionary misdeeds. It was inclined to overlook them, because of the ultimate good and the high aspiration out of which the terror resulted. That was the attitude toward the French Revolution, and again toward the Russian proletarian revolution, or at least that was the attitude when it began. But the misdeeds of the so-called National Social Revolution are devoid of any human excuse, for it lacks every concern and every love for humanity or for the idea of perfecting human society. It is a revolution of empty force or, let us say, of spiritual nihilism. It is a revolution such as has never existed, a revolution of absolute cynicism without relationship to any kind of faith and filled with lust for the degradation of men and of ideas. What it means economically may be termed anarchy, and that may leave us comparatively indifferent. But morally its purpose is extermination —the extermination of the foundations of civilization. The final meaning of its anti-Semitism is not the foolish idea of the racial purity of the German people but an assault upon Christianity itself. And even when it ridicules democracy, the contempt is really aimed at Christianity in which democracy is rooted and whose political expression it is. Freedom, truth, justice, reason, human dignity—what is the source of these ideas which are the support and mainstay of our existence and without which our spiritual life would crumble? Whence do they come if not from Christianity which has made them the law of the world? A revolution which supplants every one of these ideas with the law of force—that is the anti-Christ. And yet this is the revolution in which the European middle classes have seen their bulwark against Communism for so long a time that its successes approach a complete conquest of the world.

Democracy itself was once revolution. To-day it is the greatest conservative power upon earth, conservative in the deepest sense of the word, because it is the defence and the maintenance of the shamelessly menaced ethical foundations of the Occident. But in order to do justice to this new responsibility, it must, to a certain extent, return to its revolutionary state; it cannot merely *be*, it must give battle. For without battle it will cease to *be*. A passionate desire and will are slowly evolving out of the necessity and the confusion of the moral retreat of our times: the will to concentrate and to resist, the will to call a halt, to *command* a halt, the will to defend civilization against the corrupting onward march of force. The history of religion speaks of the *ecclesia militans*, the church militant, which preceded the *ecclesia triumphans*, the church triumphant. Likewise if democracy is to triumph, it must give battle, even though it has long been weaned from the habit of combat. A militant democracy is the need of the day, a democracy freed of all self-doubt, a democracy that knows what it ·vants, namely, victory—the victory of civilization over barbarism!

This victory will not be paid for too dearly with the sacrifice of an exaggerated humanity, namely, that patience which endureth all things—even the determination to terrorize humanity. Never can humanity permit itself such extreme patience; least of all at a critical time of battle such as ours. Democracy's concept of freedom must never include the freedom to destroy democracy; never must it give its deadly enemies freedom of speech and of deed. If I say that, you will reply: That is the very problem which freedom sets itself! No, I reply, its first problem is self-preservation. But the very fact that there can be a difference of opinion on this question is proof that freedom is debatable, that it has become a problem. Or rather it has become evident that freedom has always been a problem. The crisis of democracy is, in truth, the crisis of freedom; and the salvation of democracy from the hostile attack which threatens it will only be possible through an honest solution of the problems of freedom.

Everyone who speaks of the conditions which freedom must impose upon itself for its own sake, of a voluntary restriction and a social self-discipline of freedom, must be prepared for accusations of treachery toward freedom and democracy. And yet I believe that the people who are the first and the most vociferous with such reproaches are by no means the most valuable or the most unselfish friends of freedom. The solution of the problem of freedom is made the more difficult because there are three different attitudes toward freedom. It has real enemies—and with them it is easy to deal. It has real friends— and among them we would all like to be counted. But in between are its false friends, and they create disorder because, consciously or unconsciously, they confuse the love of freedom with an interest in freedom, with their particular interest. They shout "Democracy is in danger" whenever freedom is advised to place itself under a wholesome social discipline. And yet it is a fact that democracy can only be saved by means of a liberty ripe with wisdom, that has outgrown the stage of unsocial libertinism.

A personal interest in freedom is not a real love of freedom. Otherwise, certain elements in the democracies of Europe would not associate themselves with the arch-enemies of freedom and prepare the most terrible victories for them at the expense of their own countries. If they had a genuinely disinterested love of freedom, they would prefer to accept a social regulation of freedom, which alone can help freedom to survive liberalism.

That these two, liberalism and freedom, are identical, and that the one will stand or fall with the other, is a false pretence of Fascism—one of the many—but a particularly malicious one. Let us not succumb to it. Liberalism, spiritually and economically, is the form which life took at a given period; it marked the spirit of those times. And times changed. But freedom is an immortal idea, which does not age with the spirit of the times and vanish, and he who maintains that freedom will fall with the forms of liberalism is not its friend. Freedom is not served but harmed and, consciously or unconsciously, we are playing the game of its enemies, when we deny that freedom to-day should assume severer and more binding social forms than were appropriate in the *laissez faire* period of our fathers and grandfathers.

We have tried to discover what democracy is: it is the human adjustment between a logical contrast, the reconciliation of freedom and equality, of individual values and the demands of society. This adjustment, however, is never completely and finally attained; it remains a problem that humanity must solve again and again. And we feel that to-day in the relationship of freedom and equality, the centre of gravity has moved toward the side of equality and economic justice, away from the individual and toward the social. Social democracy is now the order of the day. If democracy is to hold its own, it must do so through socially established freedom, which rescues the individual values by friendly and willing concessions to equality; through an economic justice which ties all of democracy's children closely to it. Only then can democracy resist the assault of a dehumanized spirit of violence, and fulfil its great conservative task, to preserve the Christian foundations of occidental life, and to protect civilization against barbarism.

I am one who never expected in former years to be called upon to make statements and efforts such as these. As a writer, it is and always will be my natural function to reserve my energies for that free service of humanity which we call art. It is not by chance that we speak of the arts as "free"; for art is the sphere of free thought, of free contemplation and formulation. Politics, on the other hand, is the field of decision, of opinion and volition. Is it not, therefore, significant and symptomatic that to-day an artist whose native concern is the right, the good and true, should feel obligated to apply these standards to political and social questions: that he should seek to unite his thoughts with the political will of the times because he feels that he cannot fulfil his human responsibilities if he refuses to do this? Is not this political endeavour of the spirit, inadequate as it may be, an example of that voluntary limitation of freedom for social purposes of which I have been speaking? And is not this voluntary limitation a moral one?

I have discussed truth, justice, Christian civilization, democracy. In my purely aesthetically determined youth, it would never have occurred to me to deal in such terms. Today I pronounce them with a wholly unexpected rapture. For the position of the spirit has changed upon earth in a peculiar way. Civilization is in retreat. A period of lawlessness and anarchy reigns over public opinion. But for that very reason, paradoxical as it may be, the spirit has entered upon a moral epoch, let us say an epoch of simplification and of humble-minded distinctions between good and evil. Yes, we know once more what is good and what is evil. Evil has been revealed to us in such crassness and meanness that our eyes have opened to the dignity and the simple beauty of the good. Once more we have taken it to heart and deem it no slight to our intellectual pride to confess it.

That, if you like, is a rejuvenation of the spirit, and I have often thought that this period of spiritual rejuvenation and simplification, this moral epoch, in which we have entered, might well be the great hour of America. That is what I really meant to convey when I stated in other contexts that the preservation and guidance of our occidental cultural heritage would devolve upon America during these European dark ages. Because of its youth and moral vigour, because the soul of this country is still close to the biblical and the monumental, America is attuned to the spiritual needs of the hour and seems called to assert itself in the present situation with a natural authority. To do this would not indicate presumption but an independence and a moral self-reliance which have become morally necessary to this country and which could contribute to the recovery of Europe. May America stand forth in an abandoned and ethically leaderless world as the strong and unswerving protector of the good and the godly in mankind. I salute America as a country that is conscious of its own human inadequacy but knows what is good and what is evil; that despises force and untruth; a country that perseveres in a faith which is sound and utterly necessary to life—faith in goodness, in freedom and truth, in justice and in peace.

Jacques Maritain

Professor of Philosophy, Catholic Institute of Paris;
Institute of Medieval Studies of Toronto

THE CONQUEST OF FREEDOM[1]

I. FREEDOM OF INDEPENDENCE AND FREEDOM OF CHOICE

IN this essay I shall not treat of free will or freedom of
choice. The existence and value of this kind of freedom
are, however, taken for granted by all I shall say. That is
why I shall first give a few brief indications in their regard.
The freedom I shall treat of subsequently is the freedom of
independence and of exultation, which can be called also—in
a Paulinian but not Kantian sense—freedom of autonomy, or
also, freedom of expansion of the human person. It takes for
granted the existence of freedom of choice in us, but it is
substantially distinct from it.

A badly constructed philosophical theory that falsifies the
reflective operation by which the mind of man knows itself
explicitly can counteract and paralyze the primary and natural
operations of spontaneous consciousness. As long as we are not
victims of this accident each of us knows very well *that* he
possesses freedom of choice, that is to say, that if we betray
a friend, risk our property to aid some unfortunate, decide to
become a banker, monk, or soldier, these kinds of acts are what
they are only because we have involved therein our personality
and have arranged that they be so rather than not. But each
of us knows very poorly *wherein* freedom of choice lies. This

[1] Translated by Harry McNeill and Emmanuel Chapman, Professors of Philosophy, Fordham University.

obscurity of spontaneous consciousness, unable to bring forth what is implicit in the matter, enables philosophers, and especially savants who philosophize without knowing it, frequently to becloud the question.

Philosophers professing absolute intellectualism cannot understand the existence of free will because in their eyes intelligence not only precedes will, but precedes it in the manner of a divinity apart, which touches the will without being touched by it and without receiving from it any qualifying action. Hence the domain of formal or specifying determination (what is called the *ordo specificationis*) can never itself depend intrinsically upon the domain of efficiency or existential effectuation (*ordo exercitii*), and the will is reduced to a function by which the intelligence realizes ideas which in virtue of the mere object they represent appear best to the subject. Such was the position of the great metaphysicians of the classic age.

Pure empiricists likewise cannot understand the existence of free will, because, recognizing only sensory sequences, the idea of causality exercised upon a spirit by itself has no meaning for them. Hence, when they voice an opinion on a question, which, like that of free will, lies essentially in the ontological order, they, as metaphysicians, in spite of themselves (and bad ones at that), can only interpret the empirical results of observational science in the framework of classic mechanism inherited from Spinoza, and give themselves over, without knowing what they are doing, to the most naïve extrapolations. To the extent that science reveals dynamic elements working in our psychical activity, they see in the mere existence of these elements the proof that the same operate in a necessarily determining fashion—which is precisely what remains to be proved.

In our times Freudism offers the pseudo-metaphysical empiricist the greatest possibilities for illusion. I have shown elsewhere that it is very important to distinguish most clearly between the psycho-analytic method, which opens to investigation in the unconscious new roads of the greatest interest, and the philosophy (unconscious of itself) that Freud has sought

in crass empiricism, thereby leaving the field of his competence
and giving full rein to his dreams. The fact, revealed by
psycho-analysis, that there are unconscious motivations which
the subject obeys without knowing them furnishes in no manner,
as some would imagine, an argument against free will, for free
will begins with intellectual judgment and consciousness. To
the extent that unconscious motivation makes us act automatically, there is no question of free will; and to the extent that
it gives rise to a conscious judgment, the question is whether
or not at this moment it fashions this judgment, or by means
of free choice is rendered decisively motivating by this judgment. In other words, the question is whether unconscious
motivations are necessarily determining or simply contributing,
and it is clear that the mere fact of their existence is not
sufficient to decide the question.

In general, human free will does not exclude but presupposes the vast and complex dynamism of instincts, tendencies, psycho-physical dispositions, acquired habits, and
hereditary traits, and it is at the top point where this dynamism
emerges in the world of spirit that freedom of choice is exercised,
to give or withhold decisive efficacy to the inclinations and
urges of nature. It follows from this that freedom, as well as
responsibility, is capable of a multiplicity of degrees of which
the author of being alone is judge. It does not follow from this
that freedom does not exist—on the contrary! If it admits of
degrees, then it exists.

The efforts of eminent scientists, like Professor Compton,
to link indeterminist theories of modern physics to our natural
belief in free will may be highly significant and stimulating to
the mind and efficacious in eliminating many prejudices, but
I do not think that a strict proof providing this belief with an
unshakable intellectual basis can be found in that direction.
The direction to follow is metaphysical. It brings us to formulas
like those of M. Bergson: "Our motivations are what we
make them;" "Our reasons are determined for us only at the
moment that they become determining; that is, at the moment
when the act is virtually accomplished." But it is not by an
irrational philosophy of pure becoming, it is by a philosophy

of being and intelligence like that of St. Thomas Aquinas that
such formulas receive their full significance and demonstrative
value.

Spirit as such implies a sort of infinity; its faculty of desire
of itself seeks a good which satisfies absolutely, therefore a good
without limit, and we cannot have any desire which is not
comprehended in this general desire for happiness. But as soon
as reflection occurs, our intelligence, confronted with goods
that are not the Good, and judging them so, brings into
actuality the radical determination that our appetite for
happiness possesses in regard to everything which is not happiness itself. Efficacious motivation of an intelligent being can be
only a practical judgment: and this judgment owes to the will
the whole of its efficaciousness; it is will, impelled by its own
upredictable initiative towards the good presented to it by
such and such a judgment, that gives this judgment the power
of specifying the will efficaciously.

The free act, in which the intelligence and will involve and
envelop each other vitally, is thus like an instantaneous flash
in which the active and dominating indetermination of the will
operates in regard to the judgment itself which determines it;
the will can do nothing without an intellectual judgment; and
it is will that makes itself determined by judgment and by
this judgment rather than by another one.

Far from being a simple function of the intelligence, by
which the latter realizes ideas which in virtue of their mere
object appear best, the will is an original spiritual energy of
infinite capacity which has control over·the intelligence and its
judgments in the order of practical choice and makes what
the will wants appear best to the subject *here and now*. What
constitutes the real mystery of free will is that while essentially
needing intellectual specification, the exercise of the will has
primacy over the latter and holds it under its active and
dominating indetermination because the will alone can give it
existential efficacy.

After this preliminary explanation of freedom of choice
I shall now discuss the freedom of independence.

II. FREEDOM OF INDEPENDENCE AND THE ASPIRATIONS
OF THE PERSON

Human personality is a great metaphysical mystery. We know that an essential characteristic of a civilization worthy of the name is meaning and respect for the dignity of the human person. We know that to defend the rights and freedom of the human person we must be willing to sacrifice our most precious possessions and our lives. What values, then, deserving of such sacrifice, are enveloped in the personality of man? What do we mean precisely when we speak of the human person? When we say that a man is a person, we do not mean merely that he is an individual, in the sense that an atom, a blade of grass, a fly, or an elephant is an individual. Man is an individual who holds himself in hand by his intelligence and his will; he exists not merely in a physical fashion. He has spiritual super-existence through knowledge and love, so that he is, in a way, a universe in himself, a microcosmos, in which the great universe in its entirety can be encompassed through knowledge. By love he can give himself completely to beings who are to him, as it were, other selves. For this relation no equivalent can be found in the physical world. The human person possesses these characteristics because in the last analysis man, this flesh and these perishable bones which are animated and activated by a divine fire, exists "from the womb to the grave" by virtue of the existence itself of his soul, which dominates time and death. Spirit is the root of personality. The notion of personality thus involves that of totality and independence; no matter how poor and crushed a person may be, he is a whole, and as a person, subsistent in an independent manner. To say that a man is a person is to say that in the depth of his being he is more a whole than a part and more independent than servile. It is to say that he is a minute fragment of matter that is at the same time a universe, a beggar who participates in the absolute being, mortal flesh whose value is eternal, and a bit of straw into which heaven enters. It is this metaphysical mystery that religious thought designates when it says that the person is the image of God. The value of the person, his dignity and rights, belong to the order of things naturally sacred which bear the imprint of the Father of Being, and which have in him the end of their movement.

Freedom of spontaneity, on the other hand, is not, as free will, a power of choice that transcends all necessity, even interior necessity and all determinism. It does not imply the absence of necessity but merely the absence of constraint. It is the power of acting by virtue of its own internal inclination and without undergoing the coaction imposed by an exterior agent.

This kind of freedom admits of all sorts of degrees, from the spontaneity of the electron turning "freely" around a nucleus, that is, without deviating from its path by the interference of a foreign particle, to the spontaneity of the grass in the fields which grows "freely" and of the bird that flies "freely," that is, obeying only the internal necessities of their nature. When freedom of spontaneity passes the threshold of the spirit and is the spontaneity of a spiritual nature, it becomes properly freedom of independence. To this extent it does not consist merely in following the inclination of nature but in being or making oneself actively the sufficient principle of one's own operation; in other words, in perfecting oneself as an indivisible whole in the act one brings about. This is why freedom of independence exists only in beings which also have free will, and presupposes the exercise of free will in order to arrive at its end.

If the proper sign of personality consists, as I have just said, in the fact of being independent, of being a whole, it is clear that personality and freedom of independence are related and inseparable. In the scale of being they increase together; at the summit of being, God is person in pure act and freedom of independence in pure act. He is so personal that His existence is His very act of knowing and loving, and He is so independent that while causing all things, He Himself is absolutely without cause, his essence being his very act of existence.

In each of us personality and freedom of independence increase together. For man is a being in movement. If he does not augment, he has nothing, and he loses what he had; he must fight for his being. The entire history of his fortunes and misfortunes is the history of his effort to win together with his own personality, freedom of independence. He is called to the conquest of freedom.

Two basic truths must be noted here. The first is that the human being, though a person and therefore independent because he is a spirit, is, however, by nature at the lowest degree of perfection and independence because he is a spirit united substantially with matter and implacably subject to a bodily condition. Secondly, no matter how miserable, how poor, how enslaved and humiliated he may be, the aspirations of personality in him remain unconquerable; and they tend as such, in the life of each of us as in the life of the human race, toward the conquest of freedom.

The aspirations of personality are of two types. On the one hand, they come from the human person *as human* or as constituted in such a species; let us call them "connatural" to man and specifically human. On the other hand, they come from the human person *in so far as he is a person* or participating in that transcendental perfection that is personality and which is realized in God infinitely better than in us. Let us call them then "transnatural" and metaphysical aspirations.

The connatural aspirations tend to a relative freedom compatible with conditions here below, and the burden of material nature inflicts upon them from the very beginning a serious defeat because no animal is born more naked and less free than man. The struggle to win freedom in the order of social life aims to make up for this defeat.

The transnatural aspirations of the person in us seek super-human freedom, pure and simple freedom. And to whom belongs such freedom if not to Him alone who is freedom of independence itself, subsistent by itself. Man has no right to the freedom proper to God. When he aspires by a transnatural desire to this freedom, he seeks it in an "inefficacious" manner and without even knowing what it is. Thus divine transcendence imposes immediately the admission of a profound defeat on the part of these metaphysical aspirations of the person in us. However, such a defeat is not irreparable, at least if the victor descends to the aid of the vanquished. The movement to win freedom in the order of spiritual life aims precisely to make up for this defeat. But we must not hide from ourselves the fact that the point at which our reflection has now arrived is a crucial one for the human being. The least error costs dearly. In this knot capital errors, mortal for human society and the human soul, are mixed with capital truths to which are bound the life of the soul and that of society. We must work as hard as possible to distinguish truths from errors. There is a false conquest of freedom which is illusory and homicidal. There is a true conquest of freedom which provides truth and life for mankind.

In order to try to dissociate briefly one from the other, let me say that the false manner of understanding the attainment of freedom is based upon a philosophy called in technical language "univocalist" and "immanentist." In such a philosophy the notion of independence and freedom admits of neither internal variety nor degrees; and on the other hand God, if he exists, is conceived as a physical agent magnified *ad infinitum*; hence either he is considered *transcendent* and his *existence* is denied because he would be, as Proudhon believed, a sort of heavenly Tyrant imposing constraint and violence on all that is not his own; or, on the other hand, his *existence* is affirmed and his *transcendence* is denied—all things are considered in the manner of Spinoza or Hegel as modes or phases of his realization. In this way of thinking there is neither freedom nor autonomy except in so far as no objective rule or measure is received from a being other than oneself. And the human person claims for itself then divine freedom, so that man takes, in atheistic forms of thought and culture, the place of the God he denies, or man through pantheistic forms tries to realize in act an identity of nature with the God he imagines.

On the contrary, the true manner of understanding the attainment of freedom is based upon a philosophy of the analogy of being and divine transcendence. For this philosophy independence and freedom are realized, on the various levels of being, in several forms which are typically diverse: in God in an absolute manner, and because (being super-eminently all things) he is supreme interiority, of which all existing things are a participation; in us in a relative manner, and thanks to the privileges of spirit which, however profound may be the state of dependence in which it is placed by the very nature of things, makes itself independent by its own operation when it poses interiorly to itself by knowledge and love the law it obeys. In such a philosophy divine transcendence imposes no violence nor constraint upon creatures, but rather infuses them with goodness and spontaneity and is more internal to them than they are to themselves. It is not true that the autonomy of an intelligent creature consists in not receiving any rule or objective measure from a being other than itself. It consists in conforming to such rules and measures voluntarily because they are known to be just and true, and because of a love for truth and justice. Such is human freedom, properly speaking, to which the person tends as towards a connatural perfection; and if the person aspires also to superhuman freedom, this thirst for trans-natural perfection, whose satisfaction is not due to us, will be fully quenched only by the reception of more than is desired, and thanks to a transforming union with the Uncreated Nature. God is free from all eternity; more exactly, He is subsistent freedom. Man is not born free unless in the basic potencies of his being: he becomes free, by warring upon himself and thanks to many sorrows; by the struggle of the spirit and virtue; by exercising his freedom he wins his freedom. So that at long last a freedom better than he expected is *given* him. From the beginning to the end it is truth that liberates him.

III. TRUE AND FALSE POLITICAL EMANCIPATION

The first problem of vital importance evoked by the preceding considerations can be called the problem of true and false political emancipation. In fact, the conquest of freedom in the social and political order is the central hope characterizing the historical ideal of the last two centuries, which has constituted at once their dynamic urge, their power of truth and of illusion. What I call false political emancipation is the philosophy and the social and political practice (and the corresponding emotional orchestration) based upon the false manner of understanding the conquest of freedom that I have briefly discussed. Necessarily this engenders myths that devour the human substance. What I call true political emancipation is the philosophy and the social and political practice (and the corresponding emotional orchestration) based upon the true manner of winning freedom; this leads to no myth but to a concrete historical ideal and to a patient labour of forming and educating the human substance.

The misfortune in the eyes of a philosopher of culture is the fact that great democratic movements of modern times have sought true political emancipation under false standards. I mean that in the obscure work produced in the hearts of men and in their history we find a treasury of aspirations, efforts, and social enterprise obtained sometimes at the price of heroic sacrifices and originally directed towards the conquest of freedom—we find this treasury conceptualized in the metaphysics of the false conquest of freedom; andt o the extent that this work has been thus corrupted and deformed by a false philosophy of life, it is accompanied by error, destruction, and ravages which tend to the negation of its own vital principle and which finally make the democratic ideal seem to many minds an imposture. The spasms through which Europe is passing testify to the immense gravity of this historical phenomenon. If the true city of human rights, the true democracy, does not succeed in freeing itself from the false, if in the ordeal of fire and blood a radical purification is not brought about, Western civilization risks entering upon a night without end. If we are confident that this will not happen it is because we are confident that the necessary renovations will occur.

Truly, and even by reason of the complex and ambivalent phenomenon just referred to, the word democracy itself has become so equivocal that it would be perhaps desirable, as I have already urged several times, to find a new word to designate what I called a moment ago the true city of human rights. Moreover, the political philosophy involved therein goes largely beyond this or that classically recognized *political regime*. It is equally suitable to the *regimen mixtum*—at once monarchical, aristocratic, and democratic—which was the best regime in the mind of St. Thomas Aquinas, as well as to a strictly democratic, political regime. But we are not free to revise at will the vocabulary of concrete and historico-social matters. If a new democracy is actively realized in common consciousness and in existence, it will discover a satisfactory name for itself.

For the sake of further clarification let me say briefly that the false political emancipation (the false city of human rights) has as its principle the "anthropocentric" conception that Rousseau and Kant made out of the autonomy of the person. According to them man is free *only if he obeys himself alone*, and man is constituted by right of nature in such a state of freedom (which Rousseau considered as lost from the fact of the corruption involved in social life and which Kant relegated to the noumenal world). In a word, this is the divinization of the individual. Its logical consequences in the political and social order are threefold: In the first place, practical atheism of society (for there is no place for two gods in the world, and if the individual is practically god, God is no longer God except perhaps in a decorative way and for private use). In the second place, the theoretical and practical disappearance of the idea of the common good. In the third place, the theoretical and practical disappearance of the idea of ruler and the idea of authority falsely considered to be incompatible with freedom: and this in the political sphere (where the possessors of authority should direct men not towards the private good of other men, but towards the common good) as well as in the sphere of labour and of economics (where the technical exigencies of production demand that men work, in extremely diverse ways and proportions, for the private good of other men). By virtue of an inevitable internal dialectic this social divinization of the individual, inaugurated by bourgeois liberalism, leads to the social divinization of the State and of the anonymous mass incarnate in a Leader who is no longer a normal ruler but a sort of inhuman monster whose omnipotence is based upon myths and lies. At the same time bourgeois liberalism makes way for revolutionary totalitarianism, communist or racist, and for general slavery.

True political emancipation, on the contrary, or the true city of human rights, has as its principle a conception of the autonomy of the person in conformity with the nature of things and therefore "theocentric." According to this notion obedience, accepted for justice's sake, is not opposed to freedom. It is, on the contrary, a normal way of arriving at freedom. Man must gradually win freedom, which consists in the political and social order above all in becoming, under given historical conditions, as independent as possible of the restrictions of material nature. The human person rises above society to the extent that he is made for God and for eternal life, and owes what he is to suprasocial values. He is part of society as of a greater and better whole, to the extent that he owes to society what he is.

Thus the true city of human rights recognizes as God only one God: God himself and no created thing; and this city understands that human society, despite the diverse religious families living within it, implies a religious principle and presupposes that God is accessible to our reason and is the last end of our existence. This city is founded upon the authentic notion of the common good—which is something different from a collection of private goods, but which demands to be redistributed to individual persons; it implies the effective respect for their rights and has itself as an essential element their access to the maximum development and freedom compatible with given historical conditions. This city finally implies an authentic notion of ruler and authority.

For the true city of human rights, the possessors of authority in the political sphere are, in a democratic regime, designated by the people. They govern the people by virtue of this designation ("government by the people") and for the common good of the people ("government for the people"), but they really have the right to command; and they command free persons each of whom is called to participate concretely to a certain degree in political life and who are not abandoned like atoms but rather are grouped in organic communities from the family, which forms the natural basic community, up.

In the sphere of labour and economic relations the true city of human rights demands that the constant development of social justice compensate for the restrictions imposed upon man by the necessities (in themselves not human but technical) of labour and production. We know that to serve the private good of another man and become to this extent an organ of the same is in itself an affliction for the radical aspirations of personality, but we also know that this is a condition imposed upon men by material nature, which will last in various forms and proportions as long as the earth itself. This true city of human rights demands that, by a persevering struggle for improvement due at once to the perfection and extension of mechanical equipment and to the tension of spiritual energies transforming secular life from within the conditions of work become less and less servile and tend to a state of real deliverance for the human person. At the present stage of historical development it would seem that for certain types of workers this result can be obtained to a remarkable degree—after the catastrophe which the world is suffering to-day has brought about a reformation of economic structures and of the spirit—not only by lessening the hours of work but also by giving the workers a part in the ownership and management of the enterprise.

But here as in the political sphere the inauguration of new structures no matter how important, does not suffice. The soul of social life is fashioned by that which superbounds in it from the true internal life of individual persons, from the gift of self which that life involves and from a gratuitous generosity whose source lies in the inmost part of the heart. More concisely, good will and a relation of respect and love between persons alone can give to the *movement* of the social body a truly human character. If the person has the opportunity of being treated as such in social life and by it, and if the thankless works which this life imposes can be made easy and happy and even exalting, it is first due to the development of right and to institutions of right. But it is also and indispensably due to the development of civic friendship, with the confidence and mutual devotion this implies on the part of those who direct as well as those who carry it out. For the true city of human rights, fraternity is not a privilege of nature which flows from the natural goodness of man and which the State need only proclaim. It is the end of a slow and difficult conquest which demands virtue and sacrifice and a perpetual victory of man over himself. In this sense we can say that the heroic ideal towards which true political emancipation tends is the inauguration of a fraternal city. It is seen here how, in fact, true political emancipation depends on the Christian ferment deposited in the world and presupposes finally as the most profound stimulus evangelical love exalting things of earth civilization in their proper order.

The properties that I have just sketched were not absent from the democratic movement and hopes of modern times. They characterize, on the contrary, what was unconsciously exercised most profoundly and vitally in it. But this good seed was corrupted and vitiated by false political emancipation, and the monsters engendered by the latter grew more quickly than the authentic seed. We thus have a presentiment of the vast purifications and renovations referred to above.

IV. THE TRUE AND FALSE DEIFICATION OF MAN

There is a true and false emancipation in the political and social order. In the spiritual order there is a true and false deification of man. This is another problem of vital importance, fundamental and absolutely primary, posited by the natural instinct which impels man to win freedom.

As I have said at the beginning of this essay, by the fact that we participate in the transcendental perfection designated by the word personality, we have within us transnatural aspirations the satisfaction of which is not due to us in justice but which nevertheless torment us and tend to a superhuman freedom, freedom pure and simple—that is to say, to a divine freedom. Evidence of these aspirations for the superhuman, these desires to reach the borders of divinity, has been presented by the sages of all times.

The great spiritual errors also bear witness to these aspirations. They seek the deification of man, but by man's own forces and the development of the powers of his nature only. More often they take a pantheistic form, as can be seen in the gnostic currents of former times, in the great monistic metaphysics, and in the mysticism of quietism. It was left, however, to modern times to look for the deification of man by doing away with wisdom and breaking with God. Historically, in my opinion, the two main sources of this false deification are: (1) The immanentist conception of conscience which since the Lutheran revolution has gradually gained the ascendancy, and which demands that man within himself—"my interior freedom"—construct morality by himself alone without owing anything to law. (2) The idealist conception of science which since the Cartesian revolution has gradually gained the ascendancy and which demands that man within himself—"my self or my spirit"—construct truth by himself alone without owing anything to things. Hyper-spiritualist as it first seems, these two conceptions make science independent of being and conscience independent of law, and claim for that which is within man the kind of independence proper to God. In reality these two erroneous conceptions materialize the human soul and plunge it into external action, where by seeking its proper and only mode of realization it becomes the slave of time, matter, and the world. Science finally will be subjugated by a kind of demiurgic imperialism applied to enslave material nature to the lusts of human beings. Conscience too will be subjugated by a kind of demonic imperialism applied to "oppose oneself" in order to "pose oneself," following the phrase of Fichte, and to realize oneself by dominating others. Man, become the god of this world, will believe that he will find divine freedom for himself by being independent of God, and consequently by the radical negation of God. The false deification of man will take the atheistic form which appears in our days in an amazingly barbarous light.

It had its first experiences in the diguised atheism of orthodox Kantianism and bourgeois liberalism. After the bankruptcy of this atheism which found religion "good for the people," and after the failure of the false individualistic conquest of freedom

and personality, it was inevitable that the false deification of
man be affirmed by the open atheism of Marxist Hegelianism
which sees in religion "the opium of the people," or the open
paganism of racism which reduces religion to the idolatry of
the "soul of the people." Plebeian totalitarianism, either under
the Soviet Communist or German Nazi form, then undertakes
to lead collective man by war, forced labour, and the standard-
ization of souls to the achievement of freedom. Inevitably, from
the moment that absolute freedom, emancipation pure and
simple, divine independence, were sought in the human itself,
or in other words, from the moment that the *transnatural*
aspirations of the person were lowered into the sphere of
connatural aspirations—and by that very fact perverted and
made infinite—the social had to become deified, the things of
Caesar had to absorb monstrously the things of God, and the
pagan empire had to make itself adored.

On the contrary, the transnatural aspirations of the human
person tend normally towards God, the transcendental cause
of being, and they incite the soul to seek liberation in him.
Despite all its imperfections and blemishes such was the *élan*
of the great Hellenic wisdom. In Hindu spirituality, however,
at least if its too great proliferation, at times poisonous, is
reduced to what is most pure in it, are found the most significant
examples of states where these *transnatural* aspirations lead man
by his own action and the ascetic use of his natural powers to
turn his own nature against its own current. I think that what
in Christian language we called the "natural" mystical
experience and the highest "natural" contemplation then
reaches by the way of an entirely intellectual self-annihilation
the substance of Self, and through and in it the divine Omni-
presence.[1] This is a liberation and deliverance at one and the
same time ultimate in the order of what nature is capable of,
and not ultimate, absolutely speaking, in regard to our real
destiny and its hidden primordial truth that nature has been
made for grace. Hence this attainment of spiritual freedom is
ambivalent: true and authentic on its plane if the soul does not

---

[1] See my *Quatre essais sur l'esprit dans sa condition chornelle*, Paris, 1939. Chap.
III.

Q

stop there and it opens itself to the highest gifts; false and deceptive if the soul stops there or if it looks upon it as a necessary means, or if it takes it for deification.

There is, however, a true deification of man. *Ego dixi: dii estis*. This is called eternal life—which begins obscurely here on earth. It is as fatal to renounce perfect liberation as it is to try to reach it by the wrong ways, that is to say, by oneself alone. The transnatural aspirations are supernaturally fulfilled, and by a gift which surpasses anything we can conceive. What is grace, the theologians ask, if not a formal participation in the Divine Nature, in other terms, a deifying life received from God.

The mystery of this is that the supreme freedom and independence of man are won by the supreme spiritual realization of his dependence, his dependence on a Being who being life itself vivifies, and being freedom itself liberates, all who participate in His essence. This kind of dependence is not one of external constraint, as is the case of one physical agent in regard to another physical agent. The more he realizes it the more does man participate in the nature of the Absolute. Men who have become something of God participate in the freedom of Him who cannot be contained by anything. By losing themselves they have won a mysterious and disappropriated personality which makes them act by virtue of that which they are eternally in the Uncreated Essence. Born of spirit they are like spirit free. To tell the truth, they have won nothing, and they have received all. While they worked and suffered to attain freedom, it gave itself to them. The true conquest of supreme and absolute freedom is to be made free by Subsistent Freedom and to consent freely to it. The true deification of man consists in opening himself to the gift which the Absolute gives of itself, and the descent of the divine plenitude into the intelligent creature. What I am saying is that this is all the work of love. Law protects freedom and teaches us to practise it. When love follows the path of law it leads through law to emancipation from all servitude, even the servitude of the law. I have often quoted, and I wish to quote again, the text from the *Summa contra Gentiles* where St. Thomas comments on St. Paul, which

I regard as one of the great texts absolutely fundamental for the spiritual constitution of humanity.

> We must observe [St. Thomas says] that the sons of God are led by the divine Spirit, not as though they were slaves, but as being free. For, since to be free is to be cause of one's own actions, we are said to do freely what we do of ourselves. Now this is what we do willingly: and what we do unwillingly, we do, not freely but under compulsion. This compulsion may be absolute, when the cause is wholly extraneous, and the patient contributes nothing to the action, for instance, when a man is compelled to move by force; or it may be partly voluntary, as when a man is willing to do or suffer that which is less opposed to his will, in order that which is more opposed thereto. Now, the sanctifying Spirit inclines us to act in such a way as to make us act willingly, inasmuch as He causes us to be lovers of God. Hence the sons of God are led by the Holy Ghost to act freely and for love, not slavishly and for fear: wherefore the Apostle says (Rom. 8: 15): *You have not received the Spirit of bondage again in fear; but you have received the spirit of adoption of sons.*
>
> Now the will is by its essence directed to that which is truly good: so that when, either through passion or through an evil habit or disposition, a man turns away from what is truly good, he acts slavishly, in so far as he is led by something extraneous, *if we consider the natural direction of the will;* but if we consider the act of the will, *as inclined here and now towards an apparent good,* he acts freely when he follows the passion or evil habit, but he acts slavishly if, while his will remains the same, he refrains from what he desires through fear of the law which forbids the fulfilment of his desire. Accordingly, when the divine Spirit by love inclines the will to the true good to which it is naturally directed, He removes both the servitude [the heteronomy, as we would say to-day] whereby a man, the slave of passion and sin, acts against the order of the will, and the servitude whereby a man acts against the inclination of his will, and in obedience to the law, as the slave and not the friend of the law. Wherefore the Apostle says (II Cor. 3 : 17): *Where the Spirit of the Lord is, there is liberty,* and (Gal. 5 : 18): *If you are led by the Spirit you are not under the law.*[1]

Great is the distance between the imperfect liberation whereby the highest techniques of natural spirituality oblige nature to satisfy in some way the transnatural aspirations of the human

---

[1] St. Thomas, *Summa contra Gentiles*, iv. 22.

person, and the perfect freedom whereby the supernatural gift
the Divine Personality gives of itself to the created personality
more than fulfils these aspirations. While leaving intact the
distinction of natures, love, which at the end of spiritual growth
creates this perfect freedom, also makes man become a god by
participation. At the same time, far from enclosing itself in an
altogether intellectual contemplation which does away with
action, the freedom we mean lives by a contemplation which,
since it proceeds from love, superabounds in action and pene-
trates to that which is most intimate in the world. The heroism
it implies does not retreat into the sacred; it spills over into
the profane and sanctifies it. Detached from perfection in
perfection itself, because it wants more to love than to be
without fault, it awakens, more and more, good will and
brotherly love.

To return to the distinction between the social temporal and
the spiritual, the things which belong to Caesar and those which
belong to God, I should point out, finally, that the false deification of man results, as we have seen, in the confusion of the
temporal and the spiritual, a perverse adoration of the social,
and temporal relativities erected into an absolute; conversely,
the true deification of man, because it is accomplished by the
grace of the incarnation and draws to itself all that is human,
demands of divine things that they descend into the most
profound depths of the human, and insists that the political
and social order, while remaining essential distinct from the
spiritual, be pervaded and intrinsically super-elevated by the
current which flows into souls from the Absolute. In the degree,
small as it might be in fact, that things are this way, in that
degree the historical march of civilization in the attainment of
relative freedom, which responds to the *connatural* aspirations of
human personality, is in accord and in mutual concourse with
the supra-historical movement of the soul in the conquest of
absolute freedom, which responds, in transcending divinely,
to the *transnatural* aspirations of the person as a person.

Bertrand Russell

William James Lecturer, Harvard University

FREEDOM AND GOVERNMENT

LOGICALLY, freedom and government might seem to be antitheses, since compulsion is of the essence of government. Anarchists, of whom Kropotkin is the intellectually most respectable, have, on this ground, advocated a complete absence of government. They have believed that such collective decisions as are necessary can be adopted unanimously, without any need of powers of coercion vested in a majority or aristocracy or monarch. But history is not encouraging to this view. The two most important examples of its embodiment in a constitution—the kingdom of Poland and the League of Nations—both came to a bad end. Anarchism, however attractive, is rejected as a method of regulating the internal affairs of a State except by a few idealistic dreamers. Per contra, except by a few idealistic dreamers it is accepted as the only method of regulating international affairs. The same mentality that insists most strongly on the necessity of subjecting the individual to the State insists simultaneously on the complete independence of the sovereign State from all external control. Logically, such a view is untenable. If anarchy is bad nationally, it is bad internationally; if it is good internationally, it must be good nationally. For my part, I cannot believe it to be good in either sphere.

Belief in freedom, as a practical force in politics, arose out of two main sources, religion and trade. Religious minorities, wherever they had little chance of becoming majorities, turned against persecution; and traders objected to the curtailment of their profits by grants of monopolies to courtiers. The liberal philosophy that arose from these two motives was, at first, very moderate and restrained. The degree of liberty demanded by such men as Locke and Montesquieu is much less than exists in modern democratic states. Thus Montesquieu, quoting Cicero, says: "Liberty is the right of doing whatever the laws permit, and if a citizen could do what they forbid he would be no longer possessed of liberty, because all his fellow-citizens would be possessed of the same power." This may seem an inadequate degree of liberty, if it is not supplemented by some principle as to what the laws are to permit. In France, after the Revocation of the Edict of Nantes, the exercise of the Protestant religion was illegal; it cannot therefore be said that the right to do what the laws permitted conferred any effective liberty upon French Protestants.

Nevertheless, the right to do whatever the laws permit is a very important part of liberty. It was secured in England by *habeas corpus*, which was a barrier to kingly tyranny; it did not exist in France under the *ancien régime*. In our own day, Jews in Germany, kulaks in Russia, and nationalists in India, have been punished by the executive without appeal to the law courts, and therefore without proof of criminality. This sort of thing is forbidden in the American Constitution by the provision about "due process of law." Montesquieu's intention is to maintain that a man should be punished only by the law courts, and that the law courts should be independent of the executive. The American Constitution, whether deliberately or by inadvertence, has made the law courts also to some extent independent of the legislature, and in this respect has gone beyond what Montesquieu advocated in the passage quoted above. In other passages, however, he gave a wider and more constructive definition of liberty, for instance: "the political liberty of the subject is a tranquillity of mind arising from the opinion each person has of his safety. In order to have this liberty, it is requisite the government be so constituted as one man need not be afraid of another." This definition of political liberty could not be improved upon, and I shall accept it in what follows.

Political liberty, however, is only one species of a genus, and there is no reason to regard it as more desirable than other species of liberty. Political action may promote or restrict other kinds of liberty as well as the political kind; we cannot therefore judge of political action solely with reference to political freedom, even if we consider freedom the sole proper end of politics.

Freedom in general may be defined as the absence of obstacles to the realization of desires. Complete freedom is thus only possible for omnipotence; practicable freedom is a matter of degree, dependent both upon external circumstances and upon the nature of our desires. Stoicism and all kindred philosophies seek to secure freedom by the control of desires and by confining them to what the individual will can secure. Political theorists, on the contrary, for the most part concentrate on the external conditions of freedom. This may be a source of error if the subjective part of the problem is forgotten. 'If all the men guilty of crimes of violence were transported to an island and left to form a self-governing community, they would need a much more stringent form of government than is required where men are temperamentally law-abiding. Nevertheless, so long as we remember that we are making an abstraction, it is convenient and harmless to treat the objective part of the problem of freedom in isolation.

We may give the name "physical freedom" to the mastery over non-human obstacles to the realization of our desires. Modern scientific technique has increased physical freedom, but has necessitated new limitations of social freedom. To take an illustration that involves no controversial issues, motor traffic has unavoidably brought about a very much stricter control over the roads by the police than was formerly necessary. Speaking generally, the technical changes that have occurred in the world during the last hundred years have increased the effects, both intended and unintended, that one man's acts are likely to have upon another man's welfare. Montesquieu's "tranquillity of mind arising from the opinion each person has of his safety" would be by no means promoted by the removal of traffic regulations, and therefore no one protests against them in the name of liberty. But in other kinds of activity—of which the most important is war—although the same principle is applicable, various interests and passions prevent men from applying it, and lead them still to defend a degree of anarchy which may have promoted total freedom in a former age, but now has the opposite effect.

Many of the most vehement advocates of freedom have been led to more or less anarchic conclusions, because their conception of freedom was aristocratic rather than democratic. Byron's Corsairs and Giaours are free to practise murder and pillage and to allow their broken hearts to inspire a hatred of the human race, but their freedom is of a sort that cannot be generalized, since it is based upon terror. Tacitus can look back with nostalgia to the good old days of the Republic, when Roman aristocrats were free to plunder provinces with impunity. American plutocrats can demand, in the name of freedom, the right to obstruct organization among the men whose labour produces their wealth, while demanding the fullest freedom of organization for themselves. Educational reformers, who endeavour to introduce freedom into schools, require much vigilance to avoid unintentionally establishing a tyranny of muscle, under which all but the biggest children are trembling slaves. One of the strongest impulses of energetic individuals is the impulse to control and subject those who are unable to resist them, and if this impulse is left free the result is a great diminution of the total liberty of the community. When freedom is conceived democratically, the control of the impulse to tyranny is seen to be the essential and most difficult problem. The freedom of prominent individuals must be curtailed if any freedom is to be secured for the mass of mankind.

The promotion of physical freedom may, even in the most freedom-loving communities, in some degree override the desire for political freedom. Take, for example, the construction of roads. Even if everybody wants them, everybody would prefer the expense to be borne by someone else. The only device for distributing the burden fairly is taxation, and a man cannot be allowed to escape taxation by professing an indifference to roads. Yet his objection might be genuine: the philosopher Lao-tse held that roads corrupt primitive innocence, and there is no reason why he should not have modern disciples. If, however, a conscience clause were introduced to meet their case, it is to be feared that the number of Lao-tse's disciples would increase with inconvenient rapidity when the financial advantages of the anti-road creed became evident. In a democracy, just as much as in a tyranny, taxes have to be paid by those who object to the purposes for which they are collected. It is only by a mystical identification of the majority with the community that democracy can be held to involve liberty. It is a means to liberty if the majority are lovers of liberty; if not, not.

Eighteenth-century advocates of liberty thought always of isolated individuals rather than of organizations; many of them, like Rousseau, were even actively hostile to freedom of organization. In the modern world it is organizations that raise the difficult problems. Legislators have to consider two questions: for what purposes may organizations be formed? And what may they legally do in pursuance of their purposes? These questions have been fought out in connection with trade unions, which at first were everywhere illegal, then were permitted to exist provided they did nothing to further their objects, then, very gradually, were permitted first one activity and then another. At every stage the legal mind viewed the process with grave suspicion, and was only forced to yield by the pressure of democratic opinion. In the case of trade unions, most of those who were most in favour of freedom advocated the removal of legal restrictions, in spite of the fact that these restrictions were defended in the name of freedom by employers who wished to retain their monopoly of economic power. Nevertheless, it has always been clear that the power of trade unions *might* become a genuine menace to freedom.

The rise of fascism brought about, in its early stages, an exactly opposite situation. Here it was the reactionaries who favoured freedom of organization and the progressives who opposed it. The first step in a fascist movement is the combination under an energetic leader of a number of men who possess more than the average share of leisure, brutality, and stupidity. The next step is to fascinate fools and muzzle the intelligent, by emotional excitement on the one hand and terrorism on the other. This technique is as old as the hills; it was practised in almost every Greek city, and the moderns have only enlarged its scale. But what I am concerned with is the reaction of modern liberal sentiment to this new attack on liberty. Does the principle of free speech require us to put no obstacle in the way of those who advocate its suppression? Does the principle of toleration require us to tolerate those who advocate intolerance? Public opinion, among those who dislike fascism, is divided on these questions, and has not arrived at any clear theory from which consistent answers could be derived.

There is of course one obvious limitation upon the principle of free speech: if an act is illegal, it is logical to make it illegal to advocate it. This principle justifies the authorities in prohibiting incitement to assassination or violent revolution. But in practice this principle does not by any means cover the ground. If there is to be any personal liberty, men must be free to urge a change in the laws. Suppose a man makes a speech in favour of communism, with the implication that it is to be brought about by the ordinary processes of democracy, and suppose that, after his speech, a questioner asks whether he really believes that such changes can be secured without violent revolution. Unless he gives an affirmative answer with far more emphasis than the facts warrant, he will have, in effect, promoted revolutionary sentiment. Or suppose a fascist makes an anti-Semitic speech, urging that Jews should be subject to legal disabilities; his arguments must be such as to stimulate hatred of the Jews, and the more successful they are the more likely they are to cause violence. Imagine Mark Antony indicted for his speech in *Julius Caesar*: although it is obviously intended to cause violence, it would hardly be possible to obtain legal proof of this intention. To prohibit the advocacy of illegalities is therefore not enough; some further limitation upon the principle of free speech is necessary if incitement to violence is to be effectively prevented.

The solution of this problem has two sides: on the one hand, the ordinary citizen, if he is on the whole content with his form of government, has a right to prohibit any organized attempt to overthrow it by force and any propaganda obviously likely to promote such an attempt. But on the other hand the government must avoid such flagrant injustice or oppression as is likely to lead to violence in spite of prohibition. The Irish secured their liberties by assassination; women in England won the vote by a long series of inconvenient crimes. Such tactics ought not to have been necessary, since in each case the professed democratic principles of the government justified the aims of the rebels, and therefore seemed to excuse their methods. But when, as in the case of the fascists, the aims of the rebels are fundamentally opposed to a governmental theory accepted by the majority, and when, further, it is obvious that violence is intended to be used at a suitable moment, there is every justification for preventing the growth of organized power in the hands of a rebellious minority. For if this is not done, internal peace is jeopardized, and the kind of community that most men desire can no longer be preserved. Liberal principles will not survive of themselves; like all other principles, they require vigorous assertion when they are challenged.

Freedom of opinion is closely connected with free speech, but has a wider scope. The Inquisition made a point of investigating, by means of torture, the secret opinions that men endeavoured to keep to themselves. When men confessed to unorthodox opinions, they were punished even if it could not be proved that they had ever before given utterance to them. This practice has been revived in the dictatorial countries, Germany, Italy, and Russia. The reason, in each case, is that the government feels itself unstable. One of the most important conditions of freedom, in the matter of opinion as in other matters, is governmental security. In England, during the sixty or seventy years preceding the Great War, freedom of speech and opinion, in political matters, was almost complete, because everyone knew that no subversive opinion had a chance of success. Gilbert and Sullivan made fun of the navy and army, but the only penalty was the Queen's refusal to bestow a knighthood on Gilbert. Nowadays, they would be shot in Russia, beheaded in Germany, sent to a penal settlement in

Italy, accused of violating the Official Secrets Act in England, and investigated by a Senatorial Committee in the United States on suspicion of being in receipt of Moscow gold. The change is due to increased insecurity, which is caused by war, the fear of war, and the impoverishment due to war. And modern war is mainly due to nationalism. Until this state of affairs is changed, it is hardly to be hoped that there will be as much freedom of opinion as existed in Western countries fifty years ago.

Freedom of opinion is important for many reasons, especially because it is a necessary condition of all progress, intellectual, moral, political, and social. Where it does not exist, the *status quo* becomes stereotyped, and all originality, even the most necessary, is discouraged. Since freedom of opinion can only exist when the government thinks itself secure, it is important that the government should have the approval of the great majority of the population and should deal with discontented minorities, wherever possible, in a manner calculated to allay their discontent. A government must possess force, but cannot be a satisfactory government unless force is seldom necessary. All the kinds of freedom advocated by liberals disappear when security disappears, and security depends upon a wide diffusion of contentment. This in turn is impossible when the general level of prosperity is falling. Liberalism flourished in the nineteenth century because of economic progress; it is in eclipse now because of economic retrogression.

There can be no widespread liberty except under the reign of law, for when men are lawless only the strongest are free, and they only until they are overcome by someone still stronger. The tyrant in a lawless community is like the King of the Wood, "who slays the slayer and must himself be slain." Whoever, in the name of liberty, impairs respect for the law, incurs a grave responsibility; yet, since the law is often oppressive and incapable of being amended legally, revolution must be allowed to be sometimes necessary. The solution of this problem is not possible in abstract terms. It was solved practically in the American Revolution; but most revolutions have so weakened the respect for law that they have led to dictatorships. Perhaps a revolution can be completely successful only when those who make it are persuaded that they are defending legality against some illegal usurpation. But this requires a rare combination of fortunate circumstances, and is not possible in the case of revolutions that attempt any far-reaching change in the social structure.

The most fallacious of all the applications of the principle of liberty has been in international affairs. While it has been generally realized that liberty for the individual depends upon law, it has been thought that liberty for nations depended upon the absence of law. This is partly a historical accident, connected with the years that followed the Congress of Vienna. At that time a number of reactionary states, most of which were purely dynastic, established what was in effect an international government of Europe, and devoted their united strength to the suppression of every form of liberalism in every part of the Continent. The opposition to despotic monarchs was bound up, at that time, with the principle of nationality; democracy went hand in hand with the desire to make the boundaries of states coincide with national sentiment instead of being determined by the accidents of royal marriages or diplomatic bargains among the victors over Napoleon. It was thought that, when once national boundaries and parliamentary institutions had been established everywhere, the democracies would co-operate freely, and the causes of war would have been eliminated. In this mood of optimism, liberals completely overlooked the need for any international authority to regulate the relations between states.

But nationalism triumphant has proved, is proving, and will prove, incompatible not only with liberty, but with everything else that intelligent men have considered desirable since the Renaissance. To consider, for a moment, goods other than freedom, especially the eighteenth-century ideals of culture, education, and humanitarian enlightenment: in these matters South-eastern Europe and Latin America have lost much of what they owed to the Hapsburgs; Ireland, from nationalist sentiment, has cut itself off from European culture by Catholic education and censorship; India, from similar motives, is preparing to repudiate everything occidental. I have met

Mexican nationalists who wished to obliterate everything that their country had acquired since 1492. The conception of the unity of civilization, born in the Roman Empire, nurtured by the medieval Church, brought to maturity by the Renaissance and modern science, survives now only, and that precariously, in the Western democracies, where, it is to be feared, it will perish during this war. Elsewhere, in the name of some national hero, living or dead, the State devotes its powers to the inculcation of some national theology as crass and stupid as the superstitions of South Sea Islanders or the cannibalistic rites of the Aztecs.

If stupidity were the only defect of the modern national religions, the philosopher might shrug his shoulders and remark that the bulk of mankind have always been fools. Unfortunately, while the superstitions of savages are harmful only to themselves, those of nations equipped with scientific technique are dangerous to the whole world and, in particular, involve a grave loss of liberty, not only among the devout, but also among those who wish to remain rational. Vast expenditure on armaments, compulsory military service, and occasional wars are part of the price that has to be paid by those nations that will not accept foreign domination. The inevitable outcome of the doctrine that each nation should have unrestricted sovereignty is to compel the citizens of each nation to engage in irksome activities and to incur sacrifices, often of life itself, in order to thwart the designs of other nations. Hitler, in a sense, had already subjugated England and France, since a large part of the thoughts and actions of Englishmen and Frenchmen were determined by reference to him; and Hitler himself is a product of the previous subjugation of Germany by England and France. In a world of international anarchy individual freedom is as impossible as in a country where private violence is not restrained by the law and the police.

A complete international government, with legislative, executive, and judiciary, and a monopoly of armed force, is the most essential condition of individual liberty in a technically scientific world. Not, of course, that it will secure *complete* liberty; that, I repeat, is only possible for omnipotence, and there cannot be two omnipotent individuals in the world. The man whose desire for liberty is wholly self-centred is therefore driven, if he feels strong enough, to seek world dictatorship; but the man whose desire for liberty is social, or who feels too weak to secure more than his fair share, will seek to maximize liberty by means of law and government, and will oppose anarchic power in all its various forms.

Every man desires freedom for his own impulses, but men's impulses conflict, and therefore not all can be satisfied. There are two kinds of conflict between men's desires. In the first place, we desire more than our fair share of possessions; this can be met, in theory, by decreeing equality of distribution, as has been done by the institution of monogamy. But there is a more essential and deep-rooted conflict owing to the love of power: most human beings, though in very varying degrees, desire to control not only their own lives but also the lives of others. Most forms of control over the lives of others diminish the freedom of those who are controlled, but some increase it. The man who endows a university has power over the lives of those who profit by his benefaction, but his power is such as to liberate their own impulses. Inventors have great power, and the general tendency of inventions is to increase physical liberty. It is therefore possible for power impulses to find an outlet not incompatible with social freedom. To insure that they shall do so is a problem partly of individual psychology, partly of education, and partly of opportunity. A homicidal maniac cannot be allowed any freedom for his power impulses, but their undesirable character may be the result of bad education and lack of opportunity. Cromwell spent the first half of his career in agitation connected with draining the Fens, and the second in making himself a military dictator; in other circumstances, his power impulses might have found only the earlier beneficent outlet. If freedom is to be secure, it is essential both that useful careers shall be open to energetic men, and that harmful careers shall be closed to them. It is important also that education should develop useful forms of technical skill, and that the circumstances of childhood and youth should not be such as to generate ferocity. All these conditions are absent in totalitarian countries, where the principal means to success are sycophancy, treachery, and brutality, and where education is designed to produce a combination of submissiveness and truculence.

If freedom were the sole political desideratum, there would still, as we have seen, be need of law and government, which, in the international sphere, remain to be created. But individual freedom, however desirable, is only one among the ends of statesmanship. Among innocuous activities we admire some more than others: we praise a great poet, composer, or man of science more than we praise men who are innocent but undistinguished. Education, both general and technical, is generally conceded to be desirable, even at the cost of the liberties of both parents and children. And if we knew a way to produce a community of Shakespeares, Beethovens, and Newtons, we should probably think it worth while to do so. Freedom is too negative a conception to determine the ends of human life, or even of politics. Nevertheless, it is only in so far as the majority of men agree that other ends can be pursued in political action without arousing resistances and violences that are likely to prove disastrous. An unpopular Utopia, in so far as a benevolent dictator could realize it, would prove to be quite different from his dreams. Liberty, therefore, must always remain a *sine qua non* of other political goods.

The transition from individual to social ethics is theoretically far from simple. Most philosophers who have written on ethics have been mainly concerned with the individual. When they have been concerned also with society, they have failed to build a bridge from the individual to the community that will bear logical scrutiny. Take, for instance, the two foundations of Bentham's social philosophy: (1) every man pursues his own happiness; (2) every man ought to pursue the general happiness. Perhaps if we could submit Bentham to a *viva voce* examination, he would expand his second proposition as follows: The general happiness will be increased if every man acts in a manner likely to increase it; therefore, if I am in a governmental position, or in any way owe my own happiness to the fact that I represent the general interest, I shall endeavour to cause others to act in a way that will promote the happiness of mankind, which I can only do by means of institutions that cause the interests of the individual and those of the community to be identical. This explanation might pass muster in an ideal democracy, where no politician or official could continue to enjoy his salary unless he served the public faithfully. But it does not give any reason why, where an ideal democracy does not exist, any public man should aim at the public good. I dare say Caligula and Nero got more fun out of life than Marcus Aurelius did. One wonders what arguments Bentham would have used to them, and how long he would have been allowed to go on using them. The only argument compatible with his psychology would have been that they would come to a bad end, but they might have replied that they preferred a cheerful beginning and a bad end to drabness throughout. Bentham imagines the legislator to be in some unexplained way an incarnation of the public interest. But this is only because, in fantasy, he is the legislator, and he is in fact a benevolent man. Psycho-analysts show most people that they have unconscious vices, but in Bentham's case it was the virtues that were unconscious. In obedience to theory, he conceived of himself as wholly selfish and remained unaware of his spontaneous desire for the general happiness. Public spirit, he says (in the Table of the Springs of Action), is an absurd motive, which never actuated anyone; in fact, it is a synonym for spite. Nevertheless, he hopes to find a legislator who will seek the public good. He was young in the era of benevolent despots, which perhaps accounts for his failure of logic. However that may be, his individual psychology and his social ethics remain disparate and fundamentally inconsistent.

Of the great religions, Christianity and Buddhism, in their primitive and most vital forms, are concerned only with personal virtue, and show no interest in social and political questions. On the other hand, Confucianism is fundamentally political, and considers all virtues in relation to the welfare of the State. The result is a certain dullness and aridity, which caused it to be supplemented by Buddhism and Taoism among the more spiritually minded Chinese. Confucianism is a religion

R

for the civil service, and gave rise to the most remarkable civil service the world has ever known. But it had nothing to offer to prophets or poets or mystics: St. Francis or Dante or Pascal would have found it wholly irrelevant to their needs.

Karl Marx, as a religious leader, is analogous to both Confucius and Bentham. His ethical doctrine, in a nutshell, is this: that every man pursues the economic interest of his class, and therefore, if there is only one class, every man will pursue the general interest. This doctrine has failed to work out in practice as its adherents expected. both because men do not in fact pursue the interest of their class, and because no civilized community is possible in which there is only one class, since government and executive officials are unavoidable.

There is one method of making the public good fundamental in ethics which has been favoured by many philosophers and some politicians, namely, to endow the community with a mystical oneness and to regard the separate citizens as unreal abstractions. This view may be supported by the analogy of the human body. No man is troubled by the possibility of conflict between the different parts of his body, say the great toe and the little finger. The body has to be considered as a whole, and the interests concerned are those of the whole, not of the several members. A healthy body is a completely integrated corporative State, governed despotically by the brain. There are, no doubt, possibilities of rebellion, such as paralysis and St. Vitus's dance, but these are diseases which are exceptional. Could not the body politic be similarly integrated and similarly devoted, instinctively and harmoniously, to the welfare of the whole? The answer is merely an appeal to the facts. An individual body contains only one mind, whereas the body politic contains many, and there is no psychological mechanism by which many minds can co-operate in the same manner in which muscles controlled by a single mind co-operate. Co-operation among many minds has to be a matter of agreement, even when it is agreement to be dominated by a dictator. A further, but less fundamental, argument against those who regard a human society as an organism is that they almost invariably take a nation, rather than mankind, as the organism concerned, thus merely substituting the strife of nations for that of individuals, instead of arriving at a genuine public interest which is to be served by the whole human race.

Considered practically, not philosophically, the question is: Can the public interest ever be a force in public affairs, or must politics be always and essentially nothing but a tug-of-war between the passions of powerful individuals or groups? There are two ways in which the public interest can become practically operative: first, through the impulse of benevolence, as in Bentham; second, through the consciousness of the common man that he is too weak to stand alone, and that he can only secure that part of his political desires which he shares with other common men. An uncommon man can hope to become a dictator, but a common man can hope, at best, only to become a voter in a democracy. Common men are helpless without a leader, and as a rule follow a leader who deceives them; but there have been occasions when they have accepted the leadership of men inspired by benevolence. When this has happened, the public good has become an effective force in public affairs. To secure that it shall happen as often as possible is the practical problem for the man whose theorizing on politics is guided by a desire for the welfare of mankind.

The practical solution of this problem is difficult in the extreme, but the theoretical solution is obvious. Common men throughout the world should be made aware of the identity of their interests, wherever it exists; conflicts of interest which are apparent but not real must be shown to be illusory; real conflicts of interest, where they exist, must be removed by a change of institutions, of which the most harmful are national sovereignty and private ownership of land and raw materials; education and economic circumstances must be made such as not to generate hatred and ferocity and a desire for revenge upon the world. When all this has been achieved, co-operation will become possible with a minimum of coercion, and individual freedom will be increased as well as all other political desiderata.

To sum up: Government is a necessary but not sufficient condition for the greatest realizable degree of individual liberty;

indeed, there is need of more government than at present, not less, since an international authority is as much required as the present national states. But if government is not to be tyrannical, it must be democratic, and the democracy must feel that the common interests of mankind are more important than the conflicting interests of separate groups. To realize this state of affairs completely would be scarcely possible, but since the problem is quantitative a gradual approach may be hoped for. At present the world is moving away from all that is valued by lovers of freedom, but this movement will not last for ever. The world has oscillated many times between freedom and slavery, and the dark times in which we live are probably no more permanent than the progressive epoch that rejoiced our grandfathers.

Gaetano Salvemini

Lauro de Bosis Lecturer in the History of Italian Civilization,
Harvard University

DEMOCRACY RECONSIDERED

I "DEMOCRACY" AND "LIBERTY"

THE word "democracy" is used to indicate several inter-related but different concepts:

1. The lower strata of society, the common people, the "masses" as distinct from the "classes." We say that the middle classes occupy the space between aristocracy and democracy; that it is idle to harbour illusions on the wisdom of democracy; that democracy can be more warlike than an aristocracy.

2. That doctrine which the English call "liberalism" and which upholds the rights of the lower classes against the political and economic privileges of the upper classes. We say that democracy implies equal political rights for all citizens; that democracy teaches that there must be no hereditary privileges; that it is impossible to conciliate democracy with imperialistic practices.

3. Those political parties that hoist the democratic doctrine as their banner and claim to uphold the rights of the lower classes. We say that British democracy was defeated in the national election of 1931; that a resolution was adopted in its national convention by the democracy of a given country; that a given democracy should join hands with other democracies.

4. The institutions which conform to the democratic doctrine. We say that French democracy does not grant the

245

franchise to women; that democracy cannot work in time of war; that in the North American democracy there is a Supreme Court.

5. A country endowed with democratic institutions or its government, irrespective of whether democratic or anti-democratic parties are in power. We say that the Western democracies tried to appease Hitler by the Munich Pact; that in 1939 war broke out between dictatorial Germany and the Western democracies; that democracies cannot survive unless they show greater efficiency than the dictatorial countries.

6. The whole of the personal and political rights which a democratic constitution grants the citizens. We say that democracy vanishes if freedom of speech is abolished; that there is no use talking democracy if freedom of the press is curtailed; that without democracy there is no respect for human dignity.

7. Not all, but one of those rights that are granted by a democratic constitution. We say that freedom of speech is democracy; that universal suffrage is democracy; that a parliamentary form of government is democracy.

8. Those institutions or conditions which would prevail if the democratic doctrine were consistently carried out. We say that democracy is a most hopeful way of life; that democracy grants the same rights to men and women, to coloured and white; that democracy, according to Mazzini, is progress of all through all under the leadership of the best.

Not seldom it proves difficult to define with precision what idea one has in mind when the word democracy—or some other equivalent expression is used. We hear it said that democracy is in a state of decadence. But it is not clear whether we should understand that the masses have fallen into less satisfactory economic and political conditions, or that the exponents of the democratic doctrine have become fewer in number, or that the democratic parties are losing ground either as a result of their own errors or because the democratic doctrines have been discredited, or that democratic institutions have been wholly or only partly superseded by institutions not in conformity with the democratic doctrine. We read in the book of an English writer, who, however, was a man of great intelligence: "It has sometimes been held that democracy (a) would be no less hostile to personal liberty than other forms of government. It is true that the masses (b) may be as antagonistic to personal independence as the classes. But if it is argued that the democratic principle (c) can be hostile to liberty this is a fallacy, for it is full publicity and free discussion that are the organs of democratic government (d) and if it suppresses them democracy (e) deprives itself of the means of forming a judgment of its own affairs." In this text the word democracy is used in case (a) as equivalent to the democratic form of government or democratic institutions; in (b) the masses supplant democratic institutions; in case (c) the democratic doctrine takes the place of democratic institutions and the masses; in case (d) democratic government is what it ought to be if it corresponded faithfully to democratic doctrine; and in case (e) the masses again take the upper hand.

All these ambiguities are increased by the fact that the word democracy, like all other abstract collective words (Nation, State, Church, Fatherland, Army, Parliament, Party, Capitalism, Proletariat), is easily subjected to poetic sublimation and is endowed with a soul, a genius, a heart, and many other organs which serve us poor mortals. "Democracy" stirs up the masses, directs its parties in the political struggle; it is born, it grows, it weakens, falls ill, runs the risk of dying, or actually dies as would a person of flesh and blood. Many controversies on democracy are nothing but senseless squabblings over a mythological and non-existent being.

Finally, it is necessary to bear in mind that the word democracy is used also to indicate doctrines and activities diametrically opposed to one of the essential institutions of a democratic regime, that is to say, the right of self-government. Thus do we hear of a so-called Christian Democracy which, according to *The Catholic Encyclopædia*, has for its aim "to comfort and uplift the lower classes excluding expressly every appearance and implication of political meaning;" this democracy already existed in the time of Constantine when the clergy "began the practical work of Christian democracy" by establishing hospices for orphans, the aged, the infirm, and wayfarers. The Fascists, the Nazis, and the Communists also often and readily dub as democracy, nay more, as the "real," "true," "full," "substantial," "more honest" democracy the political regimes of present-day Italy, Germany, and Russia, because these regimes also profess to comfort and uplift the lower classes after having deprived them of the very political rights without which it is not possible to conceive of "government by the people."

The word "liberty" also labours under the disease of manifold meanings. Philosophers have spun a tremendous web of confusion around it. But we have no need of venturing on that tempestuous sea. We shall deal with the word as it has been used in the political idiom. Already in the eighteenth century Montesquieu observed that "there is no word that admits of more varied meanings, and has made more different impressions on the human mind, than that of Liberty."

> Some have taken it for the faculty of deposing a person on whom they had conferred tyrannical authority; others for the power of choosing a superior whom they are obliged to obey; others for the right of bearing arms and of being enabled therefore to use violence; others, in fine, for the privilege of being governed by a native of their own country or by their own laws. A certain nation thought for a long time that liberty consisted in the privilege of wearing long beards. Some have annexed this name to one form of government exclusive of others; those who had republican tastes applied it to this species of policy; those who had enjoyed a monarchical government gave it to monarchy. Thus they have all applied the name of liberty to the government best suited to their own customs and inclinations.

Montesquieu mentioned some of these meanings merely to introduce into his treatise, according to his custom, relief spots for the benefit of the reader. For our purpose, it will suffice to notice that the word is taken to mean:

1. The whole of the personal and political rights which a citizen enjoys under a free constitution. This meaning is analogous to that of democracy under number 6.

2. Any one of those rights, as if the whole of those rights were lost if a single one of them were discarded or curtailed. We term liberty the right of self-government, which Montesquieu termed "power of choosing a superior whom they are

obliged to obey;" this "power of a civil society or state to govern itself by its own discretion or by laws of its own making," Richard Price called "civil liberty;" and the American Declaration of 1774 stated that "the foundation of English liberty, and of all free governments, is a right in the people to participate in their legislative council."

3. National independence or self-determination, i.e. what Montesquieu defined as "the privilege of being governed by a native of their own country or by their own laws." We say that Italy and Germany gained their liberty during the nineteenth century.

Moreover, liberty no less than democracy is subject to a poetical-mythological transfiguration and in the hands of politicians not seldom is made to mean the opposite of what any honest man thinks when he uses the word. Thus Hitler and Mussolini maintain that they are endeavouring to gain liberty for their nations in international competition and that whoever hampers their nations in the conquest of their "living space" commits a crime against their liberty; in this case liberty becomes what Montesquieu described as "the right of bearing arms and of being enabled therefore to use violence."

In the title of the present paper "democracy" means "democratic doctrine" and in the pages which follow the reader will never find the words "democracy" or "liberty" transfigured or adulterated, and all confusion will be avoided between the various concepts which the words evoke.

II DEMOCRATIC AND OLIGARCHIC INSTITUTIONS

A democratic constitution grants equal rights to all citizens without discrimination of social class, creed, race, sex, or political affiliation.

Such rights fall into two categories:

1. Personal rights, that is to say, those rights which pertain to the members of the commonwealth as private individuals and which the French Constituent Assembly of 1789 termed "the rights of man:" the right to physical integrity and liberty and to be secure in one's house, papers, and effects, against

unreasonable searches and seizures; the right to choose and follow one's calling and to own and inherit property; the right to swift trial by impartial courts in accordance with known laws; freedom of thought and religion; and the right to be educated according to one's own abilities.

2. Political rights, that is to say, the rights which pertain to the individual as a member of the commonwealth and which the French Constituent Assembly of 1789 termed "the rights of the citizen:" freedom of speech, of the press, and of association; the right to participate in peaceable assemblies; the right of petition; the right to be admitted to public office according to one's talents; the right of representation or self-government, i.e. the right to change the men in power in central and local governments by the direct means of elections or through one's own representatives; and the right of resistance to unconstitutional governmental activities.

A democratic constitution must include "all" personal rights, "all" political rights, plus equality of rights among "all" citizens, plus the institutions of self-government.

Before the Reform Act of 1832, England possessed a self-governing Parliament, or a "parliamentary regime" as it is commonly called, because the House of Commons was vested with the right to turn out the Cabinet by a vote of no confidence. But the middle classes, the lower middle classes, and the lower classes were more or less thoroughly excluded from political rights, and the lower classes did not even enjoy full personal rights. British "liberties" were the privilege of an upper-class oligarchy. The characteristic feature of the British Constitution was a restricted franchise. Even after the Reform Act of 1832, the franchise remained for many years the privilege of a middle-class oligarchy. The British Constitution was democratized during the last century by the gradual extension of the franchise to all classes and by the abolition of traditional privileges, although it still retains vestiges of the old oligarchic system, such as hereditary royalty and the privileges of the Lords and of the Established Church.

The constitution of the German Empire before the War of 1914-18 granted all German citizens all personal rights, a fair measure of political rights, and even universal suffrage in the election of the Imperial Reichstag. None the less, the Empire did not have a democratic constitution. It was a federation of local States in which all classes did not share equally in the right of representation and whose executives did not depend upon the votes of the parliaments (*Landtagen*). The electorate had only the right to make their opinions known through their representatives while the Cabinets could to a large extent disregard these opinions. Thus the States forming the Imperial Federation had an oligarchic and not a democratic franchise and had representative but no self-governing parliaments. The Imperial Reichstag itself, though elected by universal suffrage, did not have the power to unseat the Chancellor by a vote of no confidence. It was a representative but not a self-governing institution. Moreover, legislation passed by the Reichstag needed the approval of an Upper House (*Bundesrath*) composed of delegates appointed by the executives of the various oligarchic and not self-governing local States. As a consequence, the constitution of the German Empire was oligarchic although it embodied universal suffrage, which is one of the indispensable features of a democratic constitution. Universal suffrage alone does not make a constitution democratic.

A parliamentary or self-governing regime may be either oligarchic or democratic. A democratic regime, besides granting equality of personal and political rights, must be parliamentary or self-governing.

In a self-governing regime the majority rules. The consent of the majority, however, does not suffice to bring a political constitution within the framework of democratic doctrine.

When the democratic movements originated, they aimed at establishing the rights of the lower-class majority against the privileges of the clergy and the nobility. After the abolition of the political privileges of these minorities a new peril arose: majorities might suppress the liberties of minorities. The democratic doctrine consequently became more complex. It came to imply not only the principle that the right to rule is vested in the majority but also the principle that the right to disagree with the majority is vested in the minority. Political

liberty is fundamentally "the right to differ." From this right
to disagree spring all other political rights of the citizen in a
democratic regime. These rights are meant not so much to
establish the power of the majority as to protect the minorities
in their right of opposition. The best test of the standards of a
democratic constitution is the provisions it makes for the protection of minorities.

Thus, a democratic constitution must include not only personal rights, political rights, and juridical equality, but respect
for the personal and political rights of the minorities.

We have spoken of the rights vested in the "majority" and
"minorities" by democratic institutions. This terminology does
not correspond to realities and should be discarded.

In all societies, political control—that is to say, administrative, military, legislative, economic, religious, moral, and intellectual leadership—is in the hands of an "organized minority,"
while the disorganized majority conforms more or less willingly
to the commands of the minority. Mosca termed "political
class" the minority controlling a given society at a given time.
This "political class" has nothing to do with a "social class"
in the Marxian sense of the term. It means the network of
managers, high officials, and influential persons who, in a given
society, control public bodies and private organizations. Such
leaders are not necessarily drawn from one single class even
though the upper strata of society do furnish the majority.
Elements from the lower social classes are admitted into the
ruling class in varying proportions.

When the political class splits up into conflicting sections,
each of which brandishes a formula of its own, one then has
"parties." Under a democratic form of government there are
parties which maintain that the existing social order cannot be
altered without impairing the welfare of those very lower
classes which bear the weight of the entire structure. Other
parties claim the monopoly of upholding the rights of the
under-privileged majority against the privileges of the upper-
class oligarchy. As a matter of fact, the latter, no less than the
former, are "organized minorities" striving for predominance.
Nor does their victory always bring about an increase in the

welfare of that majority, although victory always does bring about an increase in the welfare of any victorious minority.

Even in the most radically democratic regime the government is not run by the majority of the citizens. It is run by that party which, for the time being, is upheld by the votes of the majority. And this is the majority not of the citizens but of that single section of citizens sufficiently interested in politics to vote on election day. All parties are organized minorities that try to gain the support of the majority of the electorate, and this majority of the electorate, in its turn, is as a rule only a minority of the entire population.

We may carry even further our analysis of the minorities which compete for the right to rule. The victorious minority is composed of two parts: (1) a permanently organized machine, bossed by ward heelers, that votes solidly for the party regardless of circumstances; and (2) a flying squadron of unattached voters who are not members of any party, whose actions are unpredictable and who determine victory by voting now for this party and now for another. When the difference in voting strength between the permanent forces of the conflicting parties is not great, the victory is due to that fluctuating minority which is not regimented in any party and which may even be extremely small in numbers.

De jure, a dictatorial regime is the rule of an autocrat, an oligarchic regime is the rule of a privileged minority, and a democratic regime is the rule of the majority of the citizens. *De facto*, all political regimes are ruled by organized minorities. The autocrat could not govern millions of men if he were not surrounded by intimate advisers, party leaders, and high civil and military servants, under whom a hierarchy of minor servants assists the upper stratum of the governing class in controlling the subjects. Intimate advisers, party leaders, high civil and military servants, and minor servants have *de jure* no authority whatsoever. Sovereignty—that is, the right to make decisions and give orders—is lodged in the autocrat alone. *De facto*, the autocrat makes such decisions and issues such orders in accordance with the suggestions of the men with whom he is in touch, and the lower strata of the governing class also share to a certain extent in the authority of the higher-ups. All governments are governments by minorities. A democratic regime, no less than any other regime, is ruled by minority. And within the organized minorities or parties contending for power, there are more or less clandestine coteries that pull the strings behind the scenes. Government by majority has never existed nor is it likely ever to exist. Hence it would be correct never to speak of "majority" or "minority," but rather of "party in power" and "opposition parties."

What, then, is the difference between an autocratic regime, an oligarchic regime, and a democratic regime if all three are government by minorities?

In a dictatorial regime the minority that surrounds the dictator, and in an oligarchic regime the ruling minority, possess the monopoly of power by their own rights and have no legal responsibility toward the common herd. A democratic regime is an open field for free competition among all organized minorities or "parties" aspiring to run the government. In order to gain power or to remain in power, each minority seeks the support of the greatest possible number of citizens. All citizens, and not one class of the population alone, are entitled by universal suffrage to take part in competition if they choose to do so. Thus any section of the disorganized majority can, from time to time, give vent to its grievances and, under the leadership of one of the organized minorities of the opposition, overthrow the organized minority in power.

The existence of competing parties is essential to the working of democratic institutions. As Sir Herbert Samuel, one of the British Liberal leaders, has explained it, men and women of the same mind must have some method of acting together for their common purposes.

> Otherwise an electorate is merely a mob. Some one must frame policies, choose candidates, carry on propaganda; some one must watch the actions of the elected members; some one must mould and develop the political activities of the future. In the legislature, members supporting the same principles must work steadily together; otherwise a parliament becomes nothing more than a collection of shifting groups of individuals, and the system of representation breaks down through its own ineffectiveness. All

this can be done only by political parties. Where parties are insufficiently developed, as in India, the successful working of democratic institutions is doubtful. Where they are suppressed as in Germany, Italy and Russia, democracy is destroyed.[1]

III DICTATORIAL INSTITUTIONS

Better to understand the nature of democratic institutions one has only to observe those institutions which stand in direct opposition to them, that is, dictatorial institutions.

Under dictatorial institutions one party alone is entitled to exist. As one Fascist leader in Italy writes: "The old free State was based on two assumptions: political freedom and the party system. All parties were lawful and were permitted to exist under free rule. To-day, Fascism has entirely superseded such doctrines and practices." It is a familiar joke in Moscow that there may be any number of political parties in the Soviet Union, but under one single indispensable condition: that one party be in power and the others in jail.

All associations whose activities may be regarded as hostile to the party in power are outlawed. One man—the dictator—controls the entire machinery of government. The confidence men of the supreme master control every subordinate department of national life. Not only political associations but trade unions, charitable institutions, athletic clubs, and the like must be directed by men enjoying the confidence of the men in power. Daily papers, reviews, and all other agencies of information must be run by men subservient to the party in power. Books distasteful to the party in power are either suppressed, confiscated, or burned. Judges, public officials, and teachers are dismissed from their posts, and professional men are not allowed to carry on their professions if their political or technical activities run counter to the dictates of the party in power. Ministers of all churches must either keep silent on all matters tabooed by the party in power or join in singing the official anthems if they do not wish to be silenced or have their congregations dispersed. Elective local government is abolished, and local

[1] *Contemporary Review*, Vol. CXLVIII (1935), pp. 263-64.

bodies are run by appointees of the central government. The executive in the central government no longer depends on the legislative power. Parliament is stripped of all real authority. National elections are either abolished or reduced to a sham so as always to give a show of unanimous approval to the party in power. The personal liberty or integrity of the subjects, their property, the privacy of their homes, the right to choose their professions or their religion, are placed at the discretion of the men in power and their police. Actual or potential opponents are not tried by independent judges but by administrative or military courts and have no guarantees of a fair trial. In short, not only political but also personal rights are discarded.

Before the rise of modern dictators a political regime which not only excluded political rights but also violated the personal rights of the subject was termed a "tyranny." An "absolute," or "despotic," or "autocratic" regime was a regime having a hereditary monarch, in which no political rights were granted the subject but under which his personal rights were protected, at least to a certain extent, by fixed laws that not even the sovereign—at least in theory—was entitled to violate. Dictatorship was that form of government in which the man endowed with autocratic power was an upstart who had abolished free institutions. The Czar of Russia was an absolute monarch, whereas Napoleon I and Napoleon III were dictators.

The political institutions of present-day Germany, Italy, and Russia should be termed "tyrannies," since not only political but also personal rights have been discarded. But as a result of the moral degradation which has spread all over the world during the last twenty years, the notions of both personal and political rights have become so obscured in our minds that we no longer make any distinction between tyranny and dictatorship, and as far as Germany, Italy, and Russia are concerned, we term their political constitutions dictatorships while we should term them tyrannies.

Dictatorial or tyrannical regimes to-day are called "fascist." The term was invented in Italy soon after the War of 1914-18 to connote a political party which claimed to be both anti-democratic and anti-communist. It spread from Italy to other countries with the same meaning. Dictatorial or tyrannical regimes which do not abolish private ownership of the means of production and distribution to-day are called "fascist" in order to distinguish them from the dictatorial regime of Soviet Russia.

There is no doubt that the historical origin and the economic structure underlying the Communist dictatorship differ from those upon which are based the Fascist and Nazi dictatorships. The Communist dictatorship in Russia was set up with the aim of creating economic equality by abolishing private ownership of the means of production and of distribution, and it purports to prevent Russia from reverting to the institutions of capitalistic society. On the other hand, both the Fascist and Nazi dictatorships claim to have saved Europe from Communism and maintain that their object is to uphold private ownership, though under increasing governmental supervision. Yet many of the legislative measures by which Hitler has suppressed democratic institutions in Germany are the exact counterpart of Italian Fascist laws. And the latter are but imitations of the laws enacted in Russia by the Communist Party. Hitler ought to pay huge royalties to Mussolini, and Mussolini, in his turn, to Stalin. Thus if the historical origins and the economic aims differ, the political institutions are analogous.

Mussolini has christened his dictatorial regime a "totalitarian" regime. This word has also enjoyed great favour. A totalitarian regime demands the subject's total allegiance to one single authority: that of the dictator and the other subordinate leaders of the party in power. A democratic regime allows the citizen to harbour in his heart different loyalties: toward his family, his parish, his college, his city, his profession, his political party, his fatherland, and even international institutions, such as the Catholic Church or the proletarian Internationale. A democratic regime is not a totalitarian but a pluralistic regime.

Authority, discipline, obedience, are the passwords of dictatorial regimes. Self-reliance, discussion, co-operation, are the passwords of democratic regimes.

s

IV THE PHILOSOPHY OF DEMOCRACY

Whoever deduces the democratic doctrine from the assumption that "all men are born equal," and understands that doctrine in the sense that men are born with equal abilities, takes as a point of departure something which does not exist. The opponents of the democratic doctrine, institutions, and parties need to exert very little effort to show that that assumption is nonsensical, and that since the basis of the construction is absurd, the entire construction disintegrates.

However, one may interpret that formula not in the sense that men are born with equal abilities, but in the sense that all men, in a self-defining civilized community, are entitled to the same personal and political rights and liberties. Thus no longer does one assert a fact but a moral and juridical principle.

On what basis can this principle rest?

It rests on a fact which is demonstrated by the whole of man's experience. Men are born not with equal abilities, but with an equal ability to blunder. No person or group of persons possesses a monopoly on infallibility. There exists no social science as exact as the physical sciences. Forecasts on social life are always uncertain. There are lucky politicians and unlucky politicians. One man just happens to be reaching the door at the very moment it opens, and he enters without the slightest difficulty. Another man may knock for years, and it will never open to him. Sometimes the way out opens up by itself when the people least expect it and without their having contributed in any way to the event. Often, a political leader is deemed wise or foolish merely because he had the good or bad fortune to be in power at a time when favourable or unfavourable coincidences brought about upgrade or downgrade trends in national life. The art of government is, to a large extent, a gamble, because the prediction of social facts is, to a large extent, a gamble.

From this truth that no one is infallible and that no social class possesses a monopoly on intelligence or virtue must be drawn a conclusion to the effect that no social class ought to be vested with a monopoly on political power. Selfishness is only too natural to the human heart. If the enjoyment of political rights and consequent political power is monopolized by one section of the population and withheld from the rest, the privileged section will promote only those measures tending to increase or preserve its own wealth, influence, or prestige. Any initiative which might endanger that position will be combated or allowed to fall. The interests of the sections excluded from political power will be ignored or trampled under foot. Justice will be nothing but the interests of the stronger man as long as it is the stronger man alone who defines Justice. This is why the democratic doctrine re-vindicates for all citizens the right to organize into parties. The party whose leaders inspire the majority of the electorate with the greatest confidence goes to power. If this party fails to justify the confidence placed in it, the electorate puts another party in its place. The various possible solutions of impending problems are thus tried out one after the other. By trial and error—"muddling through," as the English say—a way out is found.

The "masses" are neither more nor less infallible than the "classes." With all the respect due to the memory of Jefferson, we can no longer allow ourselves to be deluded to-day by the idea that if the citizens are permitted free elections they will generally elect "the really good and wise" and that "a natural aristocracy" of "virtue and talents" will arise which does not labour under the drawbacks of "an artificial aristocracy, founded on wealth and birth." The wise man of Monticello lived during a period when human hopes were in the heyday of their youth. In A.D. 1940, we can no longer repeat that the composite judgment of the masses is superior to the composite judgment of the few. The composite judgment of a few or many blunderers is nothing more nor less than the composite blundering of a few or many blunderers. Democratic doctrine does not need to bind itself to outlived slogans. It needs only to assume that a working man may have more horse-sense than a millionaire and that both may blunder to the same degree.

In choosing their representatives the majority of the electorate may be wrong. They may discover soon after turning out one party that they have brought into power a party which is worse than the one that was turned out. In that case the majority of the electorate turns out the incumbent party· at the next election and either returns the first party to power or elects a third. That is why elections are held from time to time. Recurrent elections have been devised for the very purpose of enabling the citizens to correct the blunders they may have committed in former elections. Recurrent elections spring from the negation of the contention that a people is faultless.

The citizen is not a "sovereign" in the sense that he rules the country. In a representative democracy, the sovereignty of the people only means that the citizens have the right to turn out their rulers when the latter, in the opinion of the majority of the electorate, have made too many blunders. When he designates his representatives the citizen merely declares whether he is satisfied or not with prevailing conditions. If he is satisfied, he votes for the party in power.

This is much less majestic than "sovereignty." But it is still a right of great importance. The men in power are thus obliged to be ever on the alert and keep their fingers on the pulse of popular feeling in order not to be uprooted by some tornado of discontent. And when vast streams of dissatisfaction have been created, either by the mistakes or the bad luck of the party in power, an electoral landslide changes the men at the helm and a revolution is avoided. Ballots, no, bullets. No other form of government guarantees broader opportunities to all social forces wanting to have a say in the business of the community. No other form of government thwarts more effectively the establishment and enforcement of political monopolies by any organized minority. No other form of government forces a quicker adaptation to new conditions upon political classes or makes easier the wiping out of those political classes no longer fit to survive. No other form of government gives greater opportunities to assert themselves to individuals having something to say and the urge to assert themselves.

As far as the party in power is concerned, not even its members are "sovereign" in the sense that they rule the country. In that monument of common sense which is John Stuart Mill's *Considerations on Representative Government* (Chapter V), it is clearly stated that "instead of the function of governing, *for which it is radically unfit*, the proper office of a representative assembly is to watch and control the government": to throw the light of publicity on its acts; to censure them if found condemnable; to expel from office the men who compose the government if they fulfil their trust in a manner which conflicts with the deliberate sense of the country, and to be "the nation's Committee of Grievances and its Congress of Opinions."

The philosophy of dictatorship is based on the assumption that humanity is divided into two parts: the "common herd" and the "chosen few." "Some are, and must be, greater than the rest." "The best must rule the rest." But the "chosen few," the "best" must be chosen by someone. This is the business of the dictator. "Authority comes from above." The dictator is infallible. He is the predestined Man, the Saviour, the Healer, something like a Man-God who rules and exacts obedience by the force of his personal superiority over all other men and women. The dictator and his chosen few are allegedly endowed with the mysterious gift of ignoring their private interests and of being acquainted with the higher demands, not only of the present generation but also of the future ones of centuries and millennia to come. This is why the classes must rule and the masses must obey.

The Catholic Church is the most perfectly organized religious dictatorship. The Pope chooses the bishops, who, in turn, ordain the priests. Bishops and priests together form the class of the "chosen few" to whom the faithful owe unquestioning obedience. One God, one truth, one shepherd, and one flock to be guarded from sin and error. This is the logical outcome of the doctrine according to which the Pope is divinely inspired. Gregory XVI, who, upon his death in 1846, left the finances of the Church in indescribable confusion, was convinced that he was infallible even in financial matters. According to the Vatican Council, however, the Pope is infallible only when he speaks *ex cathedra*. But there are zealots who hold that whoever questions his teachings, even when not speaking *ex cathedra*, commits a sin of pride. Pius XII, in his address of August 24th, 1939, announced that the rulers of all peoples "through his voice heard the voice of Christ," that he spoke "in the name of God, of Jesus Christ, and of the Holy Ghost," and that he "brought to men the word of Jesus Christ."

Under the old absolutist monarchies, the King was not as infallible as the Pope, but he was king by divine right and enjoyed the privilege of particular assistance from Heaven. For the sincere monarchist there is something divine even in a constitutional king: "Those of us who were brought up in the Victorian period," writes an English Tory, "were taught to look on the Queen as a being perfect in wisdom and goodness. To a Victorian child it was perhaps only her sex that distinguished her from the Deity; and she was much nearer than God to her people. . . . To her subjects, if not *dea*, she was at least *diva*."[1] The consistent monarchist tolerates parliamentary institutions only as long as parliamentary majorities do not come into conflict with the plans of the sovereign, or rather of the "Crown" or the "Throne" (abstract terms are better fitted to arouse mystical feelings). When a conflict does occur, the consistent monarchist cannot fail to side with the infallible Throne.

Modern dictators are no less infallible than kings by divine right. "Mussolini is always right"—teaches the catechism of the perfect Fascist in Italy. "For the young Fascists," wrote a correspondent of the London *Times* (October 25th, 1935), "Mussolini is a God." A high official of the Department of Public Education told a French newspaperman: "Mussolini is the centre of everything. For our children Mussolini is Divine Providence. Mussolini is a hero. Mussolini is a God."[2] The Catholic Church cannot adopt this doctrine. Yet Pius XI, in December, 1926, went as far as to certify that Mussolini had been "sent by Divine Providence."

In Germany, Goering proclaims: "We Nazis believe that in political affairs Adolf Hitler is infallible, just as the Roman Catholic believes that in religious matters the Pope is infallible.

[1] O. Christi, *The Transition from Aristocracy*, pp. 202-03.
[2] *Echo de Paris*, September 30, 1935.

His will is my law." At the National Convention of the Hitler Youth Movement in February, 1937, the leader of the German Labour Front, Dr. Ley, made the following "confession of faith": "We believe that God has sent us Adolf Hitler, so that Germany may receive a foundation for its existence through all eternity." Dr. Hans Fraulk, Governor-General of German-occupied Poland, said on February 1st, 1940: "To-day the world knows that this one man [Hitler] in all history, this great shaper of German destiny, is a man truly sent to us by Almighty God." Hitler in person has made the following pronouncement: "Providence has ordained that I should be the greatest liberator of humanity. I am freeing men from the demands of a freedom and personal independence which only a few can sustain." No Pope, however, has yet given him a certificate similar to that which has been given Mussolini. But if Hitler decides to respect his concordat with the Vatican, some fine day he will get the same anointment.

One who can never aspire to such privilege is godless Stalin. But even he has his source of infallible inspiration in the Communist Manifesto. Karl Marx begot Nicolai Lenin, and Nicolai Lenin begot Joseph Stalin. In truth, the Communist doctrine does not exalt one single man above all others, but places above all other classes a collective idol, "the proletariat." The leader of the Communist Party is supposed to have received his power from "the proletariat," and not to have conquered it by his own personal strength. All that the Communists say and do is meant to heighten the prestige of that collective entity, "the proletariat," and not to swell the prestige of one individual. But sporadic tendencies toward a personal deification of Stalin appear now and then. On December 5th, 1939, the Soviet radio described Stalin as "the blazing sun of the whole earth." It is impossible to under-estimate human intelligence. So Stalin may also become an infallible God.

Whether provided with divine inspiration or not, dictators are infallible. The leader of a democratic regime says to his adversaries: "I believe I am right and that you are wrong. Let me try and see what are the results of my policies. If they prove unsatisfactory, you will then have your chance to do otherwise." The dictator says: "I am right and the results of my policies cannot but be satisfactory. Every man must be either for me or against me. Whoever declares himself against me will find himself in jail."

The basic assumption of democratic doctrine is humility. Justice Holmes used to say that a democrat is merely a person who does not imagine himself to be a god. Humility is the highway to tolerance and freedom. Intolerance in all dictatorships, be they fascist or communist, be they political or religious, springs from one source which is common to all, pride. If an infallible God were to take over the care of our happiness and salvation, the dictatorship of that God would be the most suitable political regime for ensuring the welfare of the people. Anyone opposing that infallible God would be either a fool or a wicked enemy of the community. His opposition to the infallible God would be an absurdity or a crime. In the event that he could not be convinced by propaganda, he should be put out of the way by fire or the sword. He who is convinced that he possesses the infallible secret of making men wise and happy is ever ready to kill. Robespierre was an incorruptible man who harboured an unmistakable faith in his own righteousness. There was no difference, from this standpoint, between him and the Inquisitor of whom El Greco has left us such a telling portrait. Robespierre therefore sent a great number of people to the guillotine.

The Catholic Church to-day is disarmed and therefore no longer burns heretics. It has to be satisfied with sentencing them to the eternal fires of the hereafter. Stalin, Mussolini, and Hitler are armed. They control this world, not the next. What for religious authorities is a sin is for them a crime. They therefore sentence to death.

Basically, a conflict between two moral outlooks underlies the conflict between the democratic and the dictatorial philosophies. If one likes to bully weaker people and is prepared to bow before any bully stronger than oneself, one longs for a dictator. If one does not like either to bully or be bullied, one cleaves to democratic institutions. The choice depends on the amount of respect one feels for others and for oneself.

Vilhjalmur Stefansson

Ethnologist, Geographer; Past President of the Explorers' Club

WAS LIBERTY INVENTED?

IT is common to praise the ancient Greeks. They were the first this and the greatest that. Pelion upon Ossa and coals to Newcastle may well take a back seat to lauding the Hellenes. They have been so long touted, and with so much ingenuity, that it is a triumph if we can add a leaf to their garland. In this the currently popular historians who deal with the genesis and development of human institutions may have succeeded, to judge from a 1939 article by Professor Hyde.[1] The Greeks, he says, invented liberty. He does not give a year to the invention but dates it earlier than the siege of Troy, which may have been around 1200 B.C.

Dr. Hyde's view, taken seriously, is depressing if we apply it to the chronology of Bishop Ussher; for then we have had liberty among us for half our career since Eden, and have not been getting far with it.

· But naturally Professor Hyde ignores the Bishop and uses instead, or at least implies, the time scale of the paleontologists and the anthropologists; whereupon liberty, if discovered in the second millennium B.C., will have been a human institution for only a tiny fraction of our human course; so that we may well pat ourselves on the back for the progress we have made in so short a time.

Professor Hyde does not define the term liberty except by

---

[1] Walter Woodburn Hyde, "The Origin of Liberty," *Scientific Monthly*, Vol. XLVIII (1939), pp. 519ff.

saying he uses it "in our sense of the word." The authorities he cites to prove that liberty was absent from the empires of the Nile Valley, the Fertile Crescent, and that general neighbourhood are conventional. The article, though brief, does make a sufficient case that liberty "in our sense of the word" was absent from those countries during the two or three millenniums that immediately preceded the Trojan war.

It runs through Professor Hyde's discussion not merely that he himself thinks liberty was invented but that he takes for granted his readers will agree with him. He is a distinguished historian and is, therefore, surely familiar with a large body of the most respected historical writing. So it would appear that the historians as a class, or at a minimum the school to which Professor Hyde belongs, assume that liberty, when first upon the earth, had just been discovered by some human individual or by some group of humans. To an anthropologist, or at least my variety, this permits a startling inside view of a sister discipline which we had supposed to be congenial with our own.

But perhaps we should not be startled; conflicts between disciplines are numerous in the history of science. For instance, those with college four decades behind them can remember classrooms in the same building, or at least on the same campus, where astronomers would not give the sun more than ten million years while the geologists were explaining that the earth required at least a hundred million.

A current sample of like conflict between sciences is the one between anthropology and dietetics as to whether a wholly non-vegetal diet permits good health; more specifically as to whether it contains enough Vitamin C to prevent scurvy. Here the contradictions are flung back and forth just about as they were in the 1900's between the geologists and the astronomers. Teaching in the same universities, issuing books through the same publishers, the protagonists have been challenging each other on several points, three of which we mention.

First, the dietitians make the broad claim that exclusively carnivorous food does not contain enough Vitamin C for optimum health, while the anthropologists support the equally broad contrary thesis that multitudes of people belonging to several races are known to have lived indefinitely in good average health on a diet wholly carnivorous.

More narrowly (and hedging somewhat) the dietitians have also been saying that if it is at all possible to avoid scurvy upon a non-vegetal diet, then it must be through the eating of the whole animal, particularly the "organs rich in Vitamin C" (liver, etc.). Squarely against this has been the teaching of the anthropologists that the typical hunter (at least in the northern third of North America) will have a dog team, and that instead of feeding one whole animal to his family and another whole one to his dogs he will divide each, giving those parts to the dogs which the family least covets. The records of innumerable travellers and other reporters show these less coveted portions, among most if not all hunting tribes, to include most of those organs which the dietitians have called rich in Vitamin C. So the dietitians are telling us that on such a food division as practised by, for instance, the northern Canadian Eskimos and the Athapascans, the people will develop scurvy, but that the dogs will remain in good health; while the anthropologists are declaring that both men and dogs are known to have under Eskimo and Athapasca food division good prospects of average health, and in particular that neither family nor teams will develop scurvy.

The last of our sample contradictions is: The dietitians contend that those who want to remain healthy for long periods exclusively on flesh foods must not merely eat the whole animal but must also see to it that a large part of their food is consumed raw or underdone. Here the countervailing statement of the anthropologist is that although some exclusively carnivorous people, such as the Eskimos, do cook their meat on the average less than we do, there are other wholly carnivorous people, such as the northerly Athapascans, who are meticulous about cooking—so much so that early travellers found them horrified by the sight of Europeans devouring underdone roasts and steaks.

We anthropologists know of many such conflicts with other sciences as we have with dietetics; but, speaking I know for more than just myself, I had no suspicion until reading the article by Professor Hyde that my discipline would look upon as obviously false what historians look upon as obviously true, and in such deep concerns of man as those which relate to social restraints and to freedom from them.

For apparently the historians take as axiomatic that freedom must have been invented by some man or group of men, while we feel that it cannot have been invented by humans since we must have had it already while in the process of growing human. They seem to take the absence of liberty as a natural early human condition; the invention, discovery, or first development of it as necessarily related to a "high" civilization, to one where abstract thought and broad generalization, as well as notable ingenuity and originality, had been developed. We on the other hand take as basic that early man, at least for some time after he began to fit the present definitions of *homo*, was living under a freedom broader than has ever been described by non-Utopian writers that deal with Greece.

We anthropologists feel, then, that the abridgment of liberty, and not liberty, is a human invention. We concede that the Greeks may have reinvented or rediscovered liberty, and that they probably did; but we deny the possibility that they could have been its inventors or discoverers.

Since there appear to be such fundamental differences between historical and anthropological thought upon liberty and the abridgments of liberty, it may be well to present an anthropological view in a book for which these themes are the general topics. For contrast, or at least for an introduction, we give the historian's view, as presented through the *Scientific Monthly* by Dr. Hyde.

> The fact that we Americans enjoy liberty while we imagine certain other nations do not, and the ever present fear that we may conceivably lose it ourselves, shows that we regard its acquisition as a human achievement somewhere in the past. Few of us, however, realize when the idea first appeared on earth and imagine that in some form or other it has always been here, at least since mankind began to be civilized. But we shall see that this is a fallacy and that long periods of civilized man passed without it, and that liberty was evolved late in historical times by one and only one great people—the ancient Greeks.

With this and more for an introduction, Dr. Hyde proceeds to a description of the cultures south and east of the Mediterranean and in the Mediterranean for the millenniums just before the Trojan war, continuing down to the period of the highest development of such freedom as the Greeks had. There is a parallel synopsis of histories. As we have said, a good case is made out for the absence of liberty "as we understand it" from those great empires of the Mediterranean world which are chiefly familiar to us, the Egyptians and the successive powers of the Fertile Crescent down to the Persians, with references to various other countries and powers—among them Crete, Phœnicia, Palestine, and Macedonia.

Coming back to the Greeks of his introductory paragraphs Dr. Hyde presents his claims for them as the first·people who ever had liberty. The statement is forceful, and no doubt logical upon such premises as historians of that school keep at the back of their minds. We give a not unfair, although perhaps inadequate, summary through quotations. Some of these are divided by only a few lines of text while others have paragraphs between them.

> . . . To have "invented" liberty, as I like to term it, is, to my mind, the great thing the Greeks did or could have done, beside which all their other achievements in thought, art and literature, however remarkable, were secondary. . . .
> . . . We first see the idea [of liberty] dimly adumbrated in the council of chiefs before Troy as described by Homer, but the germ was older, doubtless brought into the peninsula of Greece from the grasslands of the Danube by the ancestors of the historical Greeks who perfected it. . . .

Those who write to-day about Greek liberty depend for their material chiefly upon what the Greeks wrote, and then upon what others have written about them. From this type of study there come, no doubt usually, results as given by Professor Hyde, among them that:

> . . . . Freedom also kept the Greeks from tabus and asceticism, for their religion allowed them a sane use of nature's gifts. Their morality, like other features of their lives, was governed by "moderation." Greek ethics was a social and not a religious phenomenon. . . . There was no divine sanction to their rules

of conduct. . . . Their simple ethics freed them from any deep
sense of sin or fanaticism for unattainable perfection. The Greek
accepted life, lived here and now, and was little concerned with
doctrines of immortality. He hated death as much as we Christians
do—but for a different reason. He hated it, but did not fear it.

These deductions confirm us in that when the historians use
liberty "in our sense of the word," they are really using it as
the anthropologists do. Take my own case, for instance. In
several of my books, among them *Hunters of the Great North,
My Life with the Eskimo,* and a chapter which I contributed to
the volume *I Believe,* I have said about the Eskimos that they
had liberty and also that they had most if not all of the things
which Professor Hyde tells us about the Greeks—the only
hedging that might be required here would be on taboo. But,
perhaps through not being familiar with the historical point
of view, it did not occur to me to attribute all such things
among the Eskimos to Eskimo liberty, as Professor Hyde
attributes them among the Greeks to Greek liberty.

The Greeks had the things Professor Hyde names, and they
also had liberty; the Eskimos had the same things, and they
had liberty. There is, then, nothing in the compared or contrasted results of the students of the Greeks and of the Eskimos
that is incompatible with the idea that the traits above described, among others, may coexist with liberty.

From such works as the *Encyclopædia of the Social Sciences* it
will appear, I now realize, that Professor Hyde's conception of
the origin and nature of liberty is well known and has been
printed frequently. We may, then, consider that the case for
the Greeks has been sufficiently stated. On that assumption we
proceed to a discussion of liberty as it is found among the most
primitive peoples of to-day—those farthest back on that scale
which runs from Iron Age through Bronze and Neolithic to
Middle, Old Stone, and Pre-Stone. We take our descriptions
naturally from those men of to-day who combine the qualities
of being in their own culture farthest back from the Iron Age
and of being, through reasons of geography, history, and the
like, most nearly uninfluenced by contemporary "high" cultures. For me it is convenient to depend chiefly upon the

Eskimos, for they fit our specifications and I happen to know them through having lived with them many years as one of themselves.

Like Professor Hyde for the Greeks, we find it difficult for the Eskimo case to discuss liberty, as it were, in a vacuum. So we give a background sketch of their lives. We have to make it perhaps a little more detailed than Professor Hyde does, for he presents his argument to readers whom he knows to be familiar with Greek history and culture; we must present ours to an audience most of whom we know to be unfamiliar with the corresponding aspects of life and nature among the Eskimos.

We need in fact also a brief general introduction to our statement.

Liberty of course has a meaning chiefly in relation to its opposite, the abridgment of liberty. Biologists say that liberty has been abridged by certain animals, among them ants; but it has not been similarly contended that abridgments of freedom have been discovered among the animals biologically nearest man, his cousins (if not his ancestors) the apes.

By average scientific opinion, we have been human at least a million years. For ultra-conservatism, bring that estimate down to a hundred thousand; still man had run more than nine-tenths of his human course long before the siege of Troy. So far as the mere chances are concerned, this is plenty of time for the development of that curtailment of liberty which most of us agree was found in Egypt, Babylonia, Persia, and the rest of those countries during the millenniums immediately before Christ.

The Andaman Islanders, the Tasmanians, the Tierra del Fuegans, and the Eskimos had, all of them, spent the same 90,000 years with the same opportunity for devising institutions that fetter liberty.

American anthropologists, at a congress in 1939, passed a resolution by what the newspapers said was a unanimous vote to the effect that if there are pronounced intellectual differences between races then we have not as yet discovered what they are. *A priori*, then, the ancestors of the four groups we have named might, any or all of them, have developed such techniques for abridging liberty as chattel or wage slavery. It is equally true that, having developed the curtailment of freedom to any conceivable degree, they might have gone intò a reverse cycle—they might have rediscovered liberty, as the ancestors of the Greeks also might have and may have 10,000, 30,000 or 70,000 years before Troy.

On a basis of mere logic you would think that, with many different cultures in the world at the time of Columbus, a factual survey of the globe might have discovered a highest degree of servitude among one people, a highest development of liberty with another, and various grades between in various other countries or cultures. Those of high average freedom in 1492 might have been the descendants of a group who, one or two thousand years earlier, had a low freedom ratio; and the reverse with other groups.

What we have just stated may be called the anthropological view. In essence it is that abridgments of liberty tend to increase, both in variety and degree, as you move from simple to complex social conditions, from cultures that are "low" to those that are "high." There is an opposed popular view, that liberty goes with "advanced" culture. Then there ought to be most liberty in some such place as a university centre, like Cambridge, Massachusetts, or Ann Arbor, Michigan, and least in whatever part of the world is most remote culturally from these standards. If we could discover, contemporaneous with our university communities, others that conform to our usual description of the "Stone Age," we should (by this view) find a community where freedom was abridged a great deal more than in Cambridge.

Now it did happen to me that, after being a teaching fellow and a sort of instructor in anthropology at Harvard, I went from Cambridge to live with a Stone Age community and had a chance for a first-hand comparison of their liberties.

We of the United States were not as freedom-conscious when I left Cambridge in 1906 as most people there and elsewhere in the United States were in 1936. However, we had all recited in school, Burns on chains and slavery and Patrick Henry on the choice between liberty and death. Back in the sixth grade I was as convinced of the wrongness of British Colonial taxation as any of my Wall Street friends are to-day of the inequity of New Deal taxes. So I was, even in 1900, freedom-conscious to a degree. On my second Arctic expedition in 1910, about the first mental comparisons I made between the university town at the mouth of the Charles and the Eskimo villages at the mouth of the Coppermine were some bearing upon freedom.

It is not necessary here to prove that my associates in Cambridge, Massachusetts, were of an "advanced" culture. It is necessary to explain, at least briefly, the life in Coronation Gulf to bring out the distance in social institutions between an American college town and a Stone Age community.

A description of the culture of those Eskimos with whom I lived first during the year 1910-11 gives practically our definition of the "lowest savagery." They had no food except the tissues of animals. They used fire for cooking, as man is thought to have done in every land of the earth through many decades of centuries. They dressed exclusively in skins, as the ancestors of the North Europeans are believed to have done when England and France were in their ice ages. They used copper extensively, but merely hammered and ground into shape. For their stone implements and weapons they did not use the elaborate chipping by which we know the Late and Middle Stone Ages, and were thus in the Old Stone Age. Indeed, it has been suggested by T. A. Rickard, a student of the implements and weapons of ancient man, author of *Man and Metals* and numerous similar works, that the Coronation Gulf Eskimos were in a cultural period earlier than any of the proper Stone Ages.

The Gulf people made fire by striking together lumps of pyrite and, if they had to, by friction of wood on wood. They lived during summer in tents of undressed skins; during winter in houses of snow. Their only domestic animal was the dog, their only vehicles the sled and skin boat. For caribou and bears they used spears; for these and other animals they used the bow and arrow; for the seal they used harpoons. Their fuel was the fat of animals and so was their light.

T

Under their Stone Age way of life, these Eskimos were neither pathetic in our eyes, when we had become used to living with them, nor were they wretched in their own. They liked winter better than summer and were glad the summers, with stifling heat and swarms of biting insects, were brief. They liked the sea coast better than the treeless prairie inland; but they liked that prairie better than the woods farther south, to which they resorted only when they needed material for sledges or implements. They believed themselves to have a better country than the forest Indians, and were correct in that so far as I could judge, for I have lived with those Indians and they were, both in their own eyes and mine, a wretched people, starving more often than the Eskimos. They shivered a hundred times more, for they were as badly protected from the cold as the Eskimos were well protected—they had never developed a culture really suited to their environment, while the Eskimo culture seemed to me nearly perfect in its time and place, yielding a sense of stable security and ministering to comfort.

The Gulf Eskimos were not merely satisfied with their country and climate but also with nearly everything else. They considered meat, the tissues of animals, the finest diet in the world; they had plenty of it and were in good health on it, the best I have seen anywhere. That animals should eat vegetation and that people should eat the animals seemed to them not merely normal but desirable. They were so dressed and housed that, to judge from my experience when clothed and living similarly, they were more comfortable in winter than people usually are in New York or London. They were more free from skin troubles than we, although (or because) they knew not soap or towels and never bathed. They never washed, but their faces looked as clean as ours. Their body odours were less conspicuous than ours, no doubt in part through a Mongolian nature that is less smelly than the European, but also I think because their clothes did not capture and store up body secretions as do our fibrous undergarments. There were strong smells in their dwellings but they were smells of foods which are liked—no one finds very reprehensible the smell of a cheese if he likes its taste, and certainly we do not ordinarily find distasteful the odours of steaming coffee or grilled bacon.

The foregoing is a personal statement. In the literature concerning primitive Eskimos there are two diametrically opposed views, that they are the happiest people in the world and that they are the most wretched. A fair analysis will usually show that those who call them wretched mean that the writers think they would themselves be wretched if they were living Eskimo style; while those who call the Eskimos happy are judging objectively, by laughter and smiles and signs of contentment.

Of course there are unhappy people in Eskimo Land as there is wretchedness in Merrie England. What those mean who say the Eskimos are happy is that the average of happiness seems to be greater than what the travellers are used to when at home.

But we are supposed to discuss here not happiness but freedom, and these are not inevitably synonymous.

There are, of course, many sorts of liberty. The first, chronologically, is in a child's relation to parents and to other grownups. On this the travellers vary from saying that Eskimo children are never punished to saying that they are seldom punished, or less often than in other countries. A part of this freedom from punishment is freedom from restraint. Among the forest Indians, just to the south of Coronation Gulf, infants are strapped to a board much of the time during their first year. Our children are in cribs and cradles. The Eskimo child crawls around on the floor with a lack of restraint which, at the least, is not common among us. Our children do not get what they cry for unless we think it good for them. When the Eskimo child wants something he usually gets it, whether from our point of view it is good for him or not. To be concrete, when a two-year old child wants the scissors he is almost certain not to get them with us and almost certain to get them with the Eskimos.[1]

---

[1] On why Eskimo children are allowed to play with scissors, and why their general freedom is more than that of our children, see, for instance, the author's *My Life with the Eskimos*, pp. 395-403.

There is a like relative difference between most of a child's other freedoms when we compare Eskimo ways to ours. During the period of youth our children are told what to do, and so are the young Eskimos, but with the important difference that the punishment of recalcitrants may be and frequently is both mental and physical with us but can be only mental with the Eskimos—bad children suffer both disapproval and spanking with us; with the Eskimos there are no spankings or slaps but only the disapproval of family and associates.

In theory, marriages are equally free with us and with the Eskimos; they are upon the advice of parents and friends or on personal inclination in both cases. In practice the freedom of marrying whom you like is somewhat greater with the Eskimos. Subsequent to marriage, their freedom is definitely greater. With us the parents of a young couple are, on both sides, expected to advise them that the union should be permanent or at least should be continued for a time. With the Coronation Gulf Eskimos it did occur that parents advised either the young husband or the young wife; but this was bad form, meeting the disapproval of the community. And certainly there were many cases where a couple separated without anyone advising them against doing so—it was not considered the affair of either parents or friends.

With us the desired mate is free to say no to a proposal; that is so, too, among the Eskimos. With us freedom of saying no disappears with marriage, and we are expected to sympathize with the one who prefers to continue the union. With the Eskimos, after marriage as before, the sympathy of the community is with the one who is unwilling. A woman, or man either, has just as much right to refuse the continuance of a marriage as to refuse entering upon it.

Among the Eskimos, as with us, differences of personality are such that in one family the man has his way usually, in another the woman. We have a theory, however, that the man should control, usually or always; that the woman should have her way seldom or never. The Eskimos make no such distinction between husband and wife; neither is supposed to have any authority over the other. It is no more improper for the woman to be the stronger character than for the man to be.

From what we have just said follows the absurdity of stories that "primitive" Eskimo husbands lend their wives to other men. This can be true, and is true, only among those Eskimos who are no longer "primitive" but who have adopted the white man's religion and customs to that extent which makes wife-lending possible. The wife-lenders, then, are Eskimos who have surrendered their own belief that man and woman are equal, each without authority over the other, and have taken in its place a view based upon the Christian nuptial promise of a woman that she will obey her husband and upon the European attitude that a man should be master in his own house. This means, of course, that stories which you have read about Greenland Eskimos lending their wives to white men may very well be true; for, after all, those Eskimos have been in close association with Danes, and with other Europeans, for two hundred years. They began to adopt Christian marriage vows, through the rule of the church, so many generations ago that no doubt it seems to Greenlanders of to-day as if the obedience of wives and the lending of them had always been Greenland customs.

Sex jealousy, as we understand it, seemed unknown among the Eskimos of Coronation Gulf as recently as 1910; it is said to have become fairly common before 1930. During those twenty years perhaps half or three-fourths of the five hundred or so Coronation Eskimos had died off, through diseases introduced by the whites, while their culture had been affected materially by traders, missionaries, and particularly by Christian Eskimos who had moved in from the Mackenzie River district of north-western Canada and from Alaska. With these whites and Christian Eskimos had come the wedding pledge of obedience to the husband and the European idea that a man is the head of a household, that a woman is a kind of property, and that either husband or wife is disgraced by the "social misconduct" of the other—especially that a man can be disgraced by what his wife does.

The Coronation Eskimos, like those who have been described from other regions not strongly influenced by whites or Athapascan, Algonquin, and other Indians, were communistic anarchists. The kind and degree of their freedom will appear through a discussion of their communism and of their anarchy.

That communism means nobody owning anything is, of course, merely a device of polemics; or, if you like, any communism is a modified communism. Stone Age Eskimos owned certain things and did not own others.

In Coronation Gulf, land could not be owned. Neither could it be in the Mackenzie region to the west. The question of house ownership could not arise in the Gulf district, for there cold-weather dwellings were of snow and thereby transient. But in the Mackenzie, where houses were of earth and wood, it could arise. We digress, therefore, to explain that in the Mackenzie delta the builders owned a house as long as they dwelt in it, but lost all title when they moved out. However, there would necessarily grow up, and did grow up, a practical definition of what was meant by moving out. A family known to be on a journey, and to plan coming back, was looked upon as still in the house. There was, however, a tacit requirement that owners leave behind things to indicate they were coming back. If it was winter, and if they expected to return before spring, they would leave their belongings in the house and would close the door. But if the absence was to include the break-up, as between March, which is winter, and June, which is summer, then they would leave goods in a depot outside; for it is the nature of the Mackenzie houses that they leak and are damp in spring, which has an unfortunate effect upon most things that are Eskimo property.

If a family were planning to be away a whole year, and were to try to keep the house vacant during that time by a combination of leaving things in it and of asking that it be kept vacant, the conduct would be recognised as anti-social. Persistence in anti-social conduct is practically inconceivable on the Eskimo Stone Age cultural level. I have never heard from them, or read of them in books, that an attempt was actually made to keep a house vacant for more than a few weeks or at most a few months. The normal thing, if you were moving away, would be to think of somebody whom you liked, whose house was not as good as yours, and to suggest that he and his family be ready to move in when you move out. For it is recognized that an occupant, whether the original builder of a house or not, has at least such right over it that he could turn it over upon leaving to anyone whom he liked who happened to need it.

But the community would be the ultimate judge of whether the friend needed the house. If it were obvious that he did not need it, then (for the reasons we have mentioned, that in primitive Eskimo society you do not go against public opinion) the man who is starting on the journey would, to begin with, make no suggestion to his friend about moving in; but were he so callous to local feeling as to make the suggestion, then his friend, unless equally callous, would decline. This is another point on which we have no direct evidence—I have neither heard of nor read about a case where anyone moved into a vacated house unless his doing so met the approval of the community.

The approval of an Eskimo group may, of course, depend on friendships, or on personal liking, as with us; but in theory always, and in practice at least usually, the community approval of a family moving into a vacated house is based upon their being known to need the house.

A Mackenzie River saying has it that "There is no more sense in wanting a house that is too big for you than in wanting a coat that is too big for you." Therefore, a small family who build a large house will invite a family they like to share it with them. In practice, the wife has more of a say here than the husband, for it will be the two women, with their children, who constantly are at home while the men are out hunting. But although congeniality between the women is of more importance than between the men there may be a situation where the decision rests with, or at least is based upon, the children. If they are old enough they have strong preferences in playmates and will clamour that a family shall be invited which has the right number and kind of children.

As this paper is being written come stories from England which show that the Eskimo view of housing, never wholly alien with us, is just now much to the fore.

A friend writes from south-western England that in a way he is lucky; his country home is so small that obviously there is room in it for no more than his own family. It seems there is in his village a local committee which receives children that have been evacuated from London, studies the housing facilities of various homes in the district, studies also personal congenialities, and then by just such common-sense methods as were used by the Eskimos of Mackenzie River decides upon which householder the children shall be quartered. The chief difference seems to be one of procedure. In England the matter is formally determined by a committee formally chosen; among the Eskimos the thing happens more informally, and as it were naturally, for it is the entire community and not a selected group which makes the decision. Nor do Eskimos have set conclaves, like a New England town meeting or a Russian soviet. They just talk things over informally when they happen to meet—outdoors, within doors, in somebody's home or in the club-house. No vote is taken, but there develops a consensus of opinion. This is based upon all the factors applicable, such as whether given families are friends or strangers, whether the children involved on both sides are of ages such that they will play well together, whether a local family has no child and will, for that reason, provide a specially desirable home.

Clearly things are not wholly formal in the British arrangement. There is no doubt that, especially in small villages, public sentiment gradually makes itself felt informally in Devonshire or Cornwall much as it does at Mackenzie River or Point Barrow.

Land and houses considered, we turn next to food with the Eskimos and take a special case to bring out a general view.

There are two seals in Coronation Gulf, the "common" and the "bearded;" the common weighs usually less than a hundred pounds, the bearded several hundred. A sealer who gets a small one takes it to his wife, who skins it and cuts it up. She keeps the skin for family use and so with the fat and the lean. She may give some of the food uncooked to a neighbour, but usually she cooks as much as the size of her pot allows, and either invites the neighbours to join in a meal at her house or send portions of cooked food to families that are known to be without fresh meat.

When a hunter secures a bearded seal he does not take it home but stands on a small ice hummock with hands outstretched long enough to turn around three times slowly. All hunters who see him doing this gather, and the most influential of them cuts the seal into as many pieces as there are hunters present. This master of ceremonies gets the second last piece; so that he has been, to an extent, punished for being eminent, just as the hunter, who gets the last piece, is punished for being successful. However, in a community where no one lacks for anything as long as anyone has something, this issue is really academic.

The reward which the hunter gets for his success is that he is the hero of the hour. He is like a football player who has made a touchdown. If he consistently has better success in getting large seals than do the other hunters, he is like a player who can be relied on to make gains for his team whenever at all possible.

It is a matter of detail and not of fundamentals that there are different rules for the handling of common and bearded seals. The end result is the same; the community shares with approximate equality the benefit of any success.

We turn once more to Mackenzie River, and for an example rather than a principle, when we tell of their fishing.

A large Mackenzie family with whom I lived the winter of 1906-07, at one stage twenty-three of us, had tons and tons of fish accumulated by midwinter. Then the less successful hunters and fishers began to come in from various districts. At first we took them into our house; they ate our fish with us; their women shared in the cooking and sewing; their men and some of their women helped us in fishing. When there was no more room in our house the gathering hunters began to erect snowhouses or other dwellings in a cluster around our house. The fishing season was over, and we were getting only a few each day. The inroads of people and dog teams upon the fish pile were daily more noticeable; in a few weeks nearly all the fish were gone. At that stage the custom is to load sledges to capacity with the last of the fish and to scatter in various directions for hunting grounds that are supposed to be better. In the Mackenzie district this usually worked, for I was not able to learn that there had been a famine in the region within the memory of anyone living, or within the survival of reliable tradition.

As long as there was room, the visitors had as much right as we to bunk in our house. When the houseroom was gone the newcomers were, of course, free to build their own camps. Everybody within our house or without it was as free to use fish for men or dogs as we who had caught them. There was no chance for the most prominent man in our family, or for anyone else, to play Lord Bountiful. The people who gathered around us did admire us for the activity and success with which we had carried on the fishing; they acknowledged freely that we had done much better than they. They admired us and they liked us; but it was not in their way of thinking to be grateful to us, except as a town is grateful to a civic leader or a school to a winning ball team.

But we did have a slight degree of food ownership in the fish catch. As said, no one had to ask permission to use our fish locally nor did any have to ask permission for loading up their sleds with "our" fish when the camp finally broke up; but if a traveller came along who spent a day or two with us and then passed on, he would have to ask for fish if he wanted to take some away with him, and he would expect to pay—would pay unless we who had caught the fish said to him specially that we did not want pay.

This about freedom with dwellings and with fish in Mackenzie River is said with diffidence, in that Eskimos there had been in touch with whites—off and on, remotely, for half a century; then constantly and more intimately for the seventeen years just before I spent with them the winter of 1906-07. So their customs might have changed to some extent. I did, however, question them searchingly on how things used to be, finding evidence of change sometimes and no doubt occasionally failing to discover proof of a change that really had taken place. Therefore, we discuss here Mackenzie River only when no sample of what we are trying to bring out is available from

Coronation Gulf. Otherwise this paper is based mainly upon the Gulf Eskimos, some five hundred of whom had never seen a white man before 1910, so they cannot have suffered much change through European influence.

When a Coronation meal was being eaten you would not join unless you were invited; but you were sure to be invited. If your house was short of food you would not send a petition to another house; but the people next door knew about as much as you did about the food situation of your own family and would not think of eating without either sending you a part of their meal or else asking specially that you join them. The only modification of this procedure was that instead of sending a message to every house a woman might get one of the children to run out and shout at the top of his voice that they were about to eat. If people didn't hear the shout it was their misfortune, unless a neighbour took it upon himself to let them know.

Freedom of visiting back and forth was controlled in these Eskimo villages exactly as it is among us when we live in friendly groups. In nothing is a child better trained than in watching for signs of being not quite welcome. They learn not to shout when anybody wants to sleep. They learn to go outdoors when they notice that the house is getting too crowded. It is not merely that public opinion is so strong that no one resists it but also that everyone is taught to watch for the slightest signs of individual or collective irritation.

There were in Coronation Gulf no men or women of authority, but everyone had influence gauged by a lifetime of association. In a period of scarcity an outsider might get the impression of authority when a man said he was going inland, hunting, and everybody followed him; but if you knew the language and understood the people you would realize that they followed Brown rather than Jones because they thought his judgment better—Brown led them only in the sense of being first to announce that he would go; people followed because they thought his to be a good lead. It was like getting a Wall Street tip that a Napoleon of finance was buying a certain stock.

Not merely did the Eskimos have no chiefs but they had no

prisons or other forms of confinement, no floggings or things of that sort. There were only two forms of punishment, the disapproval of the community and death. Theoretically, the death punishment was inflicted only for that crime which is worst in the Eskimo calendar, trouble-making, and it should not be inflicted until the community was unanimous, which, in practice, meant years of discussion. The execution should be by the nearest of kin, for then a blood feud would not arise.

We discuss the vendetta only as it bears on the degree of freedom. The feud ought not to start, because a man who knew he was being discussed for execution would move away to another community. Having to do that is not as serious with them as with us, for they own no houses or other property which by its nature must be left behind; they could take with them their personal property. They would be welcome in another community even if it were known why they had come; a man would have to develop a local unpopularity before falling in line for execution.

In operation an Eskimo blood feud was similar to those of Kentucky or Sicily, except that there was no concerted effort to exterminate one of the two families involved—it was sufficient for your family to be one ahead in the score of killings. A feud usually closed by that family moving away which, at a given time, was one ahead. If they moved far enough away, the feud would die out.

The blood feud was no doubt the worst single element in the Eskimo social organization, but it was not a problem related to freedom or liberty, as these are usually understood. We have in fact described the feud chiefly to show that the question of freedom is not involved.

We have said that small animals rather than big were handled as if they were private property, but that in reality neither was private property in our sense. We have said that land could not be owned at all and that a house was not owned after our manner of ownership. Portable articles, however, were owned with the Coronation Eskimos in just our way. Their bows and arrows were as much their private property as rifles and cartridges are with our sportsmen. They owned their knives, spears, harpoons, fire implements, cooking pots—in fact, anything and everything that could be carried with you on a sledge or in a boat. And of course they owned sledges and boats as we own our cars and our power launches. And whatever you own you may sell, with the Stone Age Eskimos as with us.

Property obviously common to the whole family was never sold by husband or wife unless both were in agreement. Mature children in the family were consulted; young ones were not consulted, but they were listened to tolerantly if they expressed strong views, as through fondness of a dog or pride in a sleigh. With dog trading especially, even a young child might have considerable influence.

When the thing to be sold was clearly individual property, as a man's crooked knife or a woman's case of needles, there was also consultation at least of husband and wife; but this was looked upon more as a courtesy than a necessity. It was rare that either discouraged the sale of a thing which naturally was in the province of the other.

There was in our Stone Age community a recognized scale of prices, but it was also recognized that a special case may bring out a new value. A dog may have a standard price of two six-inch copper knives; but everybody will appreciate your being willing to exchange a dog for one knife, or even two dogs for one knife, if you have many dogs and are in special need of a knife. If you have nothing with which to buy a knife or a dog, your chances among Eskimo friends of receiving them as presents are about the same as with us among our friends. And, just as among us, you might take the knife or dog as a present but would say to yourself, or even say aloud, that you expected to pay when you were able.

We have not given a complete view of freedom among the Stone Age Eskimos of Coronation Gulf, and cannot do so, for this is a chapter and not a whole book. But the examples we have taken are fair. We might add a few things, as a mere recital. Children are free to do, if they can, the work of grown people; the grown may play children's games, by themselves or with the children, and not lose caste. Men may do women's work and women men's work. One or a few women may travel with many men, one or a few men with many women. When people are eating in two groups there may be all men in one and all women in the other; but usually there is the same number of persons in each group, so that if there are fewer women in the party there may be two or three men eating with the women.

Coronation Gulf had no exceptions to sex equality, but exceptions are known from the far west and far east. In Greenland, for instance, the rowing of the big boats was done by women, the steering by a man. Apparently there was something in the nature of disgrace to a man in having to row with the women.

This does not mean that there was no division of work. For obvious and mainly biological reasons the women looked after the children, kept house, and did the chief work of the camp, while the men hunted. There was no more disgrace, however, or impropriety, in a woman's hunting than there is with us in a woman's driving a car or piloting an airplane. If a man stayed home and looked after the children while the wife went hunting, it was always for a natural reason—that he was lame, that he was recovering from an illness, that he was snowblind, or something of that sort. You never say to a man that it is too bad he has to look after the children; what you say, and feel, is that his being lame is unfortunate.

It is not possible to find among Homer's, Plato's, or any other Greeks an approach to such complete liberty as there was among the Stone Age Eskimos of Coronation Gulf. The liberty was similar among all those Eskimos whom I have visited who were near enough to "savagery" so that I felt I could rely on what they were telling me about former days.

There seem, indeed, to be no writings for any part of the world, except perhaps a few of those on Utopias, which have ever described a human society that had more kinds of liberty or higher degrees of them than we found in 1910 among the Eskimos of Coronation Gulf.

With the Indians next south, the northerly Athapascans, liberty was on nearly as high a level when I was with them at various times between 1906 and 1912.

Roughly speaking, and of course with numerous exceptions, there was in North America a decrease of pre-Columbian liberty as you went south from its north coast, an increase of the infringements on some or most of the different liberties, until you came to a maximum of infringement, a minimum of liberty, in what we now call Mexico and Central America.

Again with numerous exceptions, the march southward, away from the Eskimos and from liberty, coincided with an advance upon districts of higher and higher culture, or at least of cultures which we speak of as higher.

Not alone in the New World but throughout the whole world it appears to be a rule, if not a law, that infractions upon liberty grow as communities grow, whether the community growth be in numbers, in culture, or in both. Such at least is the anthropological position; which does not mean that we disagree with the historians when they say that among the Greeks, and among a number of other peoples, restraints upon liberty are known to have decreased parallel with an increase in population and a growing complexity of social organization. In that connection we return to matters upon which we have touched before.

The agreement between the disciplines of anthropology and history upon liberty among the Greeks (seemingly in every respect except upon whether the Greeks invented it) leads us to ask whether we are perhaps guilty of a purely verbal dispute. Is there no issue here but the definition of a term? Have the historians so redefined liberty (even while saying with Professor Hyde that they are using it "in our sense of the word") that they can consistently speak of as having liberty people like the Greeks, for whom even the historians claim only a limited amount of freedom, and then speak of as not having liberty people like the Eskimos who, in comparison with the Greeks, had a larger number of freedoms and had many if not most of them in a higher degree?

Evidently the historians must have re-defined liberty, at least in the back of their minds; for they do speak of liberty having been invented by the Greeks.

Seemingly, then, the historian does not think it an exercise of liberty when an Eskimo group makes a decision through informal conversations during a few months and an informal arrival at a majority opinion which governs their conduct for some time thereafter; but he does think it an exercise of liberty when Republicans and Democrats campaign the United States for several months, cast a ballot on the first Tuesday after the first Monday in November, and thereby arrive at a decision which governs the United States for some time.

Or do the historians perhaps think we have liberty because we have both democratic institutions and great power as a nation, but that the Eskimos have not liberty (although their institutions are freer than any democracy) because they are not powerful enough to withstand, say, the Government of the North-west Territories of Canada or that of the Territory of Alaska? If so, the historians speak merely as of to-day.' For if they will consider the evidence they will find that the Eskimos of northernmost North America were more powerful than the Indians just south of them when white men first arrived in those districts, and that there is indication they had been more powerful than any other people of whom they had even hearsay knowledge for more centuries than the United States has yet been a free nation. We in America are more affected to-day by the actions of a country like Argentina or Hungary than the Eskimos of northern Canada were through at least a number of centuries by the conduct of the Athapascan Indians—the only people with whom there was any known chance they could come in contact.

We mentioned, when saying that the Eskimos of northern Canada had most of those things which Professor Hyde specifies as being the results of Greek liberty, that the chief, if not the only, exception would be taboo. The Greeks may not have been quite so free from taboo as the Professor intimates, or at least one sees the chance for a debate with him on it; but certainly they were freer than the Eskimos. The Greeks were not, however, freer than the Eskimos from sex taboos. There are a number of classes of taboos which we have to-day that neither the Greeks nor the Eskimos had; there is also a large and rigid class of taboos which the Eskimos do have that were less developed or absent among the Greeks.

That Eskimo taboos are a serious restriction upon freedom is not quite as true for them as it has been for the Jews at certain stages of their culture.

Eskimo food taboos, their largest single group, are not of the kind the Jews had. There is, for instance, no Eskimo concept which is nearly related to the Jewish idea that you must not use the flesh of an animal unless it splits the hoof and chews the cud, nor do the Eskimos have anything resembling kosher meat. But while the Eskimo food taboo does not resemble a Deuteronomy taboo, it does resemble the prohibitions that are imposed upon us by physicians. A doctor tells me to go easy on meat; he prescribes for you the avoidance of cocktails; to Jones he forbids a group of foods which he claims are fattening; to Brown he forbids certain breakfast cereals because (he says) they might aggravate a digestive trouble. "Doctor's orders," when of that kind, resemble superficially at least the food taboos of the Eskimos.

Our historians do not seem to feel it a notable abridgment of the liberties of the American people that tens of thousands of us are following taboos for which we have paid a doctor or which we have taken from the pages of a magazine.

The case for the closer resemblance of Eskimo food taboos to modern ones than to those of biblical Jews is strongest when we make it for sections of the Eskimo territory like Coronation Gulf that are most removed from known outside influences. The Coronation group had, so far as I discovered, only one taboo that resembled the Jewish—none of them ever ate bear livers. The rest of their taboos were individual. An old lady had said about her newborn grandson that until he killed his first caribou he must not eat marrow from the left front leg of any caribou. A father had said to his young son that until he was able to build his first good snowhouse he was never to break a marrow bone by hitting it against a stone, but must always lay it down first and hit it with the stone. A shaman had been to the moon and had learned up there that caribou would soon appear if everyone in the community (or perhaps all the

U

women in the community, or all the childless women in the community, or the left-handed men in the community, or something of that sort) would refrain from eating grouse livers. As the result of a trance a shaman had informed an expectant mother that she would have easy delivery if she walked around the house from right to left, and not from left to right, the first time she went outdoors each morning, and if at the same time she chewed on a piece of sinew, without swallowing it.

Such were the typical Coronation taboos—surely not much greater infringements on liberty than our seeing the moon over the right (or is it the left?) shoulder, not walking under a ladder, or being careful to knock on wood.

The Eskimos of the Colville section in Alaska did have a number of taboos that resembled the old Jewish ones. No child of a given sex might eat certain parts of an animal until attaining a certain age or achieving a certain goal. Specific parts of certain animals might not be eaten by a woman before marriage; there were other parts that she might not eat even after marriage until her first child was born; and there were food taboos where a woman did not attain complete freedom until after her fifth child. Even so, there might be abridgments of the same freedom if one of her children were ill, a different abridgment if two of them were ill, and still another if her brother's child was ill.

These mountain Eskimos of Alaska, and some others, had indeed developed (or borrowed) a taboo system that outsmarted Deuteronomy. But would the historians think of Jews as unfree though they had the taboos of Deuteronomy if they had also the freedoms of the Greeks? The Colville Eskimos had more freedom than the Greeks.

The anthropological part of our discussion has been upon the assumption that liberty "in our sense of the word" is that liberty of which we are thinking when we say that Hitler, Stalin, or Roosevelt are wanting to deprive us of it. We have not tried, except for mentioning the possibility of a verbal dispute, to discuss a liberty such that a Greek is free if he has it and an Eskimo is not free though he has it.

CONCLUSIONS

We state some conclusions regarding liberty, not from their having been established by this inadequate discussion but rather from the general nature of the body of anthropological facts and resulting doctrine.

If we know that man is descended from apes, or from an apelike animal, then we surely know that he cannot have invented liberty during the time he was becoming or since he became man; for you do not invent the thing you have. We believe that what man did invent was the infringement of liberty. More, we think we know he must have done so; for we seem agreed both that earlier he did not have it and that later he had it.

We think, from a comparative study of the scale- running from what we call primitive to what we call high, that there is most freedom in the lowest cultures, though with exceptions; and that there is usually least in the middle group. In the highest cultures you are watching a group of prestidigitators; for now you see liberty and now you don't.

If the Greeks are known to have rediscovered liberty, whether once or twice, it does not seem improbable that the Mexicans of 1500, if not molested by the Spaniards, might have rediscovered a liberty which their forefathers began to lose when they were at some such stage of culture as that of the Coronation Eskimos of 1910. For the probability seems to be that the ideas and devices both of liberty and of servitude have been rediscovered in various cultures in many lands.

Even with their slavery, and many repressive institutions, the Greeks did have considerable liberty during what we call their Great Age. A high civilization is, then, not necessarily low in liberty.

It may be, as Professor Hyde implies, that the Greeks had more abridgments of liberty in earlier times, before the Trojan war, than they had when they defeated the Persians. If so, they were on a rising curve of a liberty cycle at least from Homer to Alexander. Thereafter, again as Professor Hyde says, they were on a downward swing of the curve. Perhaps there has been a recent slight upward swing, say from the time when Byron went south to help them re-establish their ancient liberty (or was it their ancient glory?).

Since the average high cultures are not quite so bad, from the abridgment of liberty angle, as the majority just below them, those partial to liberty may perhaps reasonably take heart. For it is at least not incompatible with the trend of the evidence to hope that the cultures now most advanced may advance still further, and so to where it can be rightly said that there is as much freedom in the highest as in the lowest human societies.

Henry A. Wallace

Secretary of Agriculture in the Government of the United States

THE GENETIC BASIS FOR
DEMOCRACY AND FREEDOM

IN this essay I shall deal especially with the subject of "racism"—that is, the attempts of individuals in certain groups to dominate others through the building up of false racial theories in support of their claims. My discussion also will include the rôle that scientists can play in combating such false theories and preventing the use of these theories for the destruction of human liberty.

Naturally, having spent some years in the field of genetics, I would be the last person in the world to deny that heredity is an important factor in the plant and animal and human world around us. In recent years I have dealt more directly with social problems, and I have been just as greatly impressed with the part played by environment. But my experience in both these fields has given me some insight also into the misconceptions and limitations as to both heredity and environment as factors controlling the destinies of human beings.

It may be worth while to review here briefly the old question of heredity and environment, and see what is the consensus of present scientific judgment on this subject.

Marvellous progress has been made in the field of genetics in the years since Mendel's law began to be put to work by myriads of scientists unravelling problems of heredity. Our knowledge of chromosomes and genes and the way they affect the development of animals and particularly plants has been helpful in increasing the efficiency of agricultural production. Much that has been done, not only in the development of strains of livestock for the farm, but in the breeding of race horses, dogs, and other animals, is due to the concentration of desirable genes through selective breeding.

People naturally have said, "If such wonderful results can be attained with plants and animals, why not breed a superior race of humans?"

Efforts in this direction may some day be worth while, but we should recognize to-day the meagreness of our knowledge and the impossibility at present, so far as human heredity is concerned, of translating even that meagre knowledge into practice.

We know that human heredity is transmitted through the forty-eight chromosomes with which each baby starts its life. On these chromosomes, which are found in every cell of the body, are the beadlike structures called genes which in some fashion determine the various characteristics of the individual. From our genetic studies we know that in humans there are perhaps 10,000 of these genes—governing not only physical characteristics such as colour of eyes and skin, but also mental and emotional attributes. Obviously, in view of the life span of human beings and the number of genes with which we must deal, it is absurd from a scientific, to say nothing of a sociological, point of view to expect to be able to breed a new race which is superior in mental and moral as well as physical qualities, even if we had many hundreds of years in which to work.

It might be possible to concentrate on some one characteristic, such as tallness, and produce striking results in a few generations, in the way that livestock breeders have done through selective breeding with colours of coat and other physical characteristics that mark the breeds. Or we might be able to do spectacular things in the way of musical ability, which we know definitely is transmitted as a hereditary trait.

But as to the transmission of intelligence, our knowledge is still very limited. During the last three years the Department of Agriculture, in its experiment station at Beltsville, Maryland, has been studying intelligence and its associated characters in dogs, in an effort to learn to what extent these characters are inherited and how they respond to different environmental stimuli.

As measures of intelligence, six different tests have been used, these being designed to measure such characters as learning, obedience, and courage and the extent to which variations in these traits affect sheepherding ability.

Tremendous variations in intelligence, as measured by these tests, have been found to exist. Some dogs respond well to all tests and others are distinctly morons. Others respond well to one test, such as a test of courage or obedience, but fail on others. One dog passes all the tests with flying colours but for some reason is a failure when it comes to actual sheepherding. Like some humans, he is good as long as he is passing examinations, but a failure in the business world. Timidity may so affect the behaviour of an otherwise intelligent dog that it will fail completely in its other tests, yet the evidence would seem to indicate that such dogs if properly handled may do exceptionally well as sheepherders.

Experimental matings of the dogs are now in progress to determine in what way such characteristics are inherited. It is too early to know the outcome of these matings, but our results so far show that great variation exists in these traits in all breeds. It is evident from the results that breed differences do exist with respect to certain traits. In the main, however, with environment constant, we know that so far as intelligence is concerned, there is much more difference between the animals within the breed than between the breeds themselves.

Heredity is a fact, and we cannot escape its effects. But I think any geneticist worthy of the name would agree that environment is also a fact, and that we cannot truly evaluate the place of heredity unless we provide a favourable environment for the chromosomes and genes to do their work. The inherited character is the end result of the interaction of specific genetic factors, or genes, under the conditions of the environment. Years ago, when I was in college, the boys used to ask the animal husbandry professor what cross produces the best meat animal. He usually answered, "the corncrib cross"—in other words, plenty of food. That applies not only to meat animals, but also to children, and explains why good diet is so important in children's growth and development. It also explains the efforts of the Department of Agriculture to improve the diet of our under-privileged children through the Food Stamp Plan and other measures which are making the surpluses of the farms available to consumers who need them most. We feel that good feeding is more important than racial selection in improving our national stock.

Numerous experiments have been carried on by geneticists and psychologists to determine if possible the relative importance of environment and heredity, or nurture and nature. In these experiments, various tests, including that known as the I.Q. test, have been applied. One experiment, carried on in Iowa, measured the I.Q. of children born of moronic mothers so as to determine whether their I.Q. had been raised after being placed in a favourable environment. Other studies have been made with identical and fraternal twins, some pairs having been reared together and others apart.

Walter S. Neff, of the College of the City of New York, in his study of *Socio-Economic Status and Intelligence*, points out that nearly all the differences in intelligence between groups of children of the highest and lowest status is due to environment. This is his conclusion after a critical survey of the comparatively large amount of work done by various scientists. He says that "it has definitely *not* been proved that social status of the parent has anything to do with native endowment of the infant. That a positive relationship later in the life of the individual may develop is hardly denied. But all the summarized studies tend to show that low cultural environment tends to *depress* I.Q. approximately to the degree agreed to as characteristic of labourers' children, and that a high environment *raises* I.Q. correspondingly. All, then, of the twenty-point mean difference in I.Q. found to exist between children of the lowest and highest status may be accounted for entirely in environmental terms."

The truth is that, from a practical standpoint, we can do very little to improve the heredity of human beings. Most of the differences which are attributed to race are really due to social or economic background, and we know positively that social and economic background in the vast majority of cases has nothing whatever to do with heredity. In other words, there is no reason to believe that a thousand children from wealthy homes on Park Avenue in New York City will on the average have any more intelligence than a thousand children from poverty-stricken share-cropper families from the South if both are given the same food, care, and educational opportunity. There are some environments in the United States which I suspect might in certain cases cause a child sixteen years old to have an I.Q. of 60 and other environments which might cause the same child at the age of sixteen to have an I.Q. of 120. That would be an extreme example, of course, but it illustrates my point, which is that although we can do very little to improve the heredity of human beings, we can do a great deal to improve their environment.

The effect of environment on body size was brought out by studies completed recently by the Bureau of Home Economics in co-operation with the Works Progress Administration. Measurements were obtained on 147,000 boys and girls distributed in fifteen states and the District of Columbia. Thirty-six body measurements including weight were taken for every child.

It was found that these children differed in body structure from State to State. The children measured on the west coast, for instance, are on an average larger than the children measured in any other section of the country. Children of different social and economic groups were compared, and the results showed that children of a higher income level were on the average larger with respect to most measurements than children of a lower economic level. In some instances, the social and economic comparisons were made between and within regions. The results were quite illuminating. Children of the higher economic level measured on the west coast were found to be larger than the children of the lower economic level of that region. One might jump to the conclusion that the children in the wealthier families had a better heredity. But the children of the lower economic level measured on the west coast were larger than the children of the higher economic level measured in the other region to which I refer. Unless we are ready to concede that there are distinct hereditary differences among the people of our several States, or that the differences can be accounted for by selective migration, we must assume that the variations in size are due to variations in environment.

Further evidence of the effect of environment is found in observations of the Farm Security Administration concerning under-privileged farm families. Economic handicaps resulting from the tilling of submarginal land or too small acreage, from one-crop farming, and from insecurity of tenure go along with lack of education and poor health. Doubtless in some cases there are also hereditary weaknesses, but we have reason to believe that deficiencies due to remediable environmental drawbacks are far more frequent than those due to hereditary tendencies.

I have discussed the question of environment in relation to heredity at some length because it has a direct bearing on the claims concerning superior racial stock—claims that have to do not only with definite physical characteristics but also with the less tangible mental and spiritual traits.

Such claims have been put forth in Europe within the last few years as a justification for conquest and the suppression of human liberty.

The fallacies of such claims as they pertain to any one group of Europeans are readily apparent from a study of the purity of European nationalities and stocks. To show just how far from pure these stocks actually are would require a comprehensive analysis of the entire history of Europe. But even in the absence of such a detailed study, their mixed or heterozygous nature is apparent from the historical fact that conquering tribes of Huns, Turks, Mongols, and other peoples moved across the face of Europe and blended with such diverse groups as the Armenians, Finns, Slavs, Greeks, and Germans. The introduction of the African Negro slaves and the intermingling of the various local peoples of Europe also contributed to the mixture. All of this intermingling brought about not only a diversity of common physical characteristics but also the more important psychological ones. Europe has been a vast "melting pot" for the same peoples for the past two hundred years.

The racial situation in Europe is so confused that even the Nazi theorists have been appalled and have found it necessary to retreat from the concept of a Nordic body to that of a Nordic soul. Apparently it is necessary to infer that among the leaders of the Nazis there are some typical Nordic souls animating some exceedingly non-Nordic bodies.

I do not wish to give the impression that the mixing, or blending, of European stocks was undesirable. I do wish to emphasize the historical fact that it occurred, and in the light of this fact, to point out that it is sheer nonsense for anyone to talk about the purity of any European stocks. Europe gives us one of the best examples that we could have of a hetero-zygous population. In its population are gathered together most of the human genes of the world—genes that determine size; colour of skin, hair, and eyes; intelligence, craftiness, feeble-mindedness, and thousands of other characteristics.

Judging by our corn studies, which involve the actual creation of pure strains, as the Nazis apparently would like to do with human beings, it would require at least seventeen generations, or five hundred years, of the closest possible kind of breeding to get out of this conglomerate population anything approach-ing purity. Corn-breeding work has taught us that pure lines derived in this way are usually weak and require crossing in order to attain vigour. The vigour of the human race has continuously been sustained by crossings of diverse types.

It is, of course, undeniable that the idea of a racially pure stock has great emotional appeal, and that for economic and political purposes only it has been used very effectively to deceive many people. But scientists should be the last to be deceived by false racial theories based on emotional appeal and fostered for political purposes.

There is really no such thing as a pure race, in the sense in which the term is commonly used by fanatics. I like the state-ment contained in a resolution unanimously passed by the American Anthropological Association in December, 1938, which read: "Race involved the inheritance of similar physical variations by large groups of mankind, but its psychological and cultural connotations, if they exist, have not been ascertained by science."

It is not only in Europe that fallacious claims concerning mentally superior racial stocks are made. In this country, much of our thinking is based on assumptions that certain races or racial strains are mentally superior or inferior. These assumptions crop out in discussions of voting rights, of immigration policies, and of the sterilization of supposedly "inadequate" members of society. I repeat, heredity plays its part in human affairs. There are great differences between the heredity of different individuals, but as in the case of breeds of livestock developed for the same purpose, the differences between the individuals within a given nationality or group are much greater than the differences between the nationalities or groups. Most of the assumptions commonly held about superior or inferior human stock are not in accord with the findings of science.

It is encouraging therefore to discover the balanced scientific view of this question so well stated by a group of leading thinkers in the *Geneticists' Manifesto* made public in Edinburgh at the time of the Genetics Congress held there in August, 1939. This manifesto, accepting the existence of hereditary differences between human beings as a basic premise, declares that "the effective genetic improvement of mankind is dependent upon major changes in social conditions, and correlative changes in human attitudes," and that "there can be no valid basis for estimating and comparing the intrinsic worth of different individuals without economic and social conditions which provide approximately equal opportunities for all members of society instead of stratifying them from birth into classes with widely different privileges." The manifesto calls for the "removal of race prejudices and the unscientific doctrine that good or bad genes are the monopoly of particular peoples or of persons with features of a given kind." It declares that genetic improvement of the race cannot be achieved "unless there is an organization of production primarily for the benefit of consumer and worker, unless the conditions of employment are adapted to the needs of parents and especially of mothers, and unless dwellings, towns and community services generally are reshaped with the good of children as one of their main objectives." And the manifesto concludes: "The day when economic reconstruction will reach the stage where such human forces will be released is not yet, but it is the task of this generation to prepare for it, and all steps along the way will represent a gain, not only for the possibilities of the ultimate genetic improvement of man, to a degree seldom dreamed of hitherto, but at the same time, more directly, for human mastery over those more immediate evils which are so threatening our modern civilization."

Those "immediate evils" of which the manifesto speaks are all too terrifyingly real to be ignored. All of us have seen how the fallacious doctrines of racial superiority have been translated into attempts to perpetuate or seize political and economic advantage. In some countries of Europe, these attempts have been completely successful, and personal freedom—including freedom of the scientist to follow his calling unhampered—is gone. In the United States also, "racism" has reared its ugly head.

For the combating of "racism" before it sinks its poisonous fangs deep into our body politic, the scientist has both a special motive and a special responsibility. His motive comes from the fact that when personal liberty disappears scientific liberty also disappears. His responsibility comes from the fact that only he can give the people the truth. Only he can clean out the falsities which have been masquerading under the name of science in our colleges, our high schools, and our public prints. Only he can show how groundless are the claims that one race, one nation, or one class has any God-given right to rule.

To disseminate the truth about this all-important question is the first duty of the scientist. But his responsibility goes further. He should, without ceasing to be a scientist, do his best to bring about better social and economic arrangements. He should throw his weight definitely on the side of making our democracy a true democracy, so that every child and every adult may have an equal opportunity to earn and enjoy the good things of life. In doing this he will truly serve science, and he will truly serve humanity.

In this hour of world-wide crisis, it is time for men of science to act. It is time for them to band together to spread far and wide the truth about the genetic basis of democracy, and to work together for a better environment so that our political democracy and scientific freedom may survive.

Alfred North Whitehead

Professor Emeritus of Philosophy, Harvard University

ASPECTS OF FREEDOM

THE cultural history of Western civilization for the period illuminated by written records can be considered from many aspects. It can be conceived under the guise of a steady economic progression, diversified by catastrophic collapses to lower levels. Such a point of view emphasizes technology and economic organization. Alternatively, history can be conceived as a series of oscillations between worldliness and other-worldliness, or as a theatre of contest between greed and virtue or between truth and error. Such points of view emphasize religion, morality, and contemplative habits eliciting generalizations of thought. Each mode of consideration is a sort of searchlight elucidating some of the facts, and retreating the remainder into an omitted background. Of course in any history, even with a restricted topic, limited to politics or to art or to science, many points of view are in fact interwoven, each with varying grades of generality.

One of the most general philosophic notions to be used in the analysis of civilized activities is to consider the effect on social life due to the variations of emphasis between Individual Absoluteness and Individual Relativity. Here "absoluteness" means the notion of release from essential dependence on other members of the community in respect to modes of activity, while relativity means the converse fact of essential relatedness. In one of their particularizations these ideas appear in the antagonism between notions of freedom and of social organization. In another they appear in the relative importance to be ascribed to the welfare of the State and to the welfare of its individual members. The character of each epoch as to its social institutions, its jurisprudence, its notions of ideal ends within the range of practicability, depends largely upon those various patches of activity within which one or the other of these notions, individual absoluteness or individual relativity, is dominant for that epoch. No period is wholly controlled by either one of these extremes, reigning through its whole range of activities. Repression in one direction is balanced by freedom in others. Military discipline is severe. In the last resort individual soldiers are sacrificed to the army. But in many fields of human activity soldiers are left completely unfettered both by regulation and by custom. For members of university faculties the repressions and the freedoms are very different from those which obtain for soldiers.

Distribution of emphasis between absoluteness and relativity is seemingly arbitrary. Of course there is always a historical reason for the pattern. Frequently the shifting of emphasis is to be ascribed to the general tendency to revolt from the immediate past—to interchange black and white wherever we find them. Also the transformation may be a judgment upon dogmas held responsible for inherited failures. It should be one function of history to disengage such a judgment from the irritation due to transient circumstances.

More often changes in the social pattern of intellectual emphasis arise from a shift of power from one class or group of classes to another class or group of classes. For example, an oligarchic aristocratic government and a democratic government may each tend to emphasize social organization, that is to say, the relativity of individuals to the State. But governments mainly satisfying the trading and professional classes, whether nominally they be aristocratic, democratic, or absolute, emphasize personal freedom, that is to say, individual absoluteness. Governments of the latter kind have been that of Imperial Rome with its middle-class imperial agents and its middle-class Stoic lawyers and, in its happiest period, its middle-class emperors; and that of England in the eighteenth and nineteenth centuries.

With the shift of dominant classes, points of view which in one epoch are submerged, only to be detected by an occasional ripple, later emerge into the foreground of action and literary expression. Thus the various activities of each age—governmental, literary, scientific, religious, purely social—express the mentalities of various classes in the community whose influence for those topics happens to be dominant. In one of his speeches on the American Revolution, Burke exclaims, "For heaven's sake, satisfy *somebody*."

Governments are best classified by considering who are the "somebodies" they are in fact endeavouring to satisfy. Thus the English government of the first sixty years of the eighteenth century was, as to its form and its persons, aristocratic. But in policy it was endeavouring to satisfy the great merchants of the City of London and of the City of Bristol. Their dissatisfaction was the immediate source of danger. Sir Robert Walpole and William Pitt, the Great Commoner, personify the changing moods of this class, in the earlier period sick of wars, and later imperialistic.

In a period when inherited modes of life are operating with their traditional standard of efficiency, or inefficiency, the class to be actively satisfied may be relatively restricted, for example, the merchants of eighteenth-century England. The majority will then be relatively quiescent, and conservative statesmen, such as Walpole, will be anxious to do nothing to stir the depths —*Quieta non movere*. Walpole was an active reformer in respect to trade interests, otherwise a conservative.

The corresponding statesmen in France were actively concerned with the interests of the Court, whose power was based on a bureaucracy (legal, administrative, and ecclesiastical), and an army. As in contemporary England, the personnel of the whole French organization, civil and military, was aristocratic and middle class. French politics ran more smoothly, but unfortunately for France its active political element was more divorced from the main interests of the country than the active element in England, though in each country government exhibited its periods of insight and folly. The French emphasis was towards co-ordination, the English towards individual freedom. In the latter portion of this century, in England the more active class politically were the rural landowners. Note for instance the way in which, at the end of his political life, Burke hugs the improbable belief that he understood agriculture. Also the municipality of the City of London was in the earlier period an element of support for the government, and—until the excesses of the French Revolution—in the later period an element of opposition.

In the later period the oncoming industrial revolution absorbed the energies of that English industrial class whom at the earlier period the slogan "the Protestant Succession" had stirred to political activity because for them it spelled "Industrial Freedom." The mass of the people were now, towards the end of the century, stirring uneasily, as yet ignorant of the ways in which their interests were being determined, and with its better members engaged in saving their souls according to the directions of John Wesley. Finally out of this welter, after a delay caused by the wars of the French Revolution, the Victorian epoch emerged. The solution was merely temporary, and so is the planet itself.

II

In our endeavour to understand sociological change we must not concentrate too exclusively on the effect of abstract doctrine, verbally formulated and consciously assented to. Such elaborate intellectual efforts play their part in preserving or transforming or destroying. For example, the history of Europe is not to be understood without some reference to the Augustinian doctrines of original sin, of divine grace, and of the consequent mission of the Catholic Church. The history of the United States requires in addition some knowledge of the English political doctrines of the seventeenth century, and of French thought in the eighteenth century. Men are driven by their thoughts as well as by the molecules in their bodies, by intelligence and by senseless forces. Social history, however, concentrates on modes of human experience prevalent at different periods. The physical conditions are merely the background which partially controls the flux of modes and of moods. Even here we must not over-intellectualize the various types of human experience. Mankind is the animal at the head of the Primates, and cannot escape habits of mind which cling closely to habits of body.

Our consciousness does not initiate our modes of functionings. We awake to find ourselves engaged in process, immersed in satisfactions and dissatisfactions, and actively modifying, either by intensification or by attenuation or by the introduction of novel purposes. This primary procedure which is presupposed in consciousness, I will term "instinct." It is the mode of experience directly arising out of the urge of inheritance, individual and environmental. Also, after instinct and intellectual ferment have done their work, there is a decision which determines the mode of coalescence of instinct with intelligence. I will term this factor "wisdom." It is the function of wisdom to act as a modifying agency on the intellectual ferment so as to produce a self-determined issue from the given conditions. Thus for the purpose of understanding social institutions, this crude three-fold division of human nature is required: instinct, intelligence, wisdom.

But this division must not be made too sharply. After all, intellectual activity is itself an inherited factor. We do not initiate thought by an effort of self-consciousness. We find ourselves thinking, just as we find ourselves breathing and enjoying the sunset. There is a habit of day-dreaming, and a habit of thoughtful elucidation. Thus the autonomy of thought is strictly limited, often negligible, generally beyond the threshold of consciousness. The ways of thought of a nation are as much instinctive—that is to say, are subject to routine—as are its ways of emotional reaction. But most of us believe that there is a spontaneity of thought which lies beyond routine. Otherwise, the moral claim for freedom of thought is without meaning. This spontaneity of thought is, in its turn, subject to control as to its maintenance and efficiency. Such control is the judgment of the whole, attenuating or strengthening the partial flashes of self-determination. The whole determines what it wills to be, and thereby adjusts the relative importance of its own inherent flashes of spontaneity. This final determination is its wisdom or, in other words, its subjective aim as to its own nature, with its limits set by inherited factors.

Wisdom is proportional to the width of the evidence made effective in the final self-determination. The intellectual operations consist in the co-ordination of notions derived from the primary facts of instinctive experience into a logically coherent system. Those facts, whose qualitative aspects are thus co-ordinated, gain importance in the final self-determination. This intellectual co-ordination is more readily achieved when the primary facts are selected so as to dismiss the baffling aspects of things into intellectual subordination. For this reason intellectual activity is apt to flourish at the expense of wisdom. To some extent, to understand is always to exclude a background of intellectual incoherence. But wisdom is persistent pursuit of the deeper understanding, ever confronting intellectual system with the importance of its omissions. These three elements, instinct, intelligence, wisdom, cannot be torn apart. They integrate, react, and merge into hybrid factors. It is the case of the whole emerging from its parts, and the parts emerging within the whole. In judging social institutions, their rise, their culmination, and their decay, we have to estimate the types of instinct, of intelligence, and of wisdom which have co-operated with natural forces to develop the story. The folly of intelligent people, clear-headed and narrow visioned, has precipitated many catastrophes.

However far we go back in recorded history, we are within the period of the high-grade functioning of mankind, far removed from mere animal savagery. Also, within that period it would be difficult to demonstrate that mankind has improved upon its inborn mental capacity. Yet there can be no doubt that there has been an immense expansion of the outfit which the environment provides for the service of thought. This outfit can be summarized under the headings modes of communication, physical and mental, writing, preservation of documents, variety of modes of literature, critical thought, systematic thought, constructive thought, history, comparison of diverse languages, mathematical symbolism, improved technology providing physical ease. This list is obviously composed of many partially redundant and overlapping items. But it serves to remind us of the various ways in which we have at our service facilities for thought and suggestions for thought far beyond those at hand for our predecessors who lived anywhere from two to five thousand years ago. Indeed the last two hundred years has added to this outfit in a way which may create a new epoch unless mankind degenerates. Of course, a large share of this outfit had already accumulated between two and three thousand years ago. It is the brilliant use which the leading men of that millennium made of their opportunities which makes us doubt of any improvement in the native intelligence of mankind.

But the total result is that we now discern a certain simple-mindedness in the way our predecessors adjusted themselves to inherited institutions. To a far greater extent the adjustment was a matter of course, in short, it was instinctive. In the great period they discovered what we have inherited. But there was a naïvety about the discovery, a surprise. Instinctive adaptation was so pervasive that it was unnoticed. Probably the Egyptians did not know that they were governed despotically, or that the priests limited the royal power, because they had no alternative as a contrast either in fact or in imagination. They were nearer in their thoughts to the political philosophy prevalent in an anthill.

Another aspect of this fact is that in such societies, relativity is stressed rather than individual freedom. Indeed, in the earlier stages freedom is almost a meaningless notion. Action and mood both spring from an instinct based upon ancestral co-ordination. In such societies, whatever is not the outcome of inherited relativity, imposing co-ordination of action, is sheer destructive chaos. Alien groups are then evil groups. An energetic prophet hewed Agag in pieces. Unfortunately the spiritual descendants of Samuel still survive, archaic nuisances.

III

We can watch some of the episodes in the discovery of freedom. About fourteen hundred years before Christ, the Egyptian king Akhenaton evidently belonged to an advanced group who thought for themselves and made a step beyond the inherited religious notions. Such groups, with flashes of free thought, must have arisen sporadically many times before, during countless thousands of years, some successful and most of them failures. Otherwise the transition to civilization, as distinct from the mere diversity of adaptations of thoughtless customs, could never have arisen. Bees and ants have diverse social organizations; but, so far as we know, neither species is in any sense civilized. They may enjoy thoughtless adaptations of social customs. Anyhow their flashes of freedom are below the level that we can discern. But Akhenaton, having exercised his freedom, evidently had no conception of freedom as such. We have all the evidence archæology can provide that he rigidly endeavoured to impose his notions upon the thoughts and customs of the whole Egyptian nation. Apparently he failed; for there was a reaction. But reactions never restore with minute accuracy. Thus in all probability there remained a difference which the evidence before us is unable to discriminate.

A more successful group were the Hebrew prophets about eight or nine hundred years later. Spurred by the evils of their times they exercised a freedom in the expression of moral intuition, and fitted out the character of Jehovah with the results of their thoughts. Our civilization owes to them more than we can express. They constitute one of the few groups of men who decisively altered history in any intimate sense. Most spectacular upheavals merely replace one set of individuals by another analogous set; so that history is mostly a barren change of names. But the Hebrew prophets really produced a decisive qualitative alteration, and what is still more rare, a change for the better; yet the conception of freedom never entered into the point of view of the Jehovah of the prophets. Intolerance is the besetting sin of moral fervour. The first important pronouncement in which tolerance is associated with moral fervour is in the Parable of the Tares and the Wheat, some centuries later.

Subsequent examples of intolerance supervening upon the exercise of freedom are afforded by the Christian Church after its establishment by Constantine and by the Protestants under the guidance of Luther and Calvin. At the period of the Reformation mankind had begun to know better and so charity of judgment upon the Reformers begins to wear thin. But then charity is a virtue allied to tolerance, so we must be careful. All advanced thinkers, sceptical or otherwise, are apt to be intolerant, in the past and also now. On the whole, tolerance is more often found in connection with a genial orthodoxy. The apostles of modern tolerance—in so far as it exists—are Erasmus, the Quakers, and John Locke. They should be commemorated in every laboratory, in every church, and in every court of law. We must however remember that many of the greatest seventeenth-century statesmen and thinkers, including John Locke, owed their lives to the wide tolerance of the Dutch Republic.

Certainly these men were not the originators of their admirable ideas. To find the origins we must go behind them for two thousand years. So slow is translation of idea into custom. We must however first note that the examples cited have all been concerned with religion. There are other forms of behaviour, active and contemplative. The Athenians have given us the first surviving instance of the explicit recognition of the importance of tolerance in respect to varieties of social behaviour. No doubt antecedent civilizations must have provided many practical examples of it. For example, it is difficult to believe that in big metropolitan cities such as Babylon and Nineveh, there was much detailed supervision of social behaviour. On the other hand, the ways of life in Egypt seem to have been tightly organized. But the first explicit defence of social tolerance, as a requisite for high civilization, is found in the speech of Pericles as reported by Thucydides. It puts forth the conception of the organized society successfully preserving freedom of behaviour for its individual members. Fifty years later, in the same social group, Plato introduced deeper notions from which all claims for freedom must spring. His general concept of the psychic factors in the Universe stressed them as the source of all spontaneity, and ultimately as the ground of all life and motion. The human psychic activity thus contains the origins of precious harmonies within the transient world. The end of human society is to elicit such psychic energies. But spontaneity is of the essence of soul. Such in outline is the argument from Platonic modes of thought to the importance of social freedom.

Plato's own writings constitute one prolonged apology for freedom of contemplation, and for freedom for the communication of contemplative experiences. In the persistent exercise of this right Socrates and Plato lived, and it was on its behalf that Socrates died.

The establishment of freedom requires more than its mere intellectual defence. Plato above all men introduced into the world this further essential element of civilization. For he exhibited the tone of mind which alone can maintain a free society, and he expressed the reasons justifying that tone. His Dialogues are permeated with a sense of the variousness of the Universe, not to be fathomed by our intellects, and in his Seventh Epistle he expressly disclaims the possibility of an adequate philosophic system. The moral of his writings is that all points of view, reasonably coherent and in some sense with an application, have something to contribute to our understanding of the universe, and also involve omissions whereby they fail to include the totality of evident fact. The duty of tolerance is our finite homage to the abundance of inexhaustible novelty which is awaiting the future, and to the complexity of accomplished fact which exceeds our stretch of insight.

Thus two types of character must be excluded from those effectually promoting freedom. One type belongs to those who despair of attaining any measure of truth, the Sceptics. Such temperaments can obviously have no message for those who hold that thought does count. Again the pursuit of freedom with an intolerant mentality is self-defeating. For all his equipment of imagination, learning, and literary magnificence in defence of freedom, the example of Milton's life probably does as much to retard the cause as to advance it. He promotes a frame of mind of which the issue is intolerance.

The ancient world of paganism was tolerant as to creeds. Provided that your actions conformed, your speculations were unnoticed. Indeed, one mark of progress beyond purely instinctive social relations is an uneasy feeling as to the destructive effect of speculative thought. Creeds are at once the outcome of speculation and efforts to curb speculation. But they are always relevant to it. Antecedently to speculation there can be no creeds. Wherever there is a creed, there is a heretic round the corner or in his grave. Amid the great empires, Egyptian, Mesopotamian, and Hittite, and with the discovery of navigation, the intercourse between races promoted shrewd comparisons gradually broadening into speculative thought. In its beginnings this shift in human mentality must have developed slowly. Where there is no anticipation, change has to wait upon chance, and peters out amid neglect. Fortunately the Bible preserves for us fragments of the process as it affected one gifted race at a nodal point. The record has been written up by editors with the mentality of later times. Thus the task of modern scholars is analogous to an endeavour to recover the histories of Denmark and Scotland from a study of *Hamlet* and *Macbeth*. We can see initial antagonisms broadening into speculative attempts to rationalize the welter. We can watch Samuel and Agag succeeded by Solomon and the Queen of Sheba. There are the meditations of Job and his friends, the prophetical books, and the "wisdom" books of the Bible. And with a leap of six hundred years one version of the story ends with the creed of the Council at Nicæa.

IV

The episode of Greek civilization during its short phase of independence created a new situation. Speculation was explicitly recognized. It was ardently pursued. Its various modes and methods were discovered. The relation of the Greeks to their predecessors is analogous, as to stretch of time and intensity of effect, to that of the second phase of the modern industrial revolution during the last fifty years to the first phase, which in truth sprawls over the long centuries from the fifteenth century to the close of the nineteenth.

By reason of its inheritance from the episode of Hellenic culture the Roman Empire was more self-conscious than its predecessors in its treatment of the problem of liberty and of the allied problem of social institutions. So far as concerns

Western Europe, the origin of the medieval civilization must be dated from the Emperor Augustus and the journeys of Paul. For the Byzantine, Semitic, Egyptian area, the date must be pushed back to the death of Alexander the Great, and the renaissance of Greco-Egyptian learning. For the first two centuries after Augustus the former area, centred 'in Italy, was incomparably the more important. Latin literature is the translation of Hellenic culture into the medieval modes of thought, extending that period to end with the French Revolution. Throughout that whole period culture was backward looking. Lucretius, Cicero, Virgil were medievals in their relation to Hellenic literature and speculation, though they lacked the Semitic factor. After that first Latin period, the notable contributions to thought, Pagan, Christian, and Mohammedan, all derive from the eastern region, with the important exception of Augustine. Finally, the centre of culture again swings westward, as the Eastern civilization collapses under the prolonged impacts of Tartars and Turks. The notes of these three allied cultures, the Eastern, the Latin, and the later European, are scholarly learning, recurrence to Hellenic speculation restated in creedal forms, imitative literatures stressing humane aspirations, the canalization of curiosity into professional grooves, and—in the West—a new grade of intelligence exhibited in the development of a variety of social institutions. It is this last factor which has saved the progress of mankind.

The new epoch in the formation of social institutions unfolded itself very gradually. It is not yet understood in its full importance. Social philosophy has not grasped the relevant principles, so that even now each case is treated as a peculiar fact. But the problem of liberty has been transformed by it. The novelty consists in the deliberate formation of institutions, embodying purposes of special groups, and unconcerned with the general purposes of any political state, or of any embodiment of tribal unity playing the part of a state. Of course any big empire involves a coalescence of diverse tribes, customs, and modes of thought. But in the earlier examples, each subject race had its own status in the complex empire, and its ways of procedure were part of the imperial system. Also there must have been complex modes of behaviour, peculiar to the various races, inherited and tolerated as a matter of course. In the case of the smaller units such as the Greek city states, we find a condition of affairs in which all corporate action is an element in state policy. The freedom was purely individual, never corporate. All incorporation, religious or secular, was communal, or patriarchal. The saying, "Render unto Caesar the things that are Caesar's and unto God the things that are God's" was uttered by Christ in the reign of Tiberius, and not by Plato four hundred years earlier. However limited may be the original intention of the saying, very quickly God was conceived as a principle of organization in complete disjunction from Caesar.

It is interesting to speculate on the analogies and differences between the deaths of Socrates and of Paul. Both were martyrs. Socrates died because his speculative opinions were held to be subversive of the communal life. It is difficult to believe that the agents of Claudius or Nero or Galba were much concerned with Paul's speculative opinions as to the ways of God to man. Later on, Lucian's opinions were as unorthodox as Paul's. But he died in his bed. Unfortunately for Paul, as he journeyed he left behind him organized groups, indulging in activities uncoordinated with any purposes of State. Thus imperial agents were alarmed and sympathized with popular prejudice. Indeed, we know exactly what one of the best of the Roman emperors about half a century later thought of the matter. Trajan in his letter to the younger Pliny dismisses Christian theology as negligible. He is even unconcerned with the organization of Christians into groups, so long as no overt action emerges affronting the traditional association of the State with religion. Yet he recognizes that the Christians will fit into no current political philosophy, and that they represent corporate actions on the verge of the intolerable. Thus if circumstances unearth them, they are to be questioned, dismissed if possible, but punished when their actions become glaring. It is interesting to compare the Christians in the Roman Empire, from Nero to Trajan, with the communists in modern America.

Trajan shows himself as a fine statesman dealing with the faint dawn of a new epoch, not understood, and indeed not yet understood. The old organization of mankind was being affected by the influence of the new width of intellectuality due to Hellenism. Organizations mainly derived from blind inheritance, and affected by the intellect only in detail and in interpretation, are to receive the shock of other types founded primarily on the intellectual appreciation of private ends, that is to say, of ends unconcerned with the State. What Henry Osborn Taylor has termed "rational consideration" is becoming a major force in human organization. Of course, Plato and Aristotle exhibited rational consideration on a magnificent scale. But a group of thinkers do not necessarily constitute a political force. Centuries, sometimes thousands of years, have to elapse before thought can capture action. It is typical of this gap that Aristotle's manuscripts are said to have been stowed in a cellar for two hundred years, and that even to this day Plato is mainly valued as a religious mystic and a supreme literary artist. In these latter functions, Plato represents the world he inherited and not the world he created. Perhaps these constitute his best part. But he played two rôles.

The situation in the Roman Empire was in effect novel. Pericles had conceived a freedom for private actions, of a certain civilized type within narrowly restricted bounds. Plato voices the claim for contemplative freedom. But the Empire was faced with the claim for freedom of corporate action. Modern political history, from that day to this, is the confused story of the strenuous resistance of the State, and of its partial concessions. The Empire reasserted the old doctrine of the Divine Emperor; but also yielded by admitting as legal principle the Stoic doctrine of the Voice of Nature. The Middle Ages compromised with the doctrine of the two swords. In recent times the State is fighting behind its last ditch, which is the legal doctrine of sovereignty. The thought of the seventeenth and eighteenth centuries rationalized its political philosophy under the fiction of the "Original Contract." This concept proved itself formidable. It helped to dismiss the Stuarts into romance, to found the American Republic, and to bring about the French Revolution. Indeed, it was one of the most timely notions known to history. Its weakness is that it antedates the era of the importance of rational consideration, and over-estimates the political importance which at any time reason has possessed. The antagonistic doctrine was that of the "Divine Right of Kings," which is the ghost of the "Divine Emperor."

V

Political philosophy can claim no exemption from the doctrine of the golden mean. Unrestricted liberty means complete absence of any compulsory co-ordination. Human society in the absence of any compulsion is trusting to the happy co-ordination of individual emotions, purposes, affections, and actions. Civilization can only exist amid a population which in the mass does exhibit this fortunate mutual adaptation. Unfortunately a minority of adverse individual instances, when unchecked, are sufficient to upset the social structure. A few men in the whole caste of their character, and most men in some of their actions, are anti-social in respect to the peculiar type of any society possible in their time. There can be no evasion of the plain fact that compulsion is necessary and that compulsion is the restriction of liberty.

It follows that a doctrine as to the social mingling of liberty and compulsion is required. A mere unqualified demand for liberty is the issue of shallow philosophy, equally noxious with the antithetical cry for mere conformation to standard pattern. Probably there can be no one solution of this problem adapted to all the circumstances of human societies which have been and will be. We must confine ourselves to the way in which at the present day the issue is being adjusted in the Western civilization, European and American.

The organization of professions by means of self-governing institutions places the problem of liberty at a new angle. For now it is the institution which claims liberty and also exercises control. In ancient Egypt the Pharaoh decided, acting through his agents. In the modern world a variety of institutions have the power of action without immediate reference to the State. This new form of liberty which is the autonomous institution limited to special purposes was exemplified in the guilds of the Middle Ages; and that period was characterized by a remarkable growth of civilized genius. The meaning that—in England at least—was then assigned to the word "liberty" illustrates the projection of the new social structure upon the older form of customary determination. For a "liberty" did not then mean a general freedom, but a special license to a particular group to organize itself within a special field of action. For this reason "liberties" were sometimes a general nuisance.

Of course the Catholic Church was the great "liberty" which first confronted the Roman Empire, and then dominated medieval life. In its early stages it is seen in its proper theoretical relation to other autonomous societies. For example in the pagan Empire, its legal status seems to have been analogous to that of the pagan burial societies; although the status of the Church property before the age of Constantine has not yet been finally elucidated by scholars. But in the Middle Ages, the Church so towered above other institutions that it outrivalled the State itself. Accordingly its analogy to secular guilds and to other professional institutions such as universities was obscured by its greatness. The Catholic Church had another characteristic of priceless value. It was, so far as concerned Europe, universal, that is to say, Catholic. Until the approach of the Renaissance there were no European nations in the modern sense. But the Church transcended all governmental boundaries, all racial divisions and all geographic divisions. It was a standing challenge to any form of communal despotism, a universal "liberty."

VI

From the beginning of the sixteenth century this first form of institutional civilization, with its feudalism, its guilds, its universities, its Catholic Church, was in full decay. The new middle classes, whether scholars or traders, would have none of it. They were individualists. For them the universities were secondary, the monasteries were a nuisance, the Church was a nuisance, feudalism was a nuisance, the guilds were a nuisance. They wanted good order, and to be let alone with their individual activities. The great thinkers of the sixteenth and seventeenth centuries were singularly detached from universities. Erasmus wanted printers, and Baeon, Hervey, Descartes, Galileo, Leibnitz, wanted governmental patronage, or protection, more than university colleagues, mostly reactionary. When Luther, Descartes, Galileo, or Leibnitz shifted his residence, it was not to find a better university, but a more suitable government—a Duke who would protect, a Prince who would pay, or a Dutch Republic which would not ask questions. Nevertheless, the universities survived the change better than other institutions. In some ways it was a great time for them, though they shrank to the national. What finally emerged was the modern national organization of Europe with the Sovereign State dictating every form of institutional organization, as subordinate elements for its own purposes. This was a recurrence to that earlier form of human organization which showed its faint signs of decay during the period of the Roman Empire. Naturally there were great differences. For nothing is ever restored. In fact the reaction was a failure, because mankind has outgrown the simplicities of the earlier form of civilization.

The political philosophy of the modern era was a retrogression, based upon a recurrence to the philosophers and lawyers of the old classical civilizations. The Middle Ages, in the simplified form of the relations of Church with State, were considering the problem of a civilization in which men owed a divided allegiance to many intersecting institutions pursuing diverse ends. This is the real problem in a world dominated by fraternity derived from the catholic diffusion of ideas and from the international distribution of property. The solution provided by the doctrine of the sole sovereignty of the State, however grateful to Protestants and to Sovereigns, is both shocking and unworkable, a mere stick with which to beat Papists in the sixteenth and seventeenth centuries, a mere way to provide policemen for the countinghouses of merchants. But, amid this reactionary triumph of Periclean individualism in the political philosophies of the eighteenth and nineteenth centuries, there was an outcrop of institutions based upon the vigour of modern intellectual interests. These institutions, even when national, were concerned with interests impartial among the nations. These were the centuries in which science triumphed, and science is universal. Thus scientific institutions, though in form national, informally established a catholic league. Again the advance of scholarship, and of natural science, transformed the professions. It intellectualized them far beyond their stage of advance in earlier times. Professions first appear as customary activities largely modified by detached strains of theory. Theories are often wrong; and some of the earlier professional doctrines erred grievously and were maintained tenaciously. Doctrines emerged as plausible deductions, and survived as the wisdom of ancestors. Thus the older professional practice was rooted upon custom, though it was turning towards the intellectual sunlight. Here and there individuals stood out far in advance of their colleagues. For example, in the fourteen hundred years separating Galen from Vesalius, the standard of European medical practice was not to be compared with the attainments of either of these men. Also more than a century after Vesalius, Charles II of England on his deathbed was tortured by physicians employing futile remedies customary at that time. Again, as a designing engineer Leonardo da Vinci was unequalled until the advent of Vauban and James Watt. In the earlier centuries the professional influence, as a general sociological fact, was mainly a welter of bygone flashes of intelligence relapsing into customary procedures. It represented the continual lapse of intellect into instinct. But the culmination of science completely inverted the rôles of custom and intelligence in the older professions. By this inversion professional institutions have acquired an international life. Each such institution practises within its own nation, but its sources of life are world-wide. Thus loyalties stretch beyond Sovereign States.

Perhaps the most important function of these institutions is the supervision of standards of individual professional competence and of professional practice. For this purpose there is a complex interweaving of universities and more specialized institutions. The problem of freedom comes in here. For it is not opinions which are censured, but learning and ability.

Thus in the more important fields of thought, opinion is free and so are large divergencies of practice. The community is provided with objective information as to the sort of weight to be attached to individuals and as to the sort of freedom of action which may safely be granted. Whatever is done can be subjected to the test of general professional opinion, acting through this network of institutions. Further, even large freedom can now be allowed to non-professional individuals. For the great professional organizations, so long as they are efficient, should be able to demonstrate the dangers of extravagant notions. In this way, where sudden action is not in question, reason has obtained an entrenchment which should be impregnable. Indeed individual freedom, standing apart from organization, has now its indispensable rôle. For all organizations are liable to decay, and license for outside criticism is the best safeguard for the professions.

Also the sovereign State of modern legal theory has its sphere of action and its limitation. The State represents the general wisdom of the community derived from an experience broader than the topics of the various sciences. The rôle of the State is a general judgment on the activity of the various organizations. It can judge whether they welcome ability, whether they stand high among the kindred institutions throughout the world. But where the State ceases to exercise any legitimate authority is when it presumes to decide upon questions within the purview of sciences or professions.

For example, in the teaching profession it is obvious that young students cannot be subjected to the vagaries of individual teachers. In this sense, the claim for the freedom of teaching is nonsense. But the general community is very incompetent to determine either the subject matter to be taught or the permissible divergencies to be allowed or the individual competence. There can be only one appeal, and this is to general professional opinion as exhibited in the practice of accredited institutions. The appeal is catholic. The State of Tennessee did not err in upholding the principle that there are limits to the freedom of teaching in schools and colleges. But it exhibited a gross ignorance of its proper functions when it defied a professional opinion which throughout the world is practically unanimous. Even here that State is hardly to be blamed. For the current political philosophy of sovereignty is very weak as to the limitations of moral authority. Of course whoever at any moment has physical power has that power of physical compulsion, whether he be a bandit or a judge or political ruler. But moral authority is limited by competence to attain those ends whose immediate dominance is evident to enlightened wisdom. Political loyalty ceases at the frontiers of radical incapacity.

The functions of professional institutions have been considered in some detail because they constitute a clear-cut novelty within modern societies. There were faint anticipations in the ancient world, for example the schools at Athens, in particular those founded by Plato, Aristotle, and the Stoics, and elsewhere the great foundation at Alexandria. Also later the theologians of the Christian Church formed another professional group which even stretched its claim to authority beyond all bounds of good sense. It is by reason of these anticipations, and of the legal developments of the Roman and Byzantine schools of law, that the beginnings of the modern world, in respect to the problem of freedom and of moral authority, have been placed as early as Alexander and Augustus.

VII

In the immediate present, economic organization constitutes the most massive problem of human relationships. It is passing into a new phase, and presents confused outlines. Evidently something new is developing. The individualistic liberalism of the nineteenth century has collapsed, quite unexpectedly. So long as the trading middle classes were dominant as the group to be satisfied, its doctrines were self-evident. As soon as industrialism and education produced in large numbers the modern type of artisan, its whole basis was widely challenged. Again the necessity for large capital, with the aid of legal ingenuity, produced the commercial corporation with limited liability. These fictitious persons are exempt from physiological death and can only disappear by a voluntary dissolution or by bankruptcy. The introduction into the arena of this new type of "person" has considerably modified the effective meaning of the characteristic liberal doctrine of contractual freedom. It is one thing to claim such freedom as a natural right for human persons, and quite another to claim it for corporate persons. And again the notion of private property had a simple obviousness at the foot of Mount Sinai and even in the eighteenth century. When there were primitive roads, negligible drains, private wells, no elaborate system of credit, when payment meant the direct production of gold pieces, when each industry was reasonably self-contained—in fact when the world was not as it is now—then it was fairly obvious what was meant by private property, apart from any current legal fictions. To-day private property is mainly a legal fiction, and apart from such legal determination its outlines are completely indefinite. Such legal determination is probably, indeed almost certainly, the best way of arranging society. But the "voice of nature" is a faint echo when we are dealing with it. There is a striking analogy between the hazy notions of justice in Plato's Republic, and the hazy notions of private property to-day. The modern artisan, like Thrasymachus of old, is apt to define it as "the will of the stronger."

Of course these extremes as to the nature of property—simple-minded assertion and simple-minded denial—are exaggeration. The whole concept of absolute individuals with absolute rights, and with a contractual power of forming fully defined external relations, has broken down. The human being is inseparable from its environment in each occasion of its existence. The environment which the occasion inherits is immanent in it, and conversely it is immanent in the environment which it helps to transmit. The favourite doctrine of the shift from a customary basis for society to a contractual basis is founded on shallow sociology. There is no escape from customary status. This status is merely another name for the inheritance immanent in each occasion. Inevitably customary status is there, and inescapable condition. On the other hand, the inherited status is never a full determination. There is always the freedom for the determination of individual emphasis. In terms of high-grade human society, there is always the customary fact as an essential element in the meaning of every contractual obligation. There can be no contract which does not presuppose custom, and no custom leaving no loophole for spontaneous contract. It is this truth that gives vitality to the Anglo-American Common Law. It is an instrument, in the hands of skilled experts, for the interpretation of explicit contract in terms of implicit status. No code of verbal statement can ever exhaust the shifting background of presupposed fact. What does alter for dominant interest within each social system is the relative importance of the contractual and customary factors in general conscious experience. This balance, fortunate or unfortunate, largely depends on the type of social inheritance provided by that society. But contract is a mode of expression for spontaneity. Otherwise it is meaningless, a futile gesture of consciousness.

In the end nothing is effective except massively co-ordinated inheritance. Sporadic spontaneity is composed of flashes mutually thwarting each other. Ideas have to be sustained, disentangled, diffused, and co-ordinated with the background. Finally they pass into exemplification in action. The distinguishing mark of modern civilization is the number of institutions whose origin can be traced to the initial entertainment of some idea. In the ancient civilizations thought was mainly explanatory. It was only creative in respect to individual actions. But the corporate actions preceded thought. The ancient Gods, either as notions or as persons, did not create the thunderstorm, they explained it. Jehovah did not create the Hebrew tribal emotions, he explained them. He never made a covenant which initiated Hebrew history; the notion of the covenant was an explanatory idea. It was influential; but the idea arose as an explanation of the tribal history. Nevertheless it intensified a pre-existing fact. The Old Testament is on the verge of the dividing line between ancient and modern. This watershed is Hellenism. The difference is only one of proportion, of more or less. But a sufficient change of proportion makes all the difference. In the last phase of ancient life there is a haunting feeling that corporate actions ought to have originated from ideas. Thus their historical imagination unconsciously imported types of explanation of their past which were faintly relevant to their own present: explanations, fantastic, incredible, fit only for exposure by scholars. It was the shadow of the future thrown back on to the past.

Returning to the economic side of life, in the ancient world there were economic transactions between tribes and between States, and there were also the economic activities of craftsmen, merchants, and bankers. There was communal activity and individual activity. Cicero's financial worries are preserved for us in his letters to Atticus. They are very analogous to Gibbon's letters to Holroyd, which are characteristic of educated Europe in the eighteenth century. Certainly Cicero's affairs were sufficiently complex. It is not in that respect that the ancient world fell short. It would be worth sacrificing a good deal of Latin literature to know what Atticus thought of Cicero's financial position. Even after two thousand years it is difficult not to entertain a friendly anxiety on the subject. Perhaps as Cicero put his head out of the litter he had been dreaming of bankruptcy, when the sword of the soldier gave him death.

That ancient world is modern both in the physical facts which await us, and in the ripples of anxiety arising from its social intricacies. At that time the human mind was singularly powerful for the generation of ideas. To the epoch between Plato and Justinian, we can trace our philosophical ideas, our religious ideas, our legal ideas, and the model of modern governmental organization. We can recognize Pliny as he discusses whether the parents should serve on the board of governors of the Grammar School he had founded. Sidonius Apollinaris is an anticipation of many New England gentlemen, ecclesiastic and lay. But within that period the ferment of ideas had not persisted for a sufficient time to transform society by a profusion of corporations originated by explicit thought. In particular the great commercial corporations awaited modern times, the Bank of St. George at Genoa, the Bank of England, the great trading companies to India and the East. Atticus was a banker; but he was not the president of a banking corporation. Private wealth was deposited in pagan temples; but temples were corporations devoted to the customary rites of religion. The state taxes were farmed by private corporations of Roman capitalists. Here we approach modern notions. Yet after all the *publicani* were engaged in performing one of the direct services of the State. Their actions were communal and traditional with a tinge of modern modes of incorporation. No doubt many anticipations of modern commercial institutions can be found. Those times lie within the modern world. But it was modern commerce in its infancy. Indeed, the examples quoted of modern commercial activity belong to an intermediate period, and only recently has the influence of ideas produced its full economic effect. But wherever ideas are effective, there is freedom.

VIII

Unfortunately the notion of freedom has been eviscerated by the literary treatment devoted to it. Men of letters, artists in symphonies of pictorial imagination, have staged the shock of novel thought against tradition. The concept of freedom has been narrowed to the picture of contemplative people shocking their generation. When we think of freedom, we are apt to confine ourselves to freedom of thought, freedom of the press, freedom for religious opinions. Then the limitations to freedom are conceived as wholly arising from the antagonisms of our fellow-men. This is a thorough mistake. The massive habits of physical nature, its iron laws, determine the scene for the sufferings of men. Birth and death, heat, cold, hunger, separation, disease, the general impracticability of purpose, all bring their quota to imprison the souls of women and of men. Our experiences do not keep step with our hopes. The Platonic Eros, which is the soul stirring itself to life and motion, is maimed. The essence of freedom is the practicability of purpose. Mankind has chiefly suffered from the frustration of its prevalent purposes, even such as belong to the very definition of its species. The literary exposition of freedom deals mainly with the frills. The Greek myth was more to the point. Prometheus did not bring to mankind freedom of the press. He procured fire, which obediently to human purpose cooks and gives warmth. In fact, freedom of action is a primary human need. In modern thought, the expression of this truth has taken the form of "the economic interpretation of history."

The fact that the "economic interpretation" is itself a novel thought arising within the last sixty or seventy years illustrates an important sociological fact. The literary world through all ages belonged mainly to the fortunate section of mankind whose basic human wants have been amply satisfied. A few literary men have been in want throughout their lives, many have occasionally suffered. The fact shocks us. It is remembered because it is rare. The fortunate classes are oblivious to the fact that throughout the ages the masses of mankind have lived in conscious dread of such disaster—a drought, a wet summer, a bad harvest, a cattle disease, a raid of pirates. Also the basic needs when they are habitually satisfied cease to dominate thought. Delicacies of taste displace the interest in fullness of stomach. Thus the motives which stir the fortunate directing classes to conscious activity have a long-range forecast and an æsthetic tinge—power, glory, safety in the distant future, forms of government, luxury, religion, excitement, dislike of strange ways, contemplative curiosity, play. Mankind survived by evolving a peculiar excitability whereby it quickly adapts itself to novel circumstance. This instability is quickly diverted to some simple form of the more abstract interests of the minority. The great convulsions happen when the economic urge on the masses has dovetailed with some simplified ideal end. Intellect and instinct then combine, and some ancient social order passes away. But the masses of the population are always there, requiring at least a minimum of satisfaction, with their standard of life here higher and there lower, also rising or falling. Thus, even when the minority is dominant, the plain economic facts of life must be the governing force in social development. Yet, in general, the masses are intellectually quiescent, though the more ideal ends of the minority, good and bad, permeate the masses, directing policies according to the phantasies of the generations. And the primary demand for freedom is to be found in the general urge for the accomplishment of these general ends, which are fusion of ideal and economic policies,

making the stuff of history. In so far as a population is dominated by some general appetition, freedom presents no peculiar
problem to the statesman. The tribal actions are shaped
inevitably, and that group of mankind is pushed towards
accomplishment or frustration.

In modern states there is a complex problem. There are
many types of character. Freedom means that within each type
the requisite, co-ordination should be possible without the
destruction of the general ends of the whole community. Indeed, one general end is that these variously co-ordinated
groups should contribute to the complex pattern of community
life, each in virtue of its own peculiarity. In this way individuality gains the effectiveness which issues from co-ordination,
and freedom obtains power necessary for its perfection.

This is the hope of the statesman, the solution which the
long course of history is patiently disclosing. But it is not the
intuition which has nerved men to surpass the limitations of
mankind. After all, societies of primates, of animals, of life on
the earth's surface, are transient details. There is a freedom
lying beyond circumstance, derived from the direct intuition
that life can be grounded upon its absorption in what is changeless amid change. This is the freedom for which Plato was
groping, the freedom which Stoics and Christians obtained as
the gift of Hellenism. It is the freedom of that virtue directly
derived from the source of all harmony. For it is conditioned
only by its adequacy of understanding. And understanding has
this quality that, however it be led up to, it issues in the soul
freely conforming its nature to the supremacy of insight. It is
the reconciliation of freedom with the compulsion of the truth.
In this sense the captive can be free, taking as his own the
supreme insight, the indwelling persuasion towards the harmony
which is the height of existence.

INDEX

Abridgment of liberty (Stefansson), 268, 271
Absolute: freedom (Boas), 55; (Einstein), 92; immanentism (Croce), 65; individuality (Whitehead), 304; intellectualism (Maritain), 211
Absoluteness (Whitehead), 303–4
Absolutism (Beard), 22
Action (Macmurray), 181
Acton, Lord (Laski), 150, 161; 170
Adams, John (Dewey), 77
Agag (Whitehead), 309
Akhenaton (Whitehead), 309–310
Alexander the Great (Whitehead), 322
Alternative to freedom (Croce), 56, 57
American Constitution (Russell), 230; Declaration of 1774 (Salvemini), 249; Revolution (Bernstein), 44; (Russell), 236
American tariff (Laski), 155
Anarchism (Russell), 229
Anarchy (Laski), 155
Anglo-American Common Law (Whitehead), 324
Anglo-Saxon Chronicle (Beard), 20
Ant (Bergson), 38, 40
Apathy (Kingdon), 134
Aquinas, Thomas (Maritain), 220, 227
Arbitration (Laski), 158
Armaments (Laski), 153
Aristotle (Dewey), 84; (Haldane), 98; (Whitehead), 316; (Hogben), 123
Arnold, Matthew (Laski), 169
Aspiration for freedom (Croce), 64
Aspirations of the person (Maritain), 214–216
Athapascans (Stefansson), 287
Atheism (Maritain), 224
Attic Greek culture (Hogben), 123
Atticus (Whitehead), 325
Augustine (Whitehead), 314
Augustus (Whitehead), 314, 322
Autarchy (Haldane), 101
Autonomy (Maritain), 218; of the person (Maritain), 220–221; of the rational being (Anshen), 4

Bacon, Francis (Whitehead), 319
Ball, John (Beard), 15
Being (Anshen), 4
Bentham, Jeremy (Russell), 240–241
Bergson, Henri (Anshen), 4; (Maritain), 211
Beveridge, Sir William (Hogben), 126
Bill of Rights (Bernstein), 44
Biological: heredity (Dewey), 88

Bismarck (Croce), 56
Body: Human (Russell), 242; politic (Russell), 242
Bolshevism (Mann), 204; (Laski), 168
Bourgeoisie (Mann), 195
Boyle, Robert (Hogben), 126
Brinton, Crane (Beard), 13
British Constitution (Salvemini); 250
Bruening (Bernstein), 47
Buddhism (Russell), 241
Burke, Edmund (Whitehead), 305

Cæsar (Beard), 21; (Whitehead), 315
Caligula (Russell), 241
Calvin (Whitehead), 311
Calvinistic, concept of vocation (Croce), 64
Capitalism (Haldane), 103: (Laski), 167
Catholic Church (Salvemini), 261; (Whitehead), 318
Catholic Encyclopedia (Salvemini), 246
Caudwell (Haldane), 98
Cavour (Croce), 69
Censorship (Haldane), 109
Charles II (Whitehead), 320
Chattel slavery (Beard), 10
Children (Haldane),116; (Stefansson), 275–276
Choice (Maritain), 210–214; freedom of (Boas), 53
Christian: democracy (Salvemini), 246; faith (Beard), 15; churches (Hogben), 128
Christianity (Mann), 199, 200; (Russell), 241; was an impediment (Hogben), 122
Christianity and Science; conflicts between (Hogben), 123
Christians (Whitehead), 315; liberal (Hogben), 128
Chromosomes (Wallace), 294
Chukchee (Boas), 52
Church: Roman Catholic (Beard), 19
Churches (Laski), 152, 168
Cicero (Whitehead), 325; (Russell), 230
City of human rights (Maritain), 219, 221
Civilization (Laski), 150, 153–154, 157, 164, 170
Civilizations, conflict between (Laski), 163
Classless society (Haldane), 113
Claudius (Whitehead), 315
Colour, the attitude to (Laski), 149

Common: men (Russell), 243; purpose (Macmurray), 118; ideal (Laski), 167; sense (Laski), 159
Communism (Mann), 203
Communist: Dictatorship (Salvemini) 257; doctrine (Salvemini), 263; system (Croce), 70
Communist Manifesto (Salvemini), 263
Communistic anarchists (Stefansson), 278
Communists (Haldane), 96
Community (Macmurray), 187; (Mann), 198; (Hogben), 128; international (Laski), 152, 165
Comparison (Haldane), 94
Compulsion (Whitehead), 317
Comte, Auguste (Mann), 197
Concept: of freedom (Croce), 65
Concreteness of universality (Croce), 66
Conditioned reflexes (Bernstein), 43, 47
Conflict (Russell), 239
Confucianism (Russell), 241
Congress of Vienna (Russell), 237
"Connatural" aspirations of personality (Maritain), 216
Conscience (Croce), 62–63; (Maritain), 224
Consciousness (Haldane), 98; of restraint (Boas), 52
Constant, Benjamin (Mann), 194
Constantine the Great (Whitehead), 310
Constitution of the United States (Beard), 8
Constraint (Macmurray), 181
Contract (Whitehead), 324
Contractual freedom (Whitehead), 323
Co-operation (Dewey), 90; (Macmurray), 188; (Russell), 242
Corporate actions (Whitehead), 324
Correlation of contemporary knowledge (Anshen), 3
Corsairs (Russell), 232
Council of Nicaea (Whitehead), 313
Crisis of liberalism (Croce), 57–58
Cromwell, Oliver (Beard), 15; (Russell), 239
Crusades (Croce), 72
Cultural: conditions (Dewey), 87; freedom (Bernstein), 47
Culturally uniform society (Boas), 51
Culture (Dewey), 78, 88–90; European (Hogben), 130; liberal (Hogben), 129; social (Hogben), 128
Custom (Boas), 53
Customary restrictions (Haldane), 96

Dante (Haldane), 100; (Russell), 242
Darwinian hypothesis (Beard), 9–10

Darwinism (Croce), 68
Decadence of the liberal idea (Croce), 56
Declaration of Independence (Beard), 12, 16; (Dewey), 76
Declaration of the Rights of Man (Beard), 16
Democracy (Mann), 195, 200; (Maritain), 219; (Salvemini), 245–6; (Laski), 175; formal aspect of (Laski), 165; critics of (Laski), 169
Democratic and oligarchic institutions (Salvemini), 249–250
Democratic: constitution (Salvemini), 251–2; doctrine (Salvemini), 249
Dependence (Maritain), 226
Descartes (Whitehead), 319
Desire for freedom (Dewey), 75
Determinism (Macmurray), 176–178
Dickinson, G. Lowes (Hogben), 121
Dictatorial institutions (Salvemini), 255–257
Dictatorship (Macmurray), 185–186; (Laski), 166
Diderot (Anshen), 3
Diet (Stefansson), 266–267
Differentiation (Boas), 51–52; (Dewey), 89
Disarmament (Laski), 157
Discretion (Laski), 154
Disproportionate culture (Bernstein), 45
Divine: right (Beard), 16; transcendence (Maritain), 217–218
Division of labour (Einstein), 93
Due process of law (Beard), 8; (Russell), 230
Dumoyor (Mann), 197
Dutch Republic (Whitehead), 311

Economic: conditions (Dewey), 83; considerations (Dewey), 83; interpretation of history (Croce), 70; liberalism (Croce), 69; relations (Maritain), 222; restrictions (Haldane), 96; exploitation (Laski), 150; justice (Laski), 167; nationalism (Laski), 165; penetration (Laski), 169; power (Laski), 169
Edict of Nantes (Russell), 230
Education (Kingdon), 143–144; (Russell), 239
Educational: reformers (Russell), 232; system (Laski), 162
Ego (Bergson), 29–30
Emergency Powers Act (Haldane), 114
Emotions (Dewey), 80
Empiricists (Maritain), 211
Encyclopedic synthesis (Anshen), 2

End (Anshen), 5
Ends (Russell), 240
Engels (Haldane), 98
English: philosophy (Croce), 65; Royal Society (Hogben), 126
Environment (Wallace), 295–298; (Laski), 154
Epictetus (Beard), 14
Equality (Mann), 200–201; economic (Laski), 168
Erasmus (Whitehead), 311, 319
Eskimo (Boas), 51
Eskimos (Stefansson), 267; Coronation Gulf (Stefansson), 273
Essene (Hogben), 123
Ethics (Russell), 240
European: nationalities (Wallace), 298; stocks (Wallace), 298–299
Evolution (Hogben), 125
Evolutionalism (Croce), 68
Expression, opportunity of (Laski), 171
Extra-territoriality (Laski), 153

Fascism (Russell), 233; (Salvemini), 255; (Hogben), 129
Fascism, challenge of (Hogben), 130
Fascist dictatorship (Salvemini), 257
Federalist, The (Beard), 8, 21
Federation (Kingdon), 142
Feud (Stefansson), 284
Feudal system (Bernstein), 45
Feudalism (Whitehead), 318
Fichte (Maritain), 224
Fields of Freedom (Haldane), 95
Finance (Haldane), 104
Financiers (Laski), 161
Fitzjames, Stephen (Laski), 169
Food Stamp Plan (Wallace), 296
Force (Laski), 152, 163, 174
Founding Fathers (Dewey), 79, 88
Francis, Saint (Russell), 242
Franciscus e Victoria (Laski), 173
Fraternity (Maritain), 223
Fraulk, Hans (Salvemini), 263
Free: speech (Russell), 234; trade (Croce), 69; will (Macmurray), 176; (Maritain), 211–212; thought (Hogben), 120; Trade epoch (Laski), 167
Freedom (Haldane), as a capitalist, 103; as a consumer, 101; as a producer, 102; to communicate ideas and statements, 105–111; (Laski), 148, 157, 168, 171; cultural (Laski), 149, intellectual (Hogben), 122; national (Laski), 148; religious (Laski), 162
Freedom: of movement (Haldane), 99–104; of opinion (Russell), 236;

of the press (Haldane), 109; of women and children (Haldane), 115–117
French Constituent Assembly (Salvemini), 249–250,
French Revolution (Bernstein), 44–45
Freud (Maritain), 211–212
Friendship (Macmurray), 188

Galba (Whitehead), 315
Galen (Whitehead), 320
Galileo (Whitehead), 319
Genes (Wallace), 294
Genetics (Wallace), 293
Genotypes (Haldane), 97
Geographical unity (Laski), 149
German Empire, before the war of 1914–18; (Salvemini), 250–251
German philosophy (Croce), 67, 68
Giaours (Russell), 232
Gibbon, Edward (Whitehead), 325
Gilbert and Sullivan (Russell), 235
Gladstone (Hogben), 124
Glanville, Joseph (Hogben), 126
Goals (Einstein), 92
God (Maritain), 214–217, 221, 228; (Whitehead), 54
Goering, Herman (Salvemini), 262
Gold-standard (Laski), 155
Government (Russell), 243–244; (Laski), 151; democratic (Laski), 166, 168; internal functions (Laski), 156
Greek: city states (Whitehead), 315; liberty (Stefansson), 269, 286; way of life (Hogben), 121
Greeks (Stefansson), 269
Greenland Eskimos (Stefansson), 277
Gregory XVI (Salvemini), 261
Grotius (Laski), 173

Habeas Corpus (Russell), 230
Habits (Bergson), 25, 28, 32, 39
Hall (Laski), 173
Hamilton, Alexander (Beard), 8, 21
Harmony (Boas), 51
Hebrew: God (Croce), 68; prophets (Whitehead), 68
Hegel (Croce), 66; (Haldane), 98; (Maritain), 217; (Laski), 157
Hellenic wisdom (Maritain), 225
Hellenism (Whitehead), 324
Heredity (Wallace), 294
Herodotus (Beard), 13
Heroin (Haldane), 101
Hervey (Whitehead), 319
Heterozygous population (Wallace), 299
Hindu spirituality (Maritain), 225

Historicism (Croce), 65
History (Croce), 61
Hitler, Adolf (Haldane), 109; (Russell) 238; (Salvemini), 246, 257, 263; (Laski), 175
Hitlerism (Laski), 175
Holy Alliance (Laski), 156
Housing (Stefansson), 398–399
Human: idealism (Beard), 9; nature (Beard), 12–14; (Dewey), 83–84, 85–86; nature (Laski), 157; personality (Laski), 166
Humane knowledge, mission of (Hogben), 124
Humanistic teaching (Hogben), 127
Humanity (Beard), 11; (Laski), 173
Humility (Salvemini), 264
Hunger (Macmurray), 186
Huxley, Aldous (Hogben), 120
Huxley, T. H. (Hogben), 120
Hyde, Walter W. (Stefansson), 265, 266, 268–271, 291
Hymenoptera (Bergson), 40

Ideal of freedom (Croce), 58
Idealism (Laski), 160, 173
Idealist conception of science (Maritain), 224
Ideas, theory of (Bergson), 27
Illusory: constraints (Macmurray), 180–181; freedom (Macmurray), 179
Imagination (Dewey), 80
Immanentist conception of conscience (Maritain), 224
Immigration (Laski), 149
Imperial Reichstag (Salvemini), 251
Imperialism (Laski), 163, 167, 168; economic (Laski), 160
Impossible possibility (Macmurray), 182
Impulse to tyranny (Russell), 232
Independence (Laski), 171
Independence, freedom of (Maritain), 210–219
Individual: Absoluteness (Whitehead), 304–305; initiative (Boas), 54; relativity (Whitehead), 303–304; the (Croce), 66
Individualism (Whitehead), 319
Infringement on liberty (Stefansson), 287, 291
Inheritance (Mann), 198; (Whitehead), 324
Inquisition (Russell), 235
Instinct (Bergson), 38–40; (Whitehead), 307
Intelligence (Bergson), 36, 40; (Whitehead), 307–308
Interaction (Boas), 54; (Dewey), 87

Interdependence of the nations (Laski), 165
Internal: life (Maritain), 222; restrictions on freedom (Haldane), 96–97
International: anarchy (Russell), 238; authority (Russell), 237; community (Laski), 153; government (Russell), 238; government (Laski), 154; language (Hogben), 127; law (Laski), 171–172; court (Laski), 172; control (Laski), 154, 166; equality in relations (Laski), 175; pacific settlement of disputes (Laski), 164
Investing classes (Laski), 161
Inward freedom (Einstein), 93
I.Q. test (Wallace), 296
Irish Free State (Laski), 155
Isolation (Dewey), 90

Jefferson, Thomas (Beard), 17–18; (Dewey), 77, 79; (Salvemini), 259
Jesus Christ (Beard), 14
Jus gentium (Beard), 13
Justinian (Whitehead), 325

Kant (Bergson), 31; (Macmurray) 180; (Maritain), 220
Keith, Sir Arthur (Hogben), 120
Kellogg Pact (Laski), 158
Kropotkin (Russell), 229

Labour and production (Maritain), 222
Labour, International (Laski), 165
Language (Bergson), 41
Languages, teachers of (Hogben), 126
Lao-tse (Russell), 232–233
Laski, Harold (Beard), 14 n.
Law (Beard), 8; (Russell), 236; (Laski), 154, 163, 137; international (Laski), 157, 158, 164
League of Nations (Laski), 164
Legal freedom (Croce), 70
Legal restrictions (Haldane), 95, 99
Legislation (Laski), 154, 174
Leibnitz (Whitehead), 319
Leonardo da Vinci (Whitehead), 320
Lessing, G.E. (Bernstein), 49; (Croce), 67
Ley, Robert (Salvemini), 263
Libel (Haldane), 108
Liberal ideal (Croce), 56, 63, 68
Liberalism (Croce), 57; (Laski), 167
Liberty (Croce), 70; (Salvemini), 248–249
Limitation of freedom, voluntary (Mann), 208
Lincoln, Abraham (Bernstein), 43
Literature (Croce), 75
Locke, John (Russell), 230; (Whitehead), 211

Logic (Laski), 158
Louis XIV (Bernstein), 45
Love (Macmurray), 186, (Maritain), 22t, 228
Lucian (Whitehead), 315
Lucretius (Whitehead), 314
Luther, Martin (Whitehead), 311, 319

Madison (Dewey), 79
Maine, Sir Henry (Laski), 169
Man (Anshen), 1, 5, 6; (Maritain), 218
Marcus Aurelius (Beard), 14; (Russell), 241
Marriage (Haldane), 104; (Stefansson), 276
Marx, Karl (Russell), 242; (Hogben), 121
Marxian economic freedom (Bernstein), 48
Marxian socialism (Croce), 58
Marxist Belief (Dewey), 82
Marxist Hegelianism (Maritain), 225–226
Mass-production (Laski), 154
Masses, the (Croce), 60
Mazzini (Salvemini), 246; (Laski), 150, 172
Means (Anshen), 5
Mendel (Wallace), 293
Mill, John Stuart (Croce), 66; Salvemini), 361; (Laski), 148, 172
Milton (Whitehead), 312
Minorities (Salvemini), 252; National (Laski), 150; problem of (Laski), 157
Mirabeau (Bernstein), 46
Monarchist (Salvemini), 262
Montesquieu (Russell), 230; (Salvemini), 248
Moral: equality (Beard), 11–12; factor (Dewey), 81; ideal (Croce), 62, 63, 66, 67; laws (Dewey), 76–77; liberalism (Croce), 69; liberation (Croce), 64
Morality (Croce), 73; of the closed society (Bergson), 29, 40
Morals (Dewey), 84
Murray, Gilbert (Laski), 154
Mussolini (Salvemini), 249, 257, 263

Napoleon I (Beard), 21
Napoleon III (Beard), 22
Nation-state (Laski), 151, 152, 154, 155, 159, 162, 164, 165, 170, 174, 175
National sentiment (Laski), 159, 160, 168, 169
National Socialism, German (Mann), 203–204
National spirit (Laski), 170
National-state (Laski), 153

National-states, sovereign (Laski), 175;
Nationalism (Kingdon), 137–138 (Russell), 237; (Laski), 152, 157, 159, 160, 161–3, 165, 169, 170, 172, 174; economic (Laski), 163; democratic (Laski), 169; renascent (Laski), 163
Nationality, spirit of (Laski), 149
Native individual differences (Dewey), 40–41
Natural right (Beard), 16
Nature (Bergson), 27
Nazi: dictatorships (Salvemini), 257; system (Bernstein), 47
Necessity (Bergson), 27–9, 42
Neff, Walter S. (Wallace), 296
Negation of the transcendental (Croce), 65.
Nero (Russell), 241; (Whitehead), 315
Nexus: of communal relationship (Macmurray), 192; of personal relations (Macmurray), 181–185
Nietzsche (Dewey), 86
Nineteenth-century system (Laski), 154.
Non-intervention (Croce), 70

Obedience (Bergson), 33
Obligation (Bergson); binding character of, 29; composite, 32–33; definition of, 34; deriving from habits, 35; relation of instinct, 41–42
Ogden, C. K. (Hogben), 127
Oppenham (Dewey), 84
Optional Clause (Laski), 164
Organism (Bergson), 25–26, 28, 40–41
Organizations (Russell), 233
Organized minority (Salvemini), 252–254
"Original Contract" (Whitehead), 316
Oxford Liberals (Hogben), 129

Pareto (Bernstein), 45
Parliamentary government (Haldane), 113
"Parties", political (Salvemini), 252
Pascal (Russell), 242
Patriotism (Laski), 171
Paul, Saint (Whitehead), 315
Peace (Laski), 165; education for (Laski), 162; perpetual (Laski), 158
Peace Treaties of 1919 (Laski), 164
Pericles (Beard), 13; (Whitehead), 311, 316
Periods of suppressed liberty (Croce), 61
Permanent Court (Laski), 172
Persecution (Laski), 170
Personal: conflicts (Boas), 53; equality (Macmurray), 192–193; rights (Salvemini), 249

Personality (Maritain), 214, 215; aspirations of (Maritain), 216
Pessimism (Croce), 58–59
Philosophy (Croce), 73
Philosophy: of democracy (Salvemini), 258–264; of dictatorship (Salvemini), 261
Physical freedom (Russell), 231
Pico della Mirandola (Anshen), 5
Pilgrims (Beard), 15
Pitt, William (Whitehead), 305
Plato (Anshen), 5; (Whitehead), 316, 322, 323, 325, 328
Platonic: Eros (Whitehead), 326; metaphysics (Hogben), 123
Platonism (Hogben), 123, 125, 127; Secular (Hogben), 129
Pliny (Whitehead), 325
Policies (Laski), 149
Political: freedom (Dewey), 77; (Haldane), 110–113; (Russell), 230–231; English power (Laski), 155; democracy (Laski), 166
Pope Pius XII (Salvemini), 262
Power (Dewey), 85–86; (Russell), 239; (Laski), 151, 154, 165, 171; politics (Laski), 174
Prestige (Bernstein), 45–47
Price, Richard (Salvemini), 249
Prices (Stefansson), 285
Primitive: cultures (Boas), 54; society (Boas), 55
Private: property (Stefansson), 284; (Whitehead), 323
Privileged Class (Hogben), 129
Professional institutions (Whitehead), 320
Professions (Whitehead), 320
Progress (Bernstein), 43–44; (Macmurray), 191
Proletarian dictatorships (Croce), 71
Propaganda (Laski), 159, 168
Property: systems (Croce), 69
Prostitution (Haldane), 104–105
Protestant Christianity (Hogben), 123
Protestantism (Beard), 15
Proudhon (Maritain), 217
Psychoanalysis (Maritain), 212-213
Public interest (Russell), 243
Public opinion (Laski), 160
Punishment (Stefansson), 284
Puritan Christianity (Beard), 16
Puritan Revolution (Beard), 16
Puritanism (Bernstein), 47

Quakers (Whitehead), 311

Racial stock (Wallace), 298
Racism (Wallace), 301

Radio (Haldane), 109
Rationalism (Hogben), 121, 129; Liberal (Hogben), 120
Real freedom (Croce), 70; (Macmurray), 179–180
Reason (Anshen), 5; (Bergson), 37; (Hogben), 128; (Laski), 154, 159
Reconstruction, task of (Laski), 174
Religion (Macmurray), 193; of freedom (Croce), 58; social role of (Bergson), 27–29; (Laski), 168
Religious: freedom (Haldane), 95; liberty (Haldane), 114–115; unity (Laski), 149
Resistance (Bergson), 33–35
Restraints (Bernstein), 47; (Boas), 51
Revolt against custom (Boas), 53
Revolution (Bernstein), 44; (Russell), 236; (Laski), 168; French (Laski), 169
Rights political (Salvemini), 250
Robespierre (Salvemini), 264
Roman moralists (Beard), 14
Rousseau, Jean Jacques (Maritain), 220
Royal Institution (Hogben), 127

Sacco-Vanzetti case (Laski), 172
Saint-Simon (Mann), 197–199
Samuel, Sir Herbert (Salvemini), 254
Savaronola (Beard), 15
Science (Einstein), 91–93; (Maritain), 224; (Hogben), 125; modern (Laski), 154; natural (Hogben), 124
Science for the Citizen (Hogben), 123
"Science of Culture Series" (Anshen), 3
Science of nature (Dewey), 80
Scientific: endeavour (Einstein), 92; discovery (Hogben), 122; (Laski), 154; worker (Hogben), 121
Self-determination (Croce), 72; (Salvemini), 240; (Laski), 151
Self-government, local (Laski), 149
Seneca (Beard), 14
Sense (Hogben), 129
Sex equality (Stefansson), 286
Sexual freedom (Haldane), 104
Shaw, G. Bernard (Hogben), 120
Sidonius Apollinaris (Whitehead), 325
Smith, Adam (Bergson), 31; (Dewey), 84
Social: atomism (Croce), 66; democracy (Anshen), 4; (Mann), 81; divinization of the individual (Maritain), 220; dynamics (Kingdon), 133; nexus (Macmurray), 192
Social: conditions (Hogben), 122; (Laski), 165; forces (Hogben), 126
Social-temporal (Maritain), 228
Socialism (Haldane), 96; (Mann), 201–202

Socialist Party (Laski), 167
Society (Macmurray), 87; pressure
 deriving from habits (Bergson), 24–
 25; relation to individual (Bergson),
 31–33, 37
Society (Laski), 156; equal (Laski), 169
Socrates (Whitehead), 315
Sorbonne (Hogben), 123
Sorel (Bernstein), 44–45
Sovereign national state (Kingdon),
 136
Sovereign: power (Laski), 158; state
 (Laski), 152, 170, 172
Sovereignty (Laski), 157, 158, 171,
 174; (Salvemini), 260; national
 (Laski), 155; 169
Soviet Union (Haldane), 100–104
Spartacist ethic (Hogben), 123
Spencer, Herbert (Hogben), 121
Spinoza, Benedict (Haldane), 98;
 (Maritain), 211
Spiritual (Maritain), 228
Sprat (Hogben), 126
Stalin (Salvemini), 257, 263
State (Laski), 163, 168, 170
State: responsibility of the (Laski), 158;
 will of the (Laski), 166; action
 (Laski), 172; capitalist (Laski), 169;
 conception of (Laski), 173; modern
 (Laski), 152; sovereignty of (Laski),
 153
States: democratic (Laski), 169; sov-
 ereign (Laski), 163
Stoicism (Russell), 231; Stone Age
 community (Stefansson), 273
Stupidity (Russell), 238
Subjective and objective (Macmurray),
 179–180
Synthesis (Anshen), 3

Taboos (Stefansson), 288
Tacitus (Russell), 232
Taine (Bernstein), 44
Taoism (Russell), 241
Task of scholars and thinkers (Croce), 59
Taylor, Henry Osborn (Whitehead),
 316

Thought and action (Croce), 59
Thought, freedom of (Hogben), 121
Thucydides (Whitehead), 311
Tiers état (Mann), 194
Timareus (Hogben), 123
Tolerance (Hogben), 127; (Laski), 171
Totalitarian: regime (Dewey), 81;
 doctrines (Hogben), 128; movement
 (Hogben), 128
Totalitarianism (Hogben), 128
Trade unions (Russell), 233
Trajan (Whitehead), 315
"Transnatural" aspirations of person-
 ality (Maritain), 216, 225–226, 227
True and false deification of Man
 (Maritain), 223–228
True and false political emancipation
 (Maritain), 223–227
Tyrannies (Salvemini), 256

United intellectual front (Hogben),
 129
Unity of civilization (Russell), 238–239
Universities Test Acts (Hogben), 124
Unrestricted sovereignty (Russell), 238
Utilitarian individualism (Croce), 66

Values (Anshen), 2, 3; (Dewey), 82
Vauban (Whitehead), 320
Vergil (Whitehead), 314
Vesalius (Whitehead), 320
Violence (Croce), 57; (Russell), 235;
 (Hogben), 128; (Laski), 165

Walpole, Sir Robert (Whitehead), 305
Watt, James (Whitehead), 320
Weimar Constitution (Beard), 9
Wesley, John (Whitehead), 306
Wisdom (Whitehead), 307–308
Witenagemot (Beard), 21
Workers (Maritain), 222
Working classes (Laski), 161
World-community (Laski), 165, 172–
 173
World-order, A new (Laski), 174
World War (Bernstein), 46

For Product Safety Concerns and Information please contact our EU
representative GPSR@taylorandfrancis.com
Taylor & Francis Verlag GmbH, Kaufingerstraße 24, 80331 München, Germany

www.ingramcontent.com/pod-product-compliance
Ingram Content Group UK Ltd.
Pitfield, Milton Keynes, MK11 3LW, UK
UKHW021019180425
457613UK00020B/988